THE BOOKSTORE

THE
LIVING
PSALMS

by
Claus Westermann

translated by
J.R. Porter

WILLIAM B. EERDMANS PUBLISHING COMPANY
GRAND RAPIDS, MICHIGAN

Originally published as *Ausgewählte Psalmen,*
copyright © 1984 by Vandenhoeck & Ruprecht, Göttingen.

English edition copyright © 1989 by T. & T. Clark

English edition first published 1989 in the United Kingdom by
T. & T. Clark Ltd., 59 George St., Edinburgh EH2 2LQ.

This edition first published 1989 through special arrangement with
T. & T Clark by Wm. B. Eerdmans Publishing Co., 255 Jefferson Ave. SE,
Grand Rapids, MI 49503.

Library of Congress Cataloging-in-Publication Data

Westermann, Claus.
[Ausgewählte Psalmen.   English]
The living Psalms / by Claus Westermann : translated by J. R. Porter.
p.   cm.
Translation of: Ausgewählte Psalmen.
Includes index.
ISBN 0-8028-3660-7 (cloth)
ISBN 0-8028-0450-0 (paper)
1. Bible.   O.T.   Psalms—Commentaries.   I. Title.
BS1430.3.W4713   1989

223'.207—dc19   89-1588
                                                                                         CIP

TRANSLATOR'S PREFACE

In the original German volume, the author made his own translation of the psalms on which he comments. For this English edition, the translation of the psalms in the Revised Standard Version (RSV), which is generally close to the author's renderings, has been taken as the basis. It has been departed from usually only where the author preferred a different Hebrew reading or a different rendering which is of some importance for his exegesis. Other scriptural quotations are from RSV.

The author's own system of transliteration of Hebrew words has been largely retained: it will be clear to Hebraists and of small concern to others. Bibliographical references will be found in the footnotes: where English translations of German works exist these are referred to in preference to the original. The abbreviations BHK and BHS indicate respectively *Biblia Hebraica*, ed. R. Kittel, 5th edition, 1949 and *Biblia Hebraica Stuttgartensia*, edd. K. Elliger and W. Rudolph, 1976/7.

The translator wishes to express his warm appreciation to Professor Westermann who has read through the translation and made valuable suggestions for its improvement. Any remaining inadequacies are of course the responsibility of the translator alone.

AUTHOR'S FOREWORD

In 1917, Hermann Gunkel published the revised edition of his *Ausgewählte Psalmen* with the same firm, Vandenhoeck & Ruprecht in Göttingen, that published the original German edition of the present book. Gunkel's volume was followed by his great commentary on the Psalms of 1926 and his Introduction to the Psalms which appeared in 1928-33. In the foreword to his *Ausgewählte Psalmen*, he writes: 'My real purpose has been to make clear to the modern reader the nature of the piety of the psalmists, so that he may take it to heart'. As a result of my own studies of the psalms, summed up in *Lob und Klage in den Psalmen*, 1977 (English translation, *Praise and Lament in the Psalms*, 1981), it seemed desirable to show, by means of a connected commentary, how the conclusions I had reached would work out in practice. The present volume of selected psalms is the outcome. It makes no claim to completeness; purely scholarly discussion is left well in the background. The scholarly grounds for the main lines of my way of understanding the psalms will be found in the studies already mentioned. Hence I embark but rarely on discussions of technical questions of Old Testament scholarship. My purpose is only, as Gunkel also says in his foreword, 'to let the psalms speak for themselves'.

Ever since my dissertation *Das Loben Gottes in den Psalmen*, published in 1954 but begun during the Second World War and in a prison camp, the psalms have been with me throughout my academic teaching career. Thereby they have acquired for me a significance which extends far beyond the usual confines of denomination and church. The reconciling power which the psalms have so far demonstrated throughout their long history will in the future reach to the whole of endangered humanity. That God has made man in His image and likeness, so that he, as a man who realizes his human identity, can always speak to

God, in sorrow and joy alike, and can trust his Creator throughout, in all and through all – to all this the psalms give unique expression.

Claus Westermann

CONTENTS

INTRODUCTION

What is a Psalm?
A Hymn – A Prayer – a Poem

In the Old Testament psalms, there is preserved for us a literature the basic elements of which reach back to the beginnings of human existence, which received its distinctive character in the course of the history of the Israelite nation, and which, through the history of the Christian churches, has remained alive to the present day as part of the Christian Bible, from its use in Jewish and Christian worship and by its place in personal devotion. Moreover, it remains as a treasured possession of our literary culture. As such, the psalms are poems or lyrics which have survived for centuries, through changes of civilisation, religions and languages, to speak still a living word to us today. The reason for this continued vitality of the psalms is that their words are directed to God, they are prayers and appeals to Him. Certainly, prayers have changed in different religions and as those religions have developed: Christian prayers are not the same as those of the synagogue and they have also altered over the years. But the psalms transcend the differences, because they retain those fundamental aspects of man's appeal to God which remain constant over all boundaries and through all changes in patterns of prayer. Thus they may be compared with the first eleven chapters of the Bible, the primaeval history, where we find the basic constituents of human existence, which always remain unchanged. As humanity is created by God but is also limited by sin and death, so the cry to God in the psalms consists essentially of both praise and lament. These two poles of human existence never alter: 'there is a time to weep, and a time to laugh', as the wise Preacher says.

1

But it is not only these invariable characteristics of human life which make the psalms what they are: they are also prayers which have been shaped by the history of a particular people. Israel's history is mirrored in the psalms, above all in the communal laments, in the historical psalms and in many other features. Of course, the communal laments of ancient Israel cannot be simply transferred to our own situation; but they are a necessary component of the Psalter which grew out of Israel's actual history. Again, other types of psalms contain features which we cannot directly adopt as our own prayer, in particular the petitions against enemies which occur in the individual laments; but we cannot simply strike these out of the Psalter if we wish to understand it as a whole. Of necessity, the Psalter contains words which come near to us and speak to us directly and others which we find strange and distant. So there is an essential requirement for any study of the psalms which seeks to understand them intimately – we must take them as they are. This means taking the Psalter in its entirety. The different groups and categories of psalms have, through a long process, grown together into a single whole, in which every part has its place and its significance. We can only understand any particular psalm when we relate it to the whole of which it forms part.

The same considerations apply to every separate psalm: each psalm presents a developed structure and each psalm is a poetic composition. But, unlike a modern poem, it has not arisen from the mind of an individual human being but from what has happened between this human being and God. The form of the psalm is rooted in this exchange between God and man. The author of a psalm has not 'thought up' what he says in it. The appeal to God has been shaped in fixed forms long before him. His work follows a path which many have trod before him. A lament, a petition or a summons to praise has a fixed pattern and hence a psalm is a developed structure. It is like the leaf of a tree. Each leaf has the same structure but none is exactly like another. It follows that, to understand a psalm as a whole, one must start from its structure. One must begin with the whole; only in the light of the whole can an individual element be understood. The whole is not something thought up, rather its context is an event. The structure of a psalm is not the product of thought but of what has happened. In every psalm, something happens between the suppliant and the One he supplicates. This will be shown in the following discussions of various psalms.

The psalms are hymns, as is most clearly shown by their liturgical character. Hence, the true subject of the psalms is the community assembled for worship. Much has been said about the psalms as 'cultic texts'. But the often repeated statement: 'The cult is the *Sitz im Leben* of the psalms' still really tells us nothing. It all depends on what one means by 'cult'. One must beware of introducing into the psalms an already defined cultic terminology from elsewhere and, even more, of understanding the cult as an institution shut in on itself, concerned only with the 'cultic personnel' and cut off from the ordinary life of the people. Israel's worship has to be inferred first and foremost from the psalms themselves, which form part of it. The participants in this worship are not the 'cultic personnel' but the assembled congregation, in which the priests also have their special rôle. But, above all, this worship is not the function of an institution quite separate from Israel's ordinary existence; rather, it is the very centre of it, embracing every department and sector of the national life. What makes the psalms so distinctive is that they mirror the whole of that life, from the Creator, through His creation and its history, down to the personal suffering of the individual.

The Evolution of the Psalms

The psalms – though they are poems – have not evolved as literature evolves; though they are hymns, they did not come into existence as the sacral literature of the cult. The idea that a priest would sit down to write a psalm which he then had performed at the next act of worship is unthinkable for the period before the exile. However, one can perhaps say that the very latest psalms, such as Psalm 119 or the Hodayoth (a collection of hymns of praise among the Qumran texts) would have arisen in this way.

The psalms emerged from Israel's public worship. They were not first written and then sung: rather, it was the other way round. If the thesis of the oral origin of the small units in the Old Testament is correct, this would include the psalms. Most of the psalms were sung and prayed long before being written down. They were first committed to writing in the process of the growth of the whole collection. The collection of the psalms presupposes an already long, rich and varied life for them in oral tradition and in the context of worship. But why and how the psalms emerged in Israel's worship requires further explanation. Worship in Israel from the entry into Palestine, the beginning of the monarchy and the building of the Temple, until the end of the monarchy and the destruction of the Temple was fundamentally different from what we mean by worship. It was the necessary and self-evident centre of the whole national community, the centre of all its concerns, political, economic and cultural. When, in the course of worship, blessing was conveyed, then those receiving it would be blessed also in every aspect and activity of their daily lives; no part of their life would be unaffected by it. When we say that the psalms were formed in Israel's worship, we mean a worship which at that time was the heartbeat of the whole community. Israel could no more exist without worship than worship could exist without Israel. The function of this worship can best be understood as like the veins which link the heart with the whole body, conveying the life-force, which went out from worship into the people's ordinary life and flowed back from that life into worship, a process realized as the people came together for worship and returned from worship to their homes. All this is missed by any understanding of the psalms which tends to see Israel's worship (labelled as 'the cult') as an institution shut in on itself, closed to the concerns of ordinary life and directed by a cultic personnel leading its own independent existence. With such assumptions, the psalms must almost inevitably be misunderstood.

But, if worship was at the centre of Israel's common life, one consequence follows: Israel's history was part of its life or, to put it another way, Israel's life was played out in history. And if worship was the heart of the people's life, then the nation's history must be reflected in the history of its worship, that is, the worship must contain variable, as well as constant, elements, which reveal its historical development, and this in turn must be reflected to some degree in the psalms. Now the most significant division in the Psalter as a whole is between community psalms and individual psalms. The reason for this is that the history of the nation of Israel was preceded by a history of families, whose traditions are preserved in the patriarchal narratives. Patriarchal worship was very different from the worship after the settlement[1] and we already meet in it the characteristic features of the invocation of God in the psalms, lament, praise, petition, expression of trust, making a vow. These are all taken up and developed in the Psalter in the form of individual psalms, that is, psalms from the area of personal and family life. The emergence of the nation brings with it the communal psalms and from then on both types continue to exist side by side. In both, and in the relationship between them, developments occur, caused by historical developments in Israel's worship. The most important development after the settlement was the establishment of the monarchy. With it arrived the royal psalms. After the end of the monarchy, a further development occurred: now the praise of God as king moved into the foreground (Psalms 47; 93-99) and the old royal psalms were interpreted messianically.

The Psalter also frequently reflects (Psalm 89, the book of Lamentations, etc.) the profound change brought about by the collapse of the state and the disappearance of the monarchy and the Temple. Changes in the worship of the

[1] On this, see C. Westermann, *Genesis 12-36*, trans. J.J. Scullion, 1986, pp. 105-113.

post-exilic community led to far-reaching changes in the
psalms, which are all the more pronounced since our
existing Psalter was collected together at this period. To
give a single example: the psalms concerned with the state
and its polity fade into the background and only a few of
them remain in our present Psalter. It is particularly
noteworthy that communal psalms of narrative praise, to
which the category of victory song belongs, disappear
almost entirely. The contrast is now no longer between the
nation and its political enemies but between the pious and
the godless.

These brief remarks suffice to show how the history of
worship changed as the nation's history changed and how
this development is reflected in the psalms.

Psalm research at an earlier period was concerned to date
each particular psalm as exactly as possible. This was a
mistaken endeavour and led to a misunderstanding of the
evolution of the psalms. On the other hand, it is still not
sufficiently realized that, when we speak of the psalms as
emerging from worship, we mean worship as the centre of
Israel's history. Seen thus, any particular psalm, with a few
exceptions, cannot be dated precisely: what we have to
recognize is the link between the psalms and the history of
God's dealings with his people.

As has been said above, the meaning of worship as the
centre of the nation's common life is expressed in the
people's going out to worship and returning home from
worship. This is confirmed by narratives in the historical
books which record such a pilgrimage to take part in
worship. The psalms which deal with the fate of an
individual in the setting of family life are illustrated by the
story of Hannah, the mother of Samuel. The first chapter of
1 Samuel tells how she goes to the temple at Shiloh and
there vows a vow to God: 'she was deeply distressed and
prayed to the Lord and wept bitterly' . . . 'if thou wilt
indeed look on the affliction of thy maidservant, and
remember me . . . but wilt give to thy maidservant a son.'
Of her return journey we read: 'Then the woman went her
way and ate, and her countenance was longer sad.' The

psalms which deal with the fate of the nation may be illustrated from the scene in Isaiah 37: 14 f., where king Hezekiah brings into the Temple the letter threatening the downfall of Jerusalem and spreads it out before God: 'Hezekiah received the letter from the hand of the messengers, and read it; and Hezekiah went up to the house of the Lord, and spread it before the Lord. And Hezekiah prayed to the Lord.'

These two examples show clearly how worship in Israel was the centre which drew together the life of both individual and nation, the centre to which resort the childless woman (Psalm 113) and the king threatened by enemies, in order to bring their suffering before God. Of Hannah, we learn further that, after God had heard her plea and granted her a child, she returned to the temple, fulfilled her vow and expressed her joy in a psalm of thanksgiving, 1 Samuel 2.

We can only describe and understand the psalms as originating from worship when worship is seen as the unifying centre of the nation's common life. It is not always possible to utter one's plea to God in the sanctuary. It can happen outside it, when the individual or community is confronted with an occasion of joy or of distress: the sick man prays on his bed, the prisoner prays in his gaol, the man threatened by a storm prays on the ship (Psalm 107), while the victory song rises from the battlefield and a thanksgiving to God is uttered when a child is born. Prayer in public worship would lose its force without these experiences outside the sanctuary: such prayer is only given life by the movement inwards from outside and back again into daily life.

Within this movement, prayer in worship functions to bring together those many experiences of the need to invoke God and to give verbal expression to them in a way in which all can join. The secret of the language of the psalms lies in the fact that many people and many succeeding generations can recognize and utter it as their own prayer. That the psalms are to be understood in the light of this movement to and from worship is indicated by the titles later added to the psalms by those who collected them together, titles which ascribe the occasion of their composition to real-life situations, for example Psalm 3: 1, 'A Psalm of David, when he fled from Absalom his son' or Psalm 102: 1, 'A prayer of one afflicted, when he is faint and pours out his complaint before the Lord'.

Every particular psalm must be read as the product of an evolutionary development, of which the final stage is its fixation in writing as part of the entire collection of the Psalter. In its earlier stages, the psalm was the prayer of many different persons in diverse situations and its form represents the collecting together in worship of these different voices. It received its liturgical shape only after many generations, during which it was transmitted in the worshipping centre from parent to child for centuries. A specially beautiful and vivid example of this process is Psalm 107, where various experiences of delivery from mortal danger are brought together in a single psalm, which thereby became a psalm of the worshipping community.

The Collecting of the Psalms

The collecting together of the psalms was a gradual process that lasted for centuries; as a result, the succession of 150 Psalms has no logical order, which makes it extraordinarily difficult both to read and understand them. To do either satisfactorily, it is indispensable to achieve an overall view of the entire collection, because each particular psalm can only be understood in context. At the final stage, the psalms were divided into five books, Psalms 1-41; 42-72; 73-89; 80-106; 107-150, each book marked by a closing doxology; the five-fold division corresponds to the five-fold Pentateuch. But this arrangement is of little help to us, since it is plainly only mechanical and artificial. We can first arrive at the real arrangement by working backwards from the large collections to the smallest.

Larger collections are Psalms 3-41, Psalms of David, and

42-83, the Elohistic Psalter (in which the name Yahweh, Lord, is generally replaced by Elohim, God) with its appendix Psalms 89-90; within 42-83 the main part 51-71 forms another collection of Davidic psalms, only identifiable by the title.

Smaller collections were named after guilds of singers, Korah, Psalms 42-49, Asaph and others, 73-89. There is also the collection 'Songs of Ascent', Psalms 120-134.

Finally, *small groups* of psalms witness to the earliest stage, where were grouped together psalms similar in form and/ or content: the psalms celebrating the kingship of Yahweh, 93-99, psalms of praise, 103-107, the Hallelujah psalms, 111-118 and also Psalm 135 f., Psalms of David, 138-145, with, in their midst, the group of individual laments, homogeneous in form and content, 140-143. In addition, there are ample indications that the existing collection of psalms began with groups of related psalms. Thus we can and should interpret any given psalm in relation to the collection to which it originally belonged: it belongs to a category or type, that is, to a psalm group with a common form and content. These groups must now be further discussed.[2]

The Classification of the Psalms

What can be said by way of introduction is no more than provisional; it needs to be tested by the actual exegesis of the psalms. But a provisional survey is necessary, because it is from its category or type that we can recognize the class to which any given psalm of this type belongs and which gives it its character. To interpret a particular psalm, without giving attention to the class to which it belongs, is methodologically without justification. Further, each type

[2] See also C. Westermann, 'Zur Sammlung des Psalters', *Theologische Bücherei* 24, 1964, pp. 336-343.

or category has its own history, the study of which is called 'form-criticism',[3] and so each particular psalm is a link in the chain of this history. This necessarily follows from what has already been said about the history of worship in Israel, for the history of the categories of psalms belongs in the wider context of the history of prayer, in which its earlier and later developments can be detected.

Because the psalm types or categories have a history, they are not rigid patterns, into which the particular psalm must be pressed – this charge has often been levelled against form-criticism – but rather the forms share in that diversity which marks all living things. As in the natural world we can recognize the species, which yet preserves the distinctiveness of its individual members, so the single psalms belong to categories which can be shaped in a boundless variety of ways, none of which is ever quite the same.

The psalms we have can be basically classified, on the one hand, according to the two poles of praise and lament by which God is invoked but also, on the other, according to the speaker of the praise or lament, the individual or the community.

The two main groups, psalms of praise and psalms of lament, correspond to the rhythm of joy and grief which characterizes all human life, grounded as it is in human creatureliness and its limitations. Joy and grief, however, are here not human emotions which are then brought into relationship with God; rather, praising God means joy finding words, lament to God is grief's self- expression.

The division into individual and communal psalms likewise corresponds to the essential characteristics of human existence. The individual with his unique life and fate can never be completely absorbed into the community, whatever form this takes, but neither can the individual life ever break entirely free from that of the community; to some extent, the individual will always belong to a community.

[3] In German, *Formgeschichte*, the history of forms.

From these two basic divisions, there follow on four main types, from which in turn the earliest psalm collections derive: we may list them as follows, with an example of each type:

> The communal lament (Psalm 80)
> The communal psalm of praise (Psalms 124; 113)
> The individual lament (Psalm 13)
> The individual psalm of praise (Psalms 40; 103).

The communal and individual psalms of praise divide into two groups according to the grounds on which praise is uttered. If it is a question of a definite event, usually a recently experienced deliverance, the praise of God takes the form of a declaration or a narrative, the deliverance from danger is recounted (Psalms 124; 40). If such a definite occasion is not in question, but God is to be praised in the fullness of His being and His acts, the psalm takes a descriptive form (Psalms 113; 103); the occasion is then the assembling of the congregation for worship. Hence to the descriptive psalms of praise belong also the liturgical psalms, that is, those directly linked with an act of worship (for example, Psalm 118).

Only the basic psalm types have been mentioned. They permit of numerous variations: in psalms of praise, the narrative element can easily be combined with the descriptive, for example, Psalm 107, where various individual reports of an experience of deliverance flow together into congregational praise. Themes such as the expression of trust or the praise of the Creator or the summons to praise can of themselves constitute independent psalms but they can also occur in a range of other contexts. But all these variations are linked in some way with the basic types and are to be understood from them.

However, there are a number of psalms which belong to none of the basic types and show no connection with them. In each case, we have to ask whether they are psalms in the true sense at all and how it is possible to understand their place in the Psalter in the light of the basic types.

The Background of the Psalms in the
History of Religions

In his book 'Prayer', Franz Heiler undertook to investigate the phenomenon of prayer in the world's religions. This work leaves us with the impression of an extraordinarily wide range of common features, in what we call prayer, among the religions of mankind. Lament and petition, praise and thanksgiving are common to most religions which acknowledge a personal God or gods. They are the natural way of expressing man's appeal or address to a mighty and benevolent deity. So prayer in general is something that unites religions, rather than dividing them. The background of the Old Testament psalms is found in the religions of ancient Near Eastern civilisation, which, especially in the area of Semitic languages, reveals a far-reaching unity. In this sphere, forms of lament and praise to God developed that endured for centuries over a wide area. Hence it is clear that the Old Testament psalms show many relationships with similar material in the surrounding world, as the collection of A. Falkenstein and W. von Soden abundantly illustrates.[4] The same themes appear, similar structures and the same rhythmical form, including parallelism. The similarity extends to language: often identical comparisons are employed, as when God is addressed as shepherd or enemies are described as wild beasts and their attacks as laying snares. Against this far-reaching similarity, however, the differences and contrasts emerge all the more sharply. The Egyptian psalms are further from those of the Old Testament but here also there are striking similarities. Psalm 104 stands close to Akhenaten's hymn to the Sun and we also meet in Egypt the individual psalm of thanksgiving which is very like those of the Old Testament.[5] So far no psalms or psalm collections have been discovered at Ugarit but only isolated themes and

---

[4] A. Falkenstein and W. von Soden, *Sumerische und akkadische Hymnen und Gebete*, 1953.

[5] See, especially, A.M. Blackman, 'The Psalms in Egyptian Research' in ed. D.C. Simpson, *The Psalmists*, 1926, pp. 177-197.

units, which, however, do display similarities and correspondences, with what we find in the Old Testament. Thus, in the view of many scholars, Psalm 29 goes back to a Ugaritic prototype.

What has been said has been confined to the area of the ancient Near East. But, as Heiler's work abundantly demonstrates, there exist among peoples and religions, widely separated in time and space, similarities and correspondences in their prayers, which are to be accounted for by the analogous basic elements in prayer, as an appeal to God, shared by all humanity.

The Psalms in the context of the History of Prayer

In the Old Testament, we can distinguish three stages in the history of prayer. At an early stage, it consists of brief appeals, properly appeals to God, which were so much a part of daily life that we meet them only in narratives or other prose texts, where they appear as elements of the events being recounted; they arise directly from the situation in which they are uttered. Take, for instance, a shout of praise, when Jethro says: 'Blessed be the Lord, who has delivered you out of the hand of the Egyptians and out of the hand of Pharaoh!', Exodus 18: 10. Or Samson's lament in Judges 15: 18: 'Thou hast granted this great deliverance by the hand of thy servant; and shall I now die of thirst, and fall into the hands of the uncircumcised?' Or the deep sigh of David: 'O Lord, I pray thee, turn the counsel of Ahithophel into foolishness!', 2 Samuel 15: 31.

The middle stage is represented by the psalms and is closely connected with the first stage. For the psalms are for the most part composed of units which were once the kind of independent prayers that occur in the prose narratives – the appeal to God (and the cry 'O God!' can constitute a self-contained prayer), the lament or plea, the cry for help, the vow, such as that in Genesis 28: 20-22, the shout of praise as an expression of confident trust. The psalms are poetic compositions made up of such units, intended for use in worship. For example, the composition represented by a psalm of lament brings together elements whose original setting was a situation of distress or danger when a man appealed to God. The psalms mirror the collecting together in worship, the uniting centre, of many such elements from various occasions. As a poetic creation, the psalm takes up the experiences of many different people and gives expression to them, while, as a vehicle for worship, it becomes the well-tried means of expression for ever fresh experiences. The psalm, prayed together by the many worshippers, thus stands in the middle between their experiences and their appeals to God, from which it originally developed, and their returning from worship to their everyday life. Psalm 22, an elaborate lament, has its origin in the cry of a man in direst distress. The cry, 'My God, why . . . ?' did not originate in worship but was brought into it from that situation of distress. There it was transformed into a psalm for the worshipping congregation and from there, from generation to generation, it becomes part of the experiences of many others and in this way proves its worth. Only through this does the psalm composed for worship continue validly to function there.

Two consequences follow from all this. First, it becomes clear that a psalm does not spring primarily from an idea, but from an event; in every psalm something happens, and what happens is the first concern of exegesis. Secondly, it must be understood that the units, from which a psalm is fashioned, retain a relatively independent existence. They can be employed in various ways. In the construction of a psalm, one unit may receive particular emphasis and development, as the element of the praise of God's goodness does in Psalm 103, while other units may be only hinted at or ignored altogether. But also, one unit in a psalm may be developed into a complete psalm on its own: an expression of trust can grow into a psalm of trust, praise of the Creator into a creation psalm.

The third stage in the history of Old Testament prayer is the prose prayer, usually of some length, as exemplified in 1 Kings 8; Ezra 8; Nehemiah 9. There is a deep gulf between the poetic liturgical psalm and the prose prayer. In the history of Israelite worship, this gulf is the result of the destruction of the Temple, the centre of the whole national life. The rebuilt post-exilic Temple could never become such a centre to the same extent. The psalms indeed lived on but it was a shadowy existence; they could no longer completely fulfil the function they had once earlier had. The prose prayers, better suited to the late period, which now begin to appear, are evidence of this.

Bound up with the change from poetry to prose is a fundamental change in the content of prayer. Lament and praise, twin poles expressing in words joy or sorrow, are reactions to events; they presuppose something that has previously occurred. They have a spontaneous character, they are a natural reaction, as we see them in the old stories, they are utterances forced out by the circumstances of human existence. This spontaneous and responsive character of lament and praise retreats into the background during the third stage. The opposite poles are no longer lament and praise but increasingly petition and thanksgiving. But these are not natural reactions in the same way as lament and praise are; rather they are to be understood as actions performed by man. For in thanksgiving and petition man is the subject: 'we thank thee, that . . . '; 'we beseech thee, that thou wilt . . . ' But in lament and praise God is the subject: 'why art thou so far?' 'how wonderful are thy works!' Praise and lament are utterances from the heights and the depths, petition and thanksgiving are uttered on the plain. The swing of the pendulum from lament to praise is strong and deep, from petition to thanksgiving it is weaker and more restrained. Hence petition and thanksgiving can now to some extent be uttered in a single breath, so that for the first time thanksgiving and petition together constitute what is meant by 'prayer'; prayer becomes an address to God, containing thanksgiving and petition at one and the same time, and this pattern has determined our own understanding of prayer to the present day.

We can no longer undo this change from lament and praise to petition and thanksgiving, nor can we say that one is right and the other wrong. Only we must be clear that here a fundamental change has occurred, so that in this respect the prayer of the psalms is essentially different from what we understand by prayer. One sign of this change is that the psalms have no word for prayer – 'psalm' and 'psalter' are late Greek terms, derived from a musical instrument. They know only particular ways of calling on God, such as lamenting, pleading, praising. And this shows that such calling on God was still close to the situation which gave rise to it, it still had a spontaneous and natural character. It is characteristic of the later understanding of prayer, and of what prayer usually means for us, that one utters a prayer much as one performs a task, as when we just mechanically reel off the Lord's Prayer.

If the Old Testament psalms have not merely survived but remained alive and in use for thousands of years, the reason is that in them there has been preserved a way of calling on God which is spontaneous and direct and by means of which man can speak to God as he really thinks and feels.

The Psalms as Poetry

It is typical that until well into the eighteenth century the psalms were held to be prose; that seemed obvious because only the prose prayer was recognized. It was Lowth in England in his *De sacra poesi Hebraeorum* (1753) and Herder in Germany in his *Vom Geist der ebräischen Poesie* (1782) who first rediscovered the poetical character of the psalms. One should, however, qualify this statement by noting that Luther's translation of the psalms shows an instinctive feeling for the poetical form of the psalms: one may instance his translation of Psalm 90.

But how far and in what way the psalms are poetry requires careful examination, because they are poetry of a different kind from what we usually understand by the word. In the first place, its distinctive characteristic consists in the balance of sentences, what is called *parallelismus membrorum.* Two, or sometimes three, sentences are so associated together that they either repeat one another (synonymous parallelism) or one supplements the other (synthetic parallelism) or they stand in opposition to one another (antithetic parallelism). An example of the first kind is Psalm 103: 1:

'Bless the Lord, O my soul;
and all that is within me, bless his holy name!'

An example of the second is Psalm 103: 2:

'Bless the Lord, O my soul,
and forget not all his benefits.'

An example of the third is Psalm 91: 7:

'A thousand may fall at your side . . .
but it will not come near you.'

These are only the basic forms and there are many variants. A particularly artistic form, found also in Ugaritic texts, consists of three ascending clauses, as in Psalm 93: 3:

'The floods have lifted up, O Lord,
the floods have lifted up their voice,
the floods lift up their roaring.'

A similar balancing of sentences is also met with in the civilizations surrounding Israel, notably in Babylonian and Assyrian psalms. What we have is a rhythm of sentences not a rhyming of words or syllables, not determined by sound but by sense. We meet a language which is conscious that a linguistic structure consists not of words but of sentences. This corresponds to an insight that the most recent linguistic studies have re-discovered: it is not the individual word, the vocabulary, but the sentence that is the basic unit of human speech. This insight is the clue to understanding *parellismus membrorum* in the psalms and in Old Testament poetry generally. The sentences which together make a rhythm or even a rhyme are also rhythmically structured within themselves. At one time, exegetes talked much of metre and endeavoured to discover in Old Testament poetry a metrical scheme corresponding to that of Greek and Latin verse. However, a regular metre arbitrarily imposed on the text is to be distinguished sharply from the rhythmic language of the sentences themselves, which is itself inherent in what they aim to say.

What is meant by this becomes clear when we observe that the climax of many Old Testament narratives is a speech in rhythmic poetic form. In the account of the creation of humanity in Genesis 2, the words of the man when he presents to God the woman created to be his helper, 'bone of my bone and flesh of my flesh', are an example of rhythmic parallelism. Or again Nathan's accusatory exclamation to David: 'You are the man' is modelled on the rhythm of two stresses characteristic of ordinary speech. This rhythm, common to speech generally, is made up by bringing together stressed and unstressed syllables. Two sentences standing in parallel can have either a regular or irregular rhythm. Especially frequent is the pattern 3:3, as in Psalm 103: 1,2, but we also meet 2:2, as in Psalm 113: 5 f., and 4:4, as in Psalm 103: 10, depending on the content, so that in most psalms the pattern changes from one section to another. We also have a regular rhythm in three clauses, 2:2:2 and 3:3:3. Alongside, there are the irregular rhythms 3:2 or 4:2. The 3:2 pattern is commonly employed for the funeral lament, as in Amos 5: 1. Just because in one and the same psalm the rhythmic pattern frequently changes, this kind of poetry comes close to ordinary speech – it is natural, not artificial. The transition from spontaneous to controlled speech is often tenuous, and thereby there is a fixed number only of stressed syllables, as opposed to unstressed ones; the closeness of Hebrew poetry to spontaneous speech leads to a single stressed syllable being accompanied by one, two or even three unstressed ones. And in certain cases two stresses can follow immediately on one another.

In contrast to the metres of Greek and Latin, and the end-rhyme of modern, verse, the intention behind the extremely free and flexible rhythms of the psalms is not an aesthetic one – and hence the term 'poetry' for them is not altogether satisfactory – but a functional one: through these rhythms the worshipping congregation speaks and prays the psalms together. Through them, the mainly brief psalms so easily impress themselves on the worshippers' minds that, with regular recital, they take root of themselves in the memory and do not need to be learned, as we say, 'by heart'. In this manner they were able to be transmitted from generation to generation.

The Psalms – said or sung?

Psalm 150 and many other passages show that the liturgical songs of praise had an instrumental accompaniment and hence the psalms were sung. However, this was not necessarily the case with every psalm. It applies to psalms of the community, although perhaps not to all, but not necessarily to psalms of the individual. It is unlikely that individual psalms of lament were sung. In any case, we must not think of the singing of the congregational psalms of praise as like the singing of a hymn in our own services of worship. Further, we must assume that singing very closely resembled speaking, at least in pre- exilic times. Only in the second Temple do we find a picture of the singing of the psalms being undertaken by guilds of professional singers; now for the first time the psalms were sung by the choirs of these guilds. But with the destruction of the second Temple, this Temple music completely stopped; we cannot know exactly just what it was like and we have little precise information about the instruments that are mentioned. The medieval 'psalm modes' are in no way connected with the Temple music of ancient Israel; we must assume that these are far removed from it, and not only in time.

Some comments on the Titles of the Psalms

The general reader may console himself by the observation that many of the titles to the psalms have not yet been explained, in spite of long scholarly endeavour. In most cases they contribute nothing to the understanding of the psalms, since they are not contemporary with them but were added when the psalms were collected together for use in worship. All the psalms originally were without titles and twenty-four psalms still lack them.

The titles may be divided into three groups:

1. Some are names of persons or groups of persons. The personal names are intended to ascribe a psalm to one or other of the great figures of Israel's history, David, Solomon or Moses. The group names indicate guilds of Temple singers, for example the Korahites, who transmitted or performed the psalms in question.

2. The type of psalm is indicated by titles such as hymn, psalm, psalm of praise, lament and so on. The meaning of some of these titles is still unclear.

3. Other titles provide cues for the liturgical performance of the psalms and their musical accompaniment, mentioning the relevant instruments. These are intended for the choir leader or music master, who is frequently referred to in the titles. They are technical musical directions, which in the main we do not understand, since we know so little about the music of the Temple.

THE COMMUNAL PSALMS
OF LAMENT

The Texts

The Psalter preserves only a few communal psalms of lament: Psalms 44; 60 in part; 74; 79; 80 and 89. Outside the Psalter, the book of Lamentations is a collection of communal hymns of lament, though chapter 3 is an individual lament and in chapters 1, 2 and 4 the communal lament is linked with motifs from the funeral lament.

The *prophetic books* provide examples of complete communal laments in Jeremiah 14; Isaiah 63: 7-19; 64: 12; Habakkuk 1, while there are elements and reminiscences of the lament form in, for example, Amos 7: 2-5; Isaiah 26; 33; Jeremiah 3; Joel 1 f. Second Isaiah presupposes the communal lament of the period after 587 B.C. and echoes it frequently, for example 40: 27.

The *historical books* often refer to the people's lament: Exodus 32: 11- 14; Deuteronomy 9: 25-29; Joshua 7: 7-9; Judges 20: 23-26; 21: 2-4; 1 Samuel 7: 6; 1 Kings 8; 21: 9, 12. Similar references occur in the *prophetic books*, notably Joel 1-2, but also Hosea 7: 14; Isaiah 15: 2; 58: 3 ff.; Jeremiah 4: 8; 6: 26; 14: 1; 36: 6, 9; Jonah 3: 5 ff.; Micah 1: 8, 16; 5: 1.

The Lament in Worship

As we learn from these and other texts, the people's lament was characterized by its setting in an act of fasting, *ṣōm*. This was not a regularly recurring annual observance but one to which the people had to be summoned whenever the nation faced a threat of distress, danger or catastrophe. So it is on such occasions that we read of fasting and hence it is frequently mentioned in the historical books. Because all are involved in such crises, all, men, women and children, old and young alike take part in the lamentation, Joel 2: 15;

Jonah 3: 5; the summons to fast is referred to in 1 Kings 21:
9, 12; Jeremiah 36: 9; Ezekiel 21: 12; Joel 2: 16; Jonah 3: 5.
The participating congregation is sanctified, Joel 1: 14, and
various penitential actions accompany the fast, the wearing
of mourning, putting on sackcloth, Isaiah 22: 12; Jeremiah
4: 8, throwing dust and earth on the head, Joshua 7: 6;
Nehemiah 9: 1, gestures of humiliation and supplication,
and 'weeping before the Lord', Judges 20: 23-26; Jeremiah
14: 12. The lament begins in the open air, in the vineyards
and in the streets and open places of the town; then the
procession moves to the sanctuary, there 'to weep before
the Lord'.

Two different kinds of crisis are to be distinguished as
occasioning the lament; on the one hand, a political crisis,
such as war, enemy attack, destruction of the city or the
sanctuary and the deportation of the inhabitants; on the
other, natural catastrophes, such as drought, a plague of
locusts, a bad harvest or famine. It is noteworthy that
communal laments in the psalms are invariably occasioned
by enemies, while in the prophetic books, on the contrary,
they are almost always a reaction to natural catastrophes.
This difference has not yet been explained, nor has the fact
that no psalm of lament on the occasion of a pestilence has
been preserved. But we can draw some conclusions: the
category of communal psalms of lament must once have
been much more extensive than we might assume from the
scarcity of psalms of this type in the Psalter. There were
different groups of these psalms of lament, distinguished by
the different occasions they were related to, and only one of
these groups has been preserved in the Psalter. It is easy to
see why the Psalter contains only a few communal laments.
The Psalter is a collection from the post-exilic period, when
Israel was a province of a great imperial power and no
longer a state that could wage war on its own. The fast, the
setting for the communal lament, disappeared and was
supplanted, to some degree at least, by penitential liturgies
of the kind reproduced, for example, in Ezra 9. These were
no longer spontaneous reactions to particular occasions but
could be regularly repeated, as with our Ash Wednesday.

However, in one point, the communal psalms of lament retained their theological significance and probably for this reason some of them were preserved in the Psalter. They keep this significance in the Christian churches too, although, on account of their fundamentally different background, such psalms can no longer be the prayer of a Christian congregation.

When the nation finds itself hard pressed, it brings its needs before Yahweh. Because what happened in the political sphere was part of Israel's relationship with God – though this was only so up to the exile – everybody was convinced of one thing: the blow has come from Yahweh and hence only He can reverse the distress. The concern of the rites and psalms of lamentation is that God should turn again in mercy to His people. It is possible for them to entreat God for mercy because in the past He has delivered, guided and preserved His people. To that they hold fast: they recall to God His past deeds and promises. They hope for a change in their present grave circumstances, which will be brought about through God turning to them again. So the psalms of lament are one of the most important pieces of evidence for ancient Israel's understanding of history, an understanding which sees past, present and future as bound together under God's control.

Psalm 80: O Shepherd of Israel!

1   Give ear, O Shepherd of Israel,
    thou who leadest Joseph like a flock!
    Thou who art enthroned upon the cherubim, shine
        forth
2   before Ephraim, Benjamin and Manasseh!
    Stir up thy might, and come to save us!
3   Restore us, O God;
    Let thy face shine, that we may be saved!

4   O Lord of hosts, how long wilt thou punish the
        remnant of thy people?

5   Thou hast fed them with the bread of tears,
    and given them tears to drink in full measure.
6   Thou dost make us the scorn of our neighbours;
    and our enemies make mock of us.
7   Restore us, O God of hosts;
    let thy face shine, that we may be saved!
8   Thou didst bring a vine out of Egypt;
    thou didst drive out the nations and plant it.
9   Thou didst clear the way for it;
    it took deep root and filled the land.
10 The mountains were covered with its shade,
    the cedars of God with its branches;
11 it sent out its branches to the sea,
    and its shoots to the River.
12 Why then hast thou broken down its walls,
    so that all who pass along the way pluck its fruit?
13 The boar from the forest ravages it,
    and all that move in the field feed on it.

14 Turn again, O God of hosts!
    Look down from heaven, and see;
    have regard for this vine,
15a and the garden which thy right hand planted.
16 They have burned it with fire, they have cut it
        down;
    may they perish at the rebuke of thy countenance!
17 But let thy hand be upon the man of thy right
        hand,
    the son of man whom thou hast made strong for
        thyself!

18 Give us life, and we will call on thy name!
    then we will never turn back from thee.
19 Restore us, O Lord of hosts!
    let thy face shine, that we may be saved!

Text

For the title (verse 1 in the Hebrew), and all other titles, see the section on the titles of the psalms, p. 19.

In the translation of this and all other psalms, the Hebrew divine name Yahweh, *yhwh*, is rendered as 'Lord', with most English versions.

v. 1 (Heb. 2): the sign marking the end of the verse, *pasūk*, after verse 1 is to be transferred after verse 2a.

v. 4a (Heb. 5a): read 'Yahweh Sabaoth'; *'elohīm*, God, is to be omitted as a later addition.

v. 4b (Heb. 5b): 'how long wilt thou smoke (with anger, so literally *'āšanta*) at (during, in spite of) thy people's prayers?' but the Hebrew is unclear. Other proposals are: 'how long wilt thou "punish" those of thy people "who have escaped"?' or 'how long "wilt thou be deaf" to thy people's prayers?'

v. 5 (Heb. 6): the two verbs should have the first person plural suffix. *šališ* is literally a 'third part'; a large measure is meant.

v. 6 (Heb. 7): instead of *mādōn*, 'strife', *mānōd*, 'shaking' (of the head) is to be read on grounds of the parallelism; compare Psalm 44: 14 (Heb. 15).

v. 9 (Heb. 10): *pānāh* in the sense of 'to clear a way' as at Isaiah 40: 3.

v. 10 (Heb. 11): *kossū* for *kussū*. *'arzē'ēl* is 'cedars of God' as at Psalm 104: 16.

v. 13 (Heb. 14): 'ravage', the rare verb *krsm*, with four root letters. *zīz*, literally 'moving things', that is, 'animals', occurs only here and at Psalm 50: 11. The significance of the suspended ' in the third word is unclear; perhaps it marks the middle of the Psalter.

v. 15 (Heb. 16): with Gunkel, for *wekannāh* read *wegannāh*, 'and the garden'.

v. 15b is a doublet from v. 17b and thus should be omitted.

v. 16 (Heb. 17): the verbs still refer to the vine, hence read *serāfūhā* and *kesaḥ ūha*, 'they have burned it and cut it down'.

v. 18 (Heb. 19): the two halves of the verse are transposed.

v. 19 (Heb. 20): *'elohīm* is to be omitted as in v. 4.

Structure

The extended address in vv. 1c and 2a ushers in the opening petition of vv. 1, 2b and 3. To this is linked the lament of 4-6, with a resumed address, framed by the opening petition in 3 and its parallel in 7. The lament is continued in 12-13 and is followed by the petition proper in 14-15a. In between, there is the contrasting motif of 8-11: God is reminded of His past saving acts and this reminder serves to undergird the petition. To the petition is linked the 'double request' of 16-17 and the psalm concludes with a vow to praise God, v. 19, on which again follows, by way of refrain, the petition, v. 19 parallel to vv. 4 and 8; compare also v. 14.

Leaving out the repetitions, we find here the simple basic structure of the communal lament: address, lament, its contrast, petition, double request, vow of praise.

vv. 1-3: The psalm begins with an invocation, which is then repeated several times in the rest of the psalm, vv. 3, 4, 7, 14, 19. This frequently repeated invocation gives the psalm a special vividness. The function of the invocation is to make contact with God, in the same way that contact is made between men. And, as is also the case with human contacts, such an invocation addressed to God acquires a particular intensity when it springs from a situation of distress and so becomes a cry for help. In a time of dire trouble, the very calling on God's name can be a cry for help; this is what gives it intensity. From what has just been said, it is clear that addressing God and invoking Him are not the same. What God is and means, in each case, He becomes from the situation in which He is invoked. So the frequently repeated invocation confers on our psalm as a whole the character of a cry for help.

In each case, the invocation can only be understood from the psalm taken as a whole: it cannot be divorced from the situation that gives rise to it. Again, invoking God and addressing God are not the same, for the former gives expression to an awareness of separation – 'why art thou so far?'. Invocation loses its intensity as address becomes more common, something we see in the case of Babylonian psalms. Address has also replaced invocation where a prayer is made up of both petition and thanksgiving. But invocation necessarily belongs to the psalm of lament, in which the speaker calls in his distress on God as Saviour. Invocation thus understood is what is expressed by the two imperatives 'give ear!' and 'come to save us!', v. 2b.

The plea in distress is twofold throughout the Psalter: give ear! – come to save us! This twofold petition, petition in the sense of plea,[6] has the form it does because the suppliant, when he calls on God in his distress, experiences that distress as God's turning away or distancing of Himself. The possibility of deliverance depends on God turning back to him. God's saving intervention requires that He turn to the suppliant. Both invocation and twofold petition show that the divine–human relationship in the psalm is an utterly personal one. For the one who, in the psalms, calls on Him, God is truly a person; a God who can somehow be made into an object, somehow objectified, even if only in idea, simply does not exist for the suppliant.

In v. 1, the address to God is amplified; God is addressed not by name but by a divine predicate, 'Shepherd of Israel'. The comparison of God with a shepherd is carried further in the same verse, 'thou who leadest Joseph like a flock', and is also met with in two other communal laments, Psalm 74: 1 and 79: 13, 'we thy people, the flock of thy pasture'; see also Psalm 23. Confession of trust is implicit in the address to God as shepherd in our psalm: the suppliants' cry to be heard, their appeal to God to turn towards them, is addressed to the One whom Israel trusts as its shepherd. In this amplification, too, the contrasting theme of 8-11 is already implicitly anticipated; the people's plea is directed to the God it has known in the past, whom it has experienced in the past as its good shepherd and so experiences Him still – again, we may instance Psalm 23. The amplified address is made up of various elements.

[6] For the difference, see pp. 72-3

Their bringing together is not the result of a process of literary composition: rather, it is the product of the way the psalms functioned in worship through a long period, during which such amplifications could be added from quite different sources. The intention behind the amplification in the present case can easily be recognized. The invocation is amplified in order to tell what the One invoked in this crisis has meant for His people in the past, both before the settlement in Palestine (the shepherd is the one who leads 'Joseph-Israel' on his journey, Psalms 77: 15, 20; 81: 4-5) and after it (the God of the settled population is the enthroned God, represented here by the tradition of the cherub throne, 1 Samuel 4: 4; 2 Samuel 6: 2; 2 Kings 19: 15; Isaiah 37: 16; Psalm 99: 1). The petition 'come to save us' is amplified by a motif attested for a similar situation of distress in the period of the Judges, the epiphany of Judges 4-5, where God appears to the tribes to intervene on their behalf at a moment of crisis: we may also instance Habakkuk 3: 3-15; Psalms 18: 7-15; 68: 7 f., 33; 77: 16-19; 97: 2-5.

The amplification we are considering mirrors the epochs of Israel's history when Israel experienced God's help. In principle, then, it is not permissible to draw conclusions from the statements in vv. 1-2 about the date of the psalm or to claim that it originated in North Israel; at most, one can speak of the adaptation of a Northern tradition.

After the amplified invocation, v. 3 resumes the opening petition with a fresh appeal 'O God!', *'elohīm*, hence an invocation with no predicate. The cry for help is expressed in a single word *hašībēnw*, 'restore us!', which is explained by the following two verses. V. 3 recurs again, as a kind of refrain, in v. 7 at the end of the first part of the lament and, with somewhat different wording, in v. 14 at the end of the second part. But it is not simply a formal element, but in each case the context gives it a particular significance; in v. 3 it closes the invocation with an introductory petition, in vv. 7 and 14 it follows on from the lament. The threefold repetition powerfully emphasizes the petition that is linked with the invocation; the whole psalm is determined by one

basic motif 'save, O God!' (compare Psalm 118: 25). Hence
we should think of this cry 'save, O God' as an early
independent prayer, a cry for help in distress uttered
directly to God, which was preserved in the shout
'Hosannah' into New Testament times. That in v. 3a not
the verb 'save', *hōšīaʿ*, but 'restore' is used is appropriate for
the general tenor of the psalm as indicated in vv. 8–11. The
two verbs which expand the cry for help again display the
twofold structure; God turns the light of His countenance
towards men, as at Numbers 6: 24–26, and God intervenes
to deliver them – here we have the verb *hōšīaʿ*.

vv. 4–7: After the opening petition, there follows the
lament. In many psalms of lament there is no opening
petition and the lament occurs immediately after the
invocation. Here we have a lament directed to God, using
the second person singular, or a complaint against God.[7]
The lament starts where the suffering starts and the
suffering starts when God turns away. This turning away
from His people has already lasted a considerable time, as
the cry 'restore us!' itself indicates, so the lament begins
with the question 'how long?', which, together with the
other question 'why?', v. 12, characterizes the psalms of
lament. But in v. 4 only the opening remains intact, 'O
Lord of hosts, how long . . .'. Many attempts have been
made to restore the rest of the verse, but they all fail to take
account of the fact that v. 4, like v. 5, must have consisted of
two half-lines. I propose therefore:

> How long, Yahweh, wilt thine anger flame,
> wilt thou be silent before thy people's prayers?

The people, burdened with suffering, can no longer
understand why God has rejected them. They complain of
the length of their suffering with boldness and immediacy:
how long will it continue to last? yet we still hold to thee in
spite of thy wrath! Vv. 5 and 6 embody this 'how long',
they speak of what the people themselves have had to

---

[7] For the three aspects of the lament, see p. 69 f.

endure for so long (lament in the first person plural) and what they have endured at the hand of others (lament about enemies).

v. 5 is a metaphor or comparison, which is so telling because it results from a long experience of suffering. The verse speaks not so much of suffering in itself but rather of its effects. So profoundly overwhelmed is the people by its sufferings that food and drink seem no longer to offer refreshment and sustenance for daily living but only incessant torture. The same thing is said even more powerfully in Lamentations 3: 15 f.; it is echoed in Goethe's line 'Who never ate his bread in sorrow . . .'[8]

In v. 6, the accusation against God is linked with the lament about enemies, just as in v. 5 it is linked with the 'We' lament. This verse too speaks not of suffering in itself but of its effects. The sufferers have to endure scorn and mockery and this already for a long time. In the Old Testament, all suffering is suffering in community, it always brings disgrace with it. The sufferers must endure the laughter of others (v. 5 presents the contrasted theme of weeping), they must endure it when others vent their feelings against them. When both enemies and neighbours are mentioned in v. 6, it is taken for granted that nations, despite all wars and conflicts, live in community; those who are not reckoned as enemies are not 'neutrals', as we might say, but neighbours. And their mockery wounds as deeply as that of enemies. V. 6 begins 'thou dost make us . . .': what the people encounter from foes and neighbours is traced back to God, there is an aspect of suffering which results from God's turning away from His people. But precisely because of this, only one change in the situation is conceivable, that God should turn back again to His people, v.7.

vv. 8-11: The lament continues in vv. 12-13; on the 'how long?' of v. 4 there follows the 'why?' of v. 12. In between is inserted in vv. 8-11 the contrasting motif, consisting of a review of God's past saving acts and 'reproaching' the deity

---

[8] As translated by Carlyle. The original German is 'Wer nie sein Brot mit Tränen ass.'

for the contrast between then and now. It looks back to the
events the memory of which was preserved in the 'historical
Credo', to use von Rad's term, as well as in the divine
promise at the beginning of the exodus, Exodus 3: 7-8. God
is reminded of His own 'mighty acts', so that He may
remember them. The review is in two parts, God's deeds,
vv. 8-9a, and their consequences, vv. 9b-11. If one goes
behind the metaphorical language, what is referred to is the
deliverance from Egypt and the entry into Canaan, v. 8, and
then Israel's occupation of the land by means of the
expulsion of the nations, vv. 8b, 9a. There follows the
settlement and expansion of Israel in Canaan, vv. 9b-11.

All this is pictured in terms of the vine-grower at work in
his vineyard or on his vine, an image we frequently
encounter in the Bible, for example, Isaiah 5: 1-7; John 15.
God's dealings with His people are presented as a unity, as a
closed and fully integrated course of events. History
develops from the plans and actions of a Person who
controls the whole process: only as part of this process has
any given historical event significance. The unity of the
historical process corresponds to the unity of the Lord of
history, with whom it begins and ends.

Taken together, the two parts of the comparison here
give it a further meaning. It brings together God's activities
for His people in both deliverance, 8-9a, and blessing,
9b-11, and the latter is given special prominence by the
metaphor of vegetation: its growth below and above the
ground is described in extravagant language which recalls
the promises of blessing in the patriarchal narratives.

This comprehensive description of God's mighty deeds
for His people had its place not only in the historical Credo
but is also found in that review of God's saving acts which is
a regular feature of communal psalms of lament; further
examples are Psalms 44: 1-9; 74: 12-17; 83: 9-12; 85: 1-3;
126: 1-3, and we may also compare the individual lament
Psalm 22: 4-5 and Isaiah 63: 11- 14.[9] Because the present
crisis threatens to negate everything that God has done for

[9] See C. Westermann, 'Vergegenwärtigung der Geschichte in den
Psalmen', *Theologische Bücherei* 24, 1964, pp. 306-335.

His nation, the people hold up to Him all that He has done in the past and cry to him, 'Restore us!'. The aim of this recalling of past history is to influence present history, something only possible because history and divine activity are viewed as one and the same.

vv. 12-13: As we have already noted, the lament of vv. 5-7 is resumed in these verses; from the 'how long?' of the former follows on the 'why' of the latter, which in turn takes up the contrasting element of vv. 8-11 – why dost thou destroy what thou hast built? Here again the complaint against God, 12a, is linked with the lament about enemies, 12b-13. But vv. 12-13 differ from 8-11 in that the comparison in the latter is carried further in the former: God Himself has broken down the walls of His vineyard – something quite incredible – so that it can be destroyed by robbers, depicted as wild beasts.

vv. 14-15a: And again (vv. 14-15a follow on from 12-13, in the same way as v. 7 does from 4-6), those concerned can only cry to the One from whom all things come, can only cling to the wrathful God, whose doings they no longer comprehend. Vv. 14-15a differ from vv. 3 and 7, in that here the appeal to God is still expressed in picture language: oppressed and humiliated as they are, they cry to God to return to His own creation, the garden His own hand has planted – 'have regard for this vine . . .'

Once more, we observe the power and profundity of this carefully thought-out comparison, embracing as it does three aspects of a single process: first, the planting of the vineyard, v. 8, then its destruction in the immediate situation of crisis, v. 12 and finally the appeal to God to turn again for the future to what He has made, vv. 14b, 15a. We may note a particular linguistic subtlety here: the cry of vv. 3 and 7 uses the Hiphil of *šūb*, 'restore us', but in v. 14 the Qal is used, 'turn again', since now everything hangs on God's turning again to what He has made.

vv. 16-17: A double request is made in these verses, that God will both destroy the enemies and deliver His own people. We frequently meet this double request in the psalms of lament and always at the same point, after the petition and just before the conclusion. In the form in which we have it, it resembles the petition but is to be distinguished from it because it was once an independent element, having its origin in the formula of blessing and cursing, which has subsequently been taken up into the psalms. Its roots are in the thought-world of magic and originally it worked as an ex opere operato spell, without any mention of God. It could be taken over into the communal psalms of lament, including Psalm 79, because in those days a divine intervention on behalf of Israel in a political conflict could only be viewed as an intervention against Israel's enemies, for God's activity and political events were still considered inseparable. Only as prophecy developed could this outlook change. The psalms reflect an intermediate stage: when the double request was introduced there, in place of the curse there was substituted a plea for God to act, both against the enemies, v. 16, and on behalf of Israel, v. 17. In view of the parallelism between vv. 16 and 17, the 'man of thy right hand' undoubtedly means the nation of Israel, and not, as some scholars claim, the king.

vv. 18-19: The psalm ends in v. 18 with a vow of praise: this really belongs to the individual psalm of lament and is only rarely met with in the communal laments. It is a promise of loyalty, in which the invocation of God's name belongs particularly to the setting of worship, while the words 'we will never turn back from thee' concern the people's daily life. The section begins with a petition that the people may be given life and closes with the refrain of v. 19 which strikes again the chord that sounds through the whole psalm, the cry imploring God for help.

Excursus: The Comparisons in the Psalms

If one has read Psalm 80 many times, what sticks in the

mind are the two comparisons, or 'metaphors' as they are
usually called: 'Shepherd of Israel, thou who leadest Joseph
like a flock', and then 'Thou didst bring a vine out of
Egypt'. If one gives a moment's reflection to these
comparisons, one sees that they embody distinct concepts –
God the shepherd, God the vine-grower – and if these are
referred to the nation's history, we see that they reflect
respectively the period of the desert wanderings and the age
of the settlement. In the comparisons, God's activity is
closely connected with real life. Shepherd and flock, vine-
grower and vineyard form part of the reality in which those
who hear and pray the psalm actually live. What God has
done, does and will do for His people is as real, as normal
and as natural as what the shepherd does for his flock or the
vine-grower with his vineyard. The impression conveyed
by these comparisons is this: when the psalms speak of God,
they are speaking of reality.

This applies not only to Psalm 80 but also to the psalms in
general. Here are a few examples:

> Thy arrows have sunk into me, Psalm 38: 2.
> My tears have been my food day and night, Psalm 42: 3.
> As a hart longs for flowing streams, Psalm 42: 1.
> O that I had wings like a dove, Psalm 55: 6.
> I am like a lonely bird on the housetop, Psalm 102: 7.
> Their tongues are sharp swords, Psalm 56: 8.
> Put thou my tears in thy bottle! Psalm 56: 8.
> Restore our fortunes like the water-courses in the Negeb, Psalm 126: 4.
> He will hide me in his shelter in the day of trouble, Psalm 27: 5.
> In the shadow of thy wings I will take refuge, Psalm 67: 1.
> Thou hast turned for me my mourning into dancing, Psalm 30: 11.
> As a father pities his children, Psalm 103: 13.
> The snare is broken, and we have escaped, Psalm 124: 7.
> Thy steadfast love, O Lord, extends to the heavens, Psalm 36: 5.
> With thee is the fountain of life, Psalm 36: 9.

These are only a few examples; the psalms are full of such
comparisons and only a very few psalms lack them
altogether. They are usually described as metaphors or
pictorial expressions and their purpose is seen merely as
illustrating vividly what the psalms want to say. But that is
not their true purpose. All these comparisons link what

takes place between God and man in the psalms with what takes place in the real world, the world of the one who prays the psalms. This created universe, earth and sky, land and sea, the elements and the stars, plants and animals, individual human life and life in community, all these are there in the prayers of the psalms and all join in with them. We misunderstand these comparisons if we regard them as mere illustrations, as poetic or aesthetic decoration. They belong to the real life of those who hear and speak the psalms, and as such they play an essential and indispensable rôle in what the psalms show us of the divine-human relationship -confident turning to God, lament, plea and expression of trust, praise of God in all its forms. They above all invest the psalms with shining power and human intimacy: it is our own real life of which such comparisons speak.

So it is desirable, when we hear the psalms, to pay special attention to the comparisons they contain and to linger over them and meditate on them.

Lamentations 5: Renew our days!

1   Remember, O Lord, what has befallen us;
      behold, and see our disgrace!
2   Our inheritance has been turned over to strangers,
      our homes given to aliens.
3   We have become orphans, fatherless;
      our mothers have become widows.
      We must pay for the water we drink,
      the wood we get must be bought.
5   With a yoke on our necks we are hard driven;
      we are weary, we are given no rest.
6   We have given the hand to Egypt,
      and to Assyria, to get bread enough.
7   Our fathers sinned, and are no more;
      and we bear their iniquities.
8   Slaves rule over us;
      there is none to deliver us from their hand.

9   We get our bread at the peril of our lives,
     because of the sword in the wilderness.
10   Our skin is hot as an oven
     with the burning heat of famine.
11   Women were ravished in Zion,
     virgins in the towns of Judah.
12   Princes were hung up by their hands;
     no respect was shown to the elders.
13   Young men were compelled to grind at the mill;
     and boys staggered under loads of wood.
14   The old men have quit the city gate,
     the young men their music.
15   The joy of our hearts has ceased;
     our dancing has been turned to mourning.
16   The crown has fallen from our head;
     woe to us, for we have sinned!
17   For this our heart has become sick,
     for these things our eyes have grown dim,
18   for Mount Zion which lies desolate;
     jackals prowl over it.
19   But thou, O Lord, dost reign for ever;
     thy throne endures to all generations.
20   Why dost thou forget us for ever,
     why dost thou so long forsake us?
21   Restore us to thyself, O Lord!
     Renew our days as of old!
22   Or hast thou utterly rejected us?
     Art thou exceedingly angry with us?

Text

v. 2: add *nittenū*, 'were given'.
v. 5: read *hadaphānū*, 'the yoke presses on our neck'.
v. 7: add *we*, 'but'.
v. 13: with Budde, read the Niphal instead of the Qal,
       'were compelled'.
v. 19: read *we'attāh* instead of *'attāh*.
v. 21: 'that we may be restored' is a later addition.

Structure

The structure of Lamentations 5 deviates markedly from the other communal laments, so markedly in fact that one can barely reckon it among them. Only vv. 20-22 correspond unmistakeably to the communal lament: v. 20 is a lament to God, of the 'Thou' type, with its question 'Why?', and v. 22 represents the second member of the petition. Its first member, the petition to God to return again, could lie behind the long final question: is there any hope whatsoever of God turning to us? In the structure of the psalm, the oddly isolated v. 19 corresponds to the contrasting motif, 'But thou, O God . . . ', but here it only points a contrast with God's inexplicable distancing of Himself, vv. 7, 16b.

The remainder of the psalm, vv. 2-18, is a description in lament form of the disaster which has befallen Jerusalem, corresponding to the 'we' lament, but which, in a way not found elsewhere, broadens into an outburst of grief, a pouring out of the heart before God: so unrestrained is this outburst that no clear arrangement can be discerned in it.

v 1: The congregation assembled for the ceremony of lamentation, comprising the survivors of the catastrophe, brings its suffering, 1a, and its disgrace, 1b, before God. In this psalm the events are still so close that the 'outpouring of the heart' before God consists almost entirely of a narrative describing the suffering. The dull pain, bitterness and doubt which fill the survivors' hearts are brought out and brought before God in this narrative lament. God it is who can be thus approached; one can speak out to Him, spread out the heavy burden for Him to take up – 'Remember, O Lord, what has befallen us . . . '

vv. 2-18: The lament is for the city's destruction, vv. 17-18, but the city includes the fate of the living people who are implicated in the catastrophe that has befallen it. They have lost their homes and possessions, 2, and what is worse, their families, fathers and sons, 3. A life of extreme hardship is

their lot: they must pay for water and wood, 4, and beg
food from foreigners, 6; when they seek for bread they are
in constant peril of their lives, 9, and endure bodily
torment, 10. They have lost their freedom, 8, and must
suffer severely under the occupying power, 13–16a. They
are ruled by foreigners, 8, and judicial authority has been
taken from them, 14, and they are compelled to do forced
labour, 13. On the capture of the city, women were
ravished, 11, and the upper classes executed or
dishonoured, 12. All joy has gone from the city, 14b, 15–17
(15b inverts Psalm 30: 11).

When one hears these words, one feels one is living
through what they describe, so vividly and movingly is it
depicted. This can only be explained by the fact that those
who are speaking have themselves lived through it all.
Anyone who has, in our own century, experienced the
capture of a city and life under foreign occupation can
corroborate this.

In this psalm, we have one of the rare cases when we hear
from the mouth of eye-witnesses what life was like in a
conquered city: another instance is the famous lamentation
on the destruction of Ur.[10] The description has only been
handed down to us because the survivors lamented their
suffering in an act of worship, which was able to continue
after the national collapse and in spite of the destruction of
the Temple. The lament is made up from the collecting
together of individual experiences, which receive a poetic
shape that makes them a worthy vehicle for the common
experience of the assembled community: the outcome is a
picture of Jerusalem after 587 B.C., destroyed and under
enemy occupation. Because this psalm was continually
repeated in lamentation ceremonies, there is left to us a
precious fragment of history, going back to the testimony
of eye-witnesses. It is a perfect example of a first-hand
tradition, which can be traced exactly, from its beginning to
its fixation in writing, resting in turn on the continuing
tradition of a liturgical act of lamentation that has itself

[10] Translated in W. Beyerlin, *Near Eastern Religious Texts relating to the
Old Testament*, 1978, pp. 116–118.

developed from the actual events it enshrines.

vv. 7, 16b: In sharp and notable contrast to the descriptive account are the verses which speak of the sins of the fathers, v. 7, and the people's own sins, 'woe to us, for we have sinned', v. 16b. They are to be accounted for as part of the structure of the psalm of lament, as we see from Psalm 79: 8-9. God's turning away can be justified by the people's guilt; so for God to turn again to His people a confession of sin is needed. But there is an apparent contradiction between v. 7 and v. 16b. The latter is a confession of sin, indeed a spontaneous and profoundly relevant one. The present generation unites itself with the fathers, yet so that the present generation is fully conscious of it own guilt, something that is convincingly illustrated by the book of Jeremiah. By contrast, v. 7 sounds a rebellious note: the main burden of sin lies on the shoulders of our fathers and now it is we who must bear the consequences! Here we can sense a change which paved the way for the insight clearly witnessed to by Ezekiel: the individual cannot be made answerable for the sins of his fathers. So vv. 7 and 16b can be taken together, for both were certainly said and thought at the same time under the immediate impact of the destruction of 587 B.C.

vv. 19-22: The words 'But thou . . . ' refer, as opposed to the catastrophe which has just occurred, to Yahweh's reign, which is unshaken by it and endures for ever. But Yahweh also reigns from the inexplicable remoteness in which He no longer concerns Himself with His people: v. 19 is deliberately ambiguous.

There follows an element from the traditional communal lament: God reigns at such a distance that His people cannot understand why He forgets and abandons them in all they have to endure. It is because God has abandoned them that their suffering has already lasted so inexplicably long.

Next, also reflecting the language of the psalms of lament, comes the petition. Both the verbs in v. 21 plead for restoration, that things may again be as they once were.

'Restore us to thyself' means here: 'let us once more be embraced by thy mercy'.

The psalm ends uniquely with an anxious and shattering question. The question is understandable, for God's people interpret their suffering as evidence of His alienation and wrath. God's utter rejection of His people would mean their final end.

Some other Communal Psalms of Lament

Psalm 44

The psalm is structured by the contrast between God's mighty deeds on His people's behalf in the past, vv. 1-8, and the terrible present when God no longer aids them, vv. 9-16. The complaint against God is particularly sharp and bitter: 'Yet thou hast cast us off and abased us . . . ', v. 9. Hence the psalm ends with a passionate cry for help, vv. 23-26. In the middle, however, stands the protestation that, in spite of all, the nation holds fast to its God, vv. 17-18.

Psalm 74

The centre of this psalm consists of the lament over the destruction of the sanctuary, which is described in considerable detail, vv. 3-9. Instead of the review of God's activity in history, we find a unit where attention is directed to the Creator, in the course of which the battle with Chaos is portrayed in the language of myth. vv. 12-14.

Psalm 79

The occasion of Psalm 79 is the capture and destruction of Jerusalem and the desecration of the Temple. The petitions against the enemies, vv. 6, 10, 12, and the ignominy of defeat, vv. 4, 12, are especially prominent.

Psalm 89

This psalm represents a variation from the usual communal lament in that its subject is the end of the royal house and thus of the Davidic dynasty. Set in contrast is the covenant which God formerly made with David, vv. 3-4, 19-37 (compare 2 Samuel 7). On this contrasting theme the lament to God is based. Vv. 1-2, 5-18 constitute a complete psalm of praise.

Psalm 83

Psalm 83 from beginning to end is almost entirely directed against the enemies, either by way of lament or petition. In this connection, the long list of names of peoples in vv. 6-8 is noteworthy. It is possible that these are only pseudonyms for the godless who threaten the pious. If this is correct, Psalm 83 would be evidence of how the old communal laments were adapted, in late post-exilic times. to fit the opposition of the pious to the godless which marked this late period. That is quite conceivable at a date when Israel, as merely a province of a foreign empire, could no longer wage war.

COMMUNAL PSALMS OF TRUST

Psalm 123: A Song of Ascents or Pilgrimage

1   To thee I lift up my eyes,
    O thou who art enthroned in the heavens!
2   Behold, as the eyes of servants look to the hand of
        their master,
    as the eyes of a maid to the hand of her mistress,
    so our eyes look to the Lord our God,
    till he have mercy upon us.
3   Have mercy upon us, O Lord, have mercy upon
        us,
    for we have had more than enough of contempt.
4   Too long our soul has been sated
    with the scorn of those who are at ease, the
        contempt of the proud.

Text

v. 4b: 'of those who are at ease', reading *l* instead of *h*, see
         the apparatus of BHS.
         'of the proud', reading *lega' ajōnīm* with the Ketib
         and Versions, see the apparatus of BHS.

Structure

To understand the structure, it is necessary to divide the
comparison in v. 2 from the remainder and to take the
sections v. 2 and vv. 1, 3, 4 separately. If one first brackets
v. 2, then v. 1 represents a turning towards God, as in Psalm
121: 1, with the addition of an address which follows in v. 3.
The heart of the psalm is 3a with its plea to God for mercy:

the plea receives particular emphasis in Psalm 80. The ground of the plea follows in vv. 3b and 4; the ground consists of a lament to God, in which the 'we' lament is combined with the lament about enemies.

Consequently, vv. 1, 3, 4 represent an appeal to God, expanded by the elements of a turning to God, a plea to Him for mercy and the grounding of this plea in a lament. These are all units of the communal lament, but in a much reduced form; only the plea for mercy receives any emphasis. This structure, however, is altered by the comparison in v. 2, which is at the centre of the text and controls the whole of it. This central comparison makes the text a psalm of trust, for its heart is now the comparison, whose purpose is given in the words: 'till he have mercy upon us', which correspond to the element 'the certainty of a hearing'.

v. 1: The opening verse is an introduction, in which the suppliant 'lifts his eyes to God', he directs himself to Him. This 'turning to God' introduces many Babylonian psalms but this is hardly ever the case with the Old Testament psalms: Psalm 121: 1 is exceptional. The peculiarity of this introduction reflects the peculiarity of the entire psalm; it is further developed in the comparison of v. 2. The appeal proper only follows in v. 3, but in v. 1 this expansion of the address is already anticipated in the words: 'O thou who art enthroned in the heavens'. When God is here addressed as the one enthroned in heaven, the words are intentionally ambiguous, as in Lamentations 5: 19. God is addressed as the one enthroned in majesty, that is, as the king, because as such He can accomplish everything; but at the same time we detect an echo of God's remoteness. The explanation for the change from singular to plural between v. 1 and v. 2 is probably that 1a represents a turn of phrase modelled on one really belonging to the individual lament.

v. 2: The lifting of the eyes to God, v. 1, is portrayed in a comparison with a form often encountered – as, *ke* . . . so, *kēn*, 'as the eyes . . . so our eyes'. Comparisons in this form are particularly frequent in the book of Proverbs, for

example Proverbs 25: 3, 11, 13, 20, 26, 28. The comparison
begins with 'Behold . . . ', *hinnēh*; this calls attention to the
introduction of a new theme, 'pay heed!', and singles out
the comparison from its context as an independent unit
with its own particular significance. And the two halves of
the comparison, 'the eyes of servants . . . the eyes of a
maid', have the same function. The second half, the maid,
adds nothing new to the content of the verse. However, the
second half creates a parallelism which gives the
comparison greater force. Something similar occurs when
in narratives a dream is given greater weight by being one of
a pair, as we see in the Joseph story. But what lies behind the
intention of giving greater weight to the comparison? It
would have been sufficient to say: 'To thee we lift our eyes,
as servants look to their master', as in no. 195 of the Amarna
Letters: 'Our lord is the sun in heaven. And as on the rising
of the sun in heaven, so his servants wait on the words that
spring from their lord's mouth'. The intention can only be
to let the comparison speak for itself; those who pray the
psalm are to linger over the comparison. Hence, v. 2,
properly speaking, does not just explain or illustrate what is
implied by the congregation's plea for God's mercy in vv.
1, 3, 4, which would be unnecessary, but rather strengthens
and intensifies it. To be more precise: without the
comparison, the object of the plea remains wholly vague,
but, with it, it is made definite, in particular through the
phrase 'till he have mercy upon us', *'ad šejeḥonnēnū*. It is
made into a tightly knit movement from the opening
'lifting up of the eyes' to its final goal, God's turning back.
So the 'till' contrasts with the 'how long?' of the lament that
sounds in vv. 3b, 4a. This clearly articulated movement or
gradient is expressed in terms of human relationships,
master and servant, mistress and maid, which reflect the
realm of experience of those who speak the psalm. By the
conjunction of the comparison with the congregation's
appeal and God's answer, the latter becomes part of the
'real-life' situation depicted in the former. What happens
between God and man becomes authentic and human, a
reality already experienced and capable of being

experienced again – 'so . . . as'. So Psalm 123 provides the perfect example of an Old Testament comparison, in the light of which the parables of Jesus, such as that of the widow, Luke 18: 1-8, can be more clearly defined.

Support for this understanding of v. 2 comes from the fact that in it the relationship of master and servant and mistress and maid is viewed wholly positively, as in the patriarchal history and many other Old Testament passages. When it is said that servant and maid look to the *hand* of their master or mistress, what is meant is their kindly 'handling' by their superiors. Thus understood, 'to look to the hand' can be used as meaning 'to ask', compare Ecclesiasticus 33: 21: 'It is better that your children should ask from you, than that you should look to the hand of your sons'.

v. 3a: The repeated 'Have mercy upon us' or 'Be gracious to us' is the heart of the psalm. It is itself not a complete psalm but an appeal to God for mercy, that as a rule forms a single psalm unit. Psalm 123 shows that such psalm units were self-contained pleas to God independent of the liturgy, just like the cry for mercy which the sufferers addressed to Jesus as he was passing by: 'they cried aloud, "Have mercy on us, Son of David!"', Matthew 9: 27.

vv. 3b, 4: The lament is not an independent unit; it is introduced simply as a subordinate sentence, giving the grounds for the plea. Also, this two-member sentence gives the grounds for the lament only in terms of the effect of the distress on those involved and says nothing about the distress itself. The description betrays an amazing reticence; v. 3b says only, 'we can no more!', 'we have had more than enough of contempt', and v. 4 says the same somewhat more fully, listing the source of the contempt as 'those who are at ease' and 'the proud'. The expressions do not indicate exactly what is meant, but the reference has a social rather than a political context, compare Isaiah 32: 9, 11; Amos 6: 1; Zechariah 1: 15. Again, there is no indication of the nature of the distress which has provoked the cry for help. The

psalm stresses so powerfully the cry for mercy and the
certainty of God's response that everything else retreats into
the background.

Psalm 126: Those who sow in tears shall reap with shouts of joy

1. When the Lord restored the fortunes of Zion,
    we were like those who dream.
2   Then our mouth was filled with laughter,
    and our tongue with shouts of joy;
    then they said among the nations,
    'The Lord has done great things for them'.
3   Yes, the Lord has done great things for us;
    we are glad.
4   Restore our fortunes, O Lord,
    like the water-courses in the Negeb!
5   Those who sow in tears
    shall reap with shouts of joy!
6   He that goes forth weeping,
    bearing the seed for sowing,
    shall come home with shouts of joy,
    bringing his sheaves with him.

Text

v. 1:   vv. 1-3 speak of the past, not, as in Luther's
        translation, of the future.
v. 6:   read *mōsēk* for *mesek*, see the apparatus of BHS and
        Amos 9: 13.

Structure

This psalm is concerned with the fortunes of the nation and
the middle verse, v. 4, is a plea for a change in them, and so
an element of the communal lament. But as with Psalm 123,

the plea for change is so much the heart of the psalm that everything else is related and subordinate to it. Again like Psalm 123, the plea is determined by the confident trust expressed in vv. 5-6; hence we are dealing with a psalm of trust. The opening words describe an earlier divine act of deliverance. But, unlike Psalm 80: 8-11, the purpose here is not to exert influence on God, but the trust is to be confirmed by a future divine deliverance. After the plea for change in v. 4, there follows, in 5-6, an expression of certainty founded on that earlier experience, 1-3, that the present distress too will be changed by God.

The structure of the psalm corresponds to no regular psalm type: basic to it is the *single* motif, as in Psalm 123, of the plea for the removal of distress, in a framework of expressions of confidence.

vv. 1-3: Many in Germany will have in mind Luther's translation: 'When the Lord shall free Zion's prisoners, then shall we be like those who dream . . .'. But linguistic usage requires that the words look back to the past, and the Septuagint translates them in this way. Nevertheless, to translate them as future does not wholly destroy the coherence of the psalm, since vv. 4-6 speak of the future.

v. 1: Basic to the psalm is the expression *šub šebut*, as we should emend it in v. 1. It opens the review of the past in v. 1, it is taken up again in the plea for the removal of the distress in v. 4, and it is also echoed in vv. 5 and 6. This idiom, which is frequently met with, for example, in Jeremiah 31: 23, means literally 'to restore the restoration'; it represents a strengthening of the verb by a noun from the same root, and so the sense is 'to bring about a change'. Almost always, Israel is the object and God the intended subject. And generally the reference is to the restoration following the catastrophe of 587 B.C. as in Psalm 85: 1.[11] The use of this expression makes it likely, though not

[11] See the article *šub* by J. A. Soggin, edd. E. Jenni and C. Westermann, *Theologisches Handwörterbuch zum Alten Testament, II*, 1976, pp. 884-891, especially pp. 886-888, where all the relevant passages are given.

certain, that vv. 1-3 look back to the return from exile and the new beginning in the former homeland. 'We are like those who dream' – the change was so unexpected, so overwhelming, that it could hardly be grasped. This is proved by the message of Second Isaiah, whose heralding of this change in fact met with considerable scepticism and rejection.

vv. 2-3: The two opening clauses of v. 2 are in synonymous parallelism. But really they are only a single sentence, recalling the joy which then filled the entire nation. Second Isaiah's summons to rejoice and his songs of praise looking ahead to the future, for example, Isaiah 40: 9-11; 42: 10-13, were not in vain. The great time of joy has arrived, says Psalm 126: 2, and the return of Israel from exile has also made a profound impression on the surrounding world, which perceives and recognizes what Israel's God has done for His people: we may compare Exodus 18: 9. And what the others perceive is confirmed by Israel as the people praise God for His mighty deeds and recall the joy of those days.

Two contexts are to be noted here. The first is a temporal one: the Old Testament's strong historical consciousness rests on the fact that the memory of past historical events gains a new lease of life when their recalling has significance for the present, when it has an effect on the present. Such is the case here: the present severe distress, vv. 4-6, awakens the memory of God's mighty deeds in the past, in particular the mighty deed of the return from exile. This serves to strengthen confidence in God's help for the present situation. So a three-stage structure is generated in our psalm; deliverance from past distress, 1-3, a plea in present distress, 4, and the future prospect of the removal of that distress, 5-6. But the strong awareness, which is visible here, of the nation's history as a connected chain of events, is only possible because one and the same God is active in that history. This ordered historical process derives from the plans and actions of God and the nation's rôle in it is to respond to the divine activity with petition and praise.

The second context relates to content: what the nation experiences on the road of history is always something in which the nation itself, the other nations, 2b, and God all participate, and this corresponds to the three elements of the lament.

v. 4: At the centre of the psalm lies the plea to God for help, a prayer which could also exist independently. We have already met the phrase 'Restore our fortunes' in v. 1 and the repetition here chimes in with that: thou hast once before restored our fortunes! – there is an unspoken hint of the divine activity in the course of history. As in Psalm 123, a comparison is joined to the plea, 'like the water-courses in the Negeb'. The meaning is that the streams disappear in the dry season but, as R. de Vaux, writes, 'in the winter they suddenly swell up and make the land fruitful'. The comparison is with the surprising and wonderful restoration. The psalm takes it for granted that the work of God as Creator and of God as Lord of history are to be seen together: in both it is the same God who works renewal!

vv. 5–6: These two verses are in parallelism; v. 6 says the same as v. 5, only somewhat more fully. A phase of an individual's life or a phase of a nation's history may begin in deep distress, 'to sow in tears', but a miraculous transformation can bring it to a successful conclusion. These verses do not view such a transformation just as a possibility or a wishful longing; they pronounce that it will certainly happen, as the progression from v. 5 to v. 6 shows. So the end of the psalm, referring back to its beginning in vv. 1–3, becomes a declaration of confident trust, and these concluding words also depict creation and history as a single unity.

This psalm is one of the finest examples in the Old Testament of how God's ancient people throughout its history held fast to its God with utter confidence during times of dire distress, and so found in its history a meaning which could reconcile it to all disasters.

Psalm 124: The snare is broken!

1.   If it had not been the Lord who was on our side,
     let Israel now say –
2   if it had not been the Lord who was on our side,
     when men rose up against us,
3   then they would have swallowed us up alive,
     when their anger was kindled against us;
4   then the flood would have swept us away,
     the torrent would have gone over us;
5   then over us would have gone the raging waters.
6   Blessed be the Lord, who has not given us as prey to
        their teeth!
7   Our soul has escaped
     as a bird from the snare of the fowlers;
     the snare is broken, and we have escaped!
8   Our help is in the name of the Lord,
     who made heaven and earth.

Text

v. 1: Literally, 'if not Yahweh (it had been), who for us
    (was)'.
v. 3: *'azaj* = *'āz*, compare Psalm 119: 92, an Aramaism,
    as is the relative particle *še*.
v. 4: *naḥlah* for *naḥal*; 'us', *nefeš*, here is literally 'throat',
    'neck', in contrast to v. 7 where it means 'soul',
    'life'.

Structure

The strict psalm structure is not found in this text. Only in
v. 6, perhaps including v. 7, is there a psalm motif proper, a
shout of praise, 'blessed be Yahweh!', with the ground for it
in the following relative clause, 6b, and the sequel in v. 7. It
is preceded in vv. 1-5 by a repeated 'if – then' clause, not
attested elsewhere, which describes the threat and God's

intervention to avert it. V. 8 is a liturgical supplement. When we ask how the psalm developed, we must begin by observing that the central expression 'Blessed be the Lord' often occurs in narrative texts, where it is a shout of praise that expresses the immediate and appropriate reaction to a given situation, for example Exodus 18: 10. These *bārūk* clauses, 'blessed be . . . ' are among those psalm elements which once existed independently. The shout of praise has become a psalm in the true sense by the addition of the account of the preceding threat, 1-5, and the subsequent deliverance and liberation, 7. V. 7 is poetry and could therefore be the original continuation of v. 6. By contrast, vv. 1-5 is in its basic structure a prose sentence, with the striking opening 'let Israel say'. The Aramaisms point to a late date of composition.

vv. 1-5: The wholly artificial pattern 'if (not) . . . then' is an addition, more precisely a reflective expansion of the central words of the psalm in v. 6. God has not given us as a prey to their teeth, but had God not helped us, then . . . Such a reflection, carrying the thought further, 'had it not so happened, then . . . ', does not correspond to the language of the psalms, but has been made conformable to it by the by the use of parallelism and metre. Isaiah 1: 9 provides a close parallel: 'If the Lord of hosts had not left us a few survivors, we should have been like Sodom, and become like Gomorrah'. Isaiah 1: 9 is probably a later addition[12] and it corresponds in form and content to the later expansion in Psalm 124: 1-5. The construction 'if – then', *lūlēj – 'āz*, only occurs elsewhere in this sense at Psalm 119: 92, a fact which also indicates a late date.

vv. 1-2: The first sentence, 'if not . . . ', comprises two verses and four half-verses. In fact it is one single sentence and really in prose: 'If it had not been Yahweh on our side, when men rose up against us . . . ' Out of this sentence, two

---

[12] See F. Crüsemann, *Studien zur Formgeschichte von Hymnus und Danklied in Israel*, Wissenschaftliche Monographien zum Alten und Neuen Testament 32, 1969, pp. 162-164.

verses were constructed by repeating its first section, vv. 1a
and 2b, and by the addition of the words 'let Israel now say',
Apart from Psalm 129: 1, where Psalm 129: 1-2 are
constructed in much the same way as Psalm 124: 1-2, we
meet these words only at Psalm 118: 2-4, a passage which
seems to contain directions for worship. Here the words
adapt the prose sentence to the language of worship. In vv.
1-2 the distress is referred to only in very general terms, as is
the divine aid, here 'for us' in place of the usual 'with us'.
The enemies are called simply 'men', a feature otherwise
found only in individual psalms of lament or praise, for
example Psalm 56: 1; 57: 4 among others.

vv. 3-5: The following clause extends to three verses; what
it has to say is adequately summed up in v. 3a: 'then they
would have swallowed us up alive'. This prose passage is at
one place, 3b, expanded by the stock expression: 'when
their anger was kindled against us', which in content
properly belongs to 2b as the second half-line. The other
expansion is a comparison: the enemies' attack is compared
with an inundation of flood waters, as also, for example, in
Psalm 93: 3. The comparison of v. 4 is repeated in
somewhat different words in v. 5.

vv. 6-7: V. 6 contains the kernel of the psalm, a shout of
praise, or an exclamation, corresponding to our 'thank
God', 'Blessed (be) the Lord', *bārūk yhwh*, to which is added
a relative clause, setting out the ground for the shout of
praise: 'who has not given us as a prey to their teeth', which
in turn is developed in the comparison of v. 7. The shout of
praise *bārūk yhwh* with a following relative clause is a
regular and frequently occurring form, see below p. 53.

But the passages in which this form is found differ from
the shout of praise at v. 6 in two respects, and properly to
understand our psalm demands a comparison with these
other passages.[13] The first point is that all these passages,
apart from three in the Psalter, for which see below, occur

[13] See F. Crüsemann, *op. cit.*, pp. 160-168.

in narratives in the historical books. In most of them the situation is identical: we have the exclamation of someone who has just been saved from a dangerous or tense situation. The exclamation voices the sigh of relief of the one who has found deliverance or safety.

Excursus: In Genesis 24: 27, the servant who has succeeded in his mission says: 'Blessed be the Lord . . . who has not forsaken his steadfast love and his faithfulness toward my master'; in 1 Samuel 25: 32, and compare v. 39, David says when he meets Abigail: 'Blessed be the Lord . . . who sent you this day to me'; in 2 Samuel 18: 28, the messenger says to David: 'Blessed be the Lord . . . who has delivered up the men who raised their hand against my lord the king'; in Ruth 4: 14: 'Blessed be the Lord, who has not left you this day without next of kin'. To these examples may be added Genesis 14: 20; Exodus 18: 10; 2 Samuel 22: 47; 1 Kings 1: 48; 5: 7; 8: 56; 10: 9; Ezra 7: 27; 2 Chronicles 6: 4.

All these passages are reports or narratives – in this case the two cannot be distinguished – which speak of a divine act of deliverance or aid. Since all the relative clauses depend on the cry 'Blessed be God!',[14] this group of passages provides important proof for the motif 'narrative praise'.[15] This differs from what we call 'thanksgiving' in that it includes an account of what God has done and for which He is to be praised (for the difference between 'praising' and 'thanksgiving', see p. 168 f. below). But none of these passages are parts of psalms. They all occur in narratives and all have their place as an essential part of the narrative, as the reaction to something that has just happened. As such, they belong to the pre-cultic stage of prayer,[16] when the individual psalm motifs, such as the cry for help, the vow or shout of praise, still had an independent existence and were outside the cult and preceded it: indeed, we meet these

[14] See *Theologisches Handwörterbuch zum Alten Testament I*, 1971, pp. 353–376, especially pp. 355–358.
[15] For this, see C. Westermann, *Praise and Lament in the Psalms*, 1981, pp. 81–90 and 102–116.
[16] For this, see p. 13 above.

motifs in colloquial speech and in tales and romances down to our own day. Later they became a unit of the psalms. The second point in which Psalm 124: 6 differs from this parallel group of passages is that in the latter the speaker is almost always an individual, and the same remains the case even when the phenomenon under discussion becomes an element in a psalm, for example, Psalm 28: 6: 'Blessed be the Lord, *bārūk yhwh*, for he has heard the voice of my supplications' or Psalm 31: 21: 'Blessed be the Lord, for he has wondrously shown his steadfast love to me when I was beset'; other instances are Psalms 66: 20; 72: 18; 68: 19; 144: 1. These passages show that the idiom 'Blessed be the Lord . . . who has done' was originally an individual's shout of praise. Psalm 124 presents a change when this motif is made to refer to a group or the majority. Psalm 124 is thus certainly a communal psalm of praise, or perhaps a psalm of a particular group, but it does not provide a model from which we could derive a specific psalm category.[17] Rather, it is a late transformation of a motif only really suitable to an individual speaker;[18] and the same is true of Psalm 129. No doubt Israel once knew communal psalms of praise, as well as the corresponding psalms of lament, but these have not been preserved in the Psalter. The reason for their disappearance lies in the fact that the Psalter was only formed in the post-exilic period. Hence nothing can be said about the date or setting of Psalm 124, though we should think of it as rather late. Nor can we discover who are the enemies; vv. 1–3 and 6 suggest a military operation, but it is also possible that the godless are intended, as in Psalm 83. But no certain answer can be given.

The shout of praise in v. 6 compares the enemies with beasts of prey: ' . . . as prey to their teeth'. The following verse gives expression to the joy of those who have escaped, using the comparison of the net or snare of the hunter or fowler. Both comparisons occur frequently in individual laments, referring to the psalmist's enemies, the godless.

[17] For this, see the references listed in footnote 15.
[18] See F. Crüsemann, *op. cit.*, pp. 160–168.

Here the comparison is taken over by a group, which was under the severest enemy threat but now has been freed. The comparison with a bird loosed from the fowler's snare expresses particularly vividly the experience of freedom: it highlights the moment of freedom which the creature experiences. Anyone who hears or recites it can sense what is meant by the words 'as a bird'. And what is meant becomes still clearer when we further realize that Hebrew has no word for 'freedom'. Freedom belongs so absolutely to human existence that life without it is not really human life at all; and this is common to men and all living creatures.

The entire psalm, but especially the way v. 7 follows on from v. 6, shows that, for those who created and recited it, it was the experience of being set free that directed their gaze to the One who had freed them – 'If it had not been the Lord who was on our side . . . '

v. 8: The verse is a liturgical addition, which picks up again the opening of the psalm in the language of worship. It tells the hearers of the psalm that they have a helper and that this helper is the Creator, in whose hand are all things and whose help knows no bounds.

THE ROYAL PSALMS

With the royal psalms, a political institution takes its place in Israel's worship. Kingship is the only political institution in human history which is as such at the same time a sacral institution, for all kingship is in origin sacral. Kingship in the world surrounding Israel, Egypt, Mesopotamia and Canaan, differed in different areas but everywhere it was closely linked with the gods.[19] It is thus only to be expected that among the psalms we meet a group of royal psalms. They belong to two periods in the history of Israelite worship, to worship during the monarchy and after its end. But they have a different function in each of these periods. During the monarchy, they refer to the reigning king; after it, in the post-exilic period, they give expression to the expectation of a new and different king, the Messiah.

A formal category of royal psalms is not found in the Psalter; they are all different. All they have in common is that they are concerned with the king; the psalms in question are Psalms 2; 18; 20; 21; 45; 61: 6-7; 63: 11; 72; 89; 101; 132; 144. We can conclude therefore that Israel's worship never reached the point of coining an independent category of royal psalms.

A. The content of two psalms, 2 and 110, points to the accession of a new king and hence their setting is the coronation ceremony or an annual festival in which this was ritually celebrated. In them we are able to discover some of the coronation rites, the most important being a word from God to the king. Psalm 2: 6-9 is the divine promise to the monarch. The opening of Psalm 110 shows that the whole psalm is such a divine promise; hence Psalm 110 is not really a psalm but rather a royal oracle, remotely similar to the prophetic oracle of weal.

B. Another act of worship can be recognized in connection with the monarchy, the offering of prayer and

[19] See C. Westermann, 'Das sakrale Königtum', *Theologische Bücherei* 55, 1974, pp. 291-308.

praise for the king. This will have played an important rôle, since it is the commonest element in the royal psalms. Psalms 20 and 21 are linked together as respectively offering such prayer and praise. Behind Psalm 20 lies the individual lament, but considerably changed; in place of the plea for deliverance, a prayer for God's perpetual help is introduced. Behind Psalm 21 lies the narrative praise of the individual thanksgiving psalm, but instead of the report of deliverance we have the report of God's blessings to the king, vv. 3-6, and the future blessings desired for him, vv. 8-12. Psalm 72 is also a petition for the king, in the form of a wish which seeks to embrace the whole being and activity of the monarch. The first part of Psalm 132 too is a petition for the king. In Psalm 61, a petition that the king may enjoy a long life, vv. 6-7, is inserted into an otherwise unaltered individual lament. Similarly v. 11 of Psalm 63, a psalm of trust, is an addition concerned with the king; compare also Psalms 28: 8; 84: 9.

C. Psalm 18 = 2 Samuel 22 is a narrative psalm of praise or thanksgiving, in which the king himself is the speaker. Vv. 1-30 constitute an individual psalm of praise, unchanged except for an added description of an epiphany; vv. 31-50 represent a king's praise of God, or his victory song, praising the God who supports him in the field against his enemies. Traces of a similar psalm are also to be found in Psalm 144, which is made up of fragments.

D. Psalm 45 is a royal wedding song, extolling the beauty of the king and the queen, perhaps also sung at a dynastic festival.

E. Psalm 132 is a psalm for a festival celebrating both the king and Zion. In this connection, it commemorates David's bringing up the ark to Mount Zion and Nathan's promise for the dynasty.

F. Psalm 101 is a king's vow, probably on the occasion of his coronation, with respect to his behaviour, vv. 1-4, and the exercise of his office, vv. 5- 8. But a royal vow of this kind seems only to form the background of the psalm, which is quite unpolitical and does not mention any of the king's official duties. We could think of the way in which the book of Ecclesiastes is dressed up as a royal speech. The psalm is governed by the contrast between the pious man and the godless man and recalls the language of Psalm 1.

G. Psalm 89 is a communal lament, occasioned by the fall of the Davidic dynasty in 587 B.C. Vv. 38-51 comprise the communal lament; it is preceded by a recalling of Nathan's promise for David and his line, vv. 19-37 along with 3-4, functioning as the review of God's former actions, and is in turn preceded by a psalm of praise, vv. 5-18.

Something should now be said about the relationship of the royal psalms to other psalm types. Only in Psalm 89 is the *communal lament* on the occasion of the catastrophe of 587 B.C. fully integrated with a royal psalm, for the collapse of the state and the collapse of the dynasty are one and the same. A faint echo of the communal lament can be heard in Psalm 2, although there it is not the distress caused by an enemy victory which is described, but rather a threat from the nations, vv. 1-3, which, however, will be neutralized by God's promise to the king, vv. 4-9.

The petition for the king is sometimes added or adapted to the *individual lament*, Psalms 20; 61; 63; 72.

A royal victory song is linked with the *individual psalm of praise* in Psalm 18, while in Psalm 21 what is said in praise of the king is an adaptation of it.

The royal wedding song of Psalm 45 shows no connection with other psalm types.

The whole of Psalm 110 represents the *royal oracle*, a divine word addressed to the king in the course of worship, probably by a cultic prophet; the oracle is found also in Psalm 2: 6-9 and presupposed by Psalm 20: 6. A specially significant rôle is played in it by Nathan's promise, which we meet in Psalms 132: 11-12 and 89: 19-37.

Background in the History of Religions

Kingship as it was introduced into Israel had already existed for centuries and millennia among Israel's neighbours. Moreover, it is a type of leadership known throughout the entire world. It follows therefore that governmental organization, centred on the court, and rituals associated with kingship, everywhere displayed many common features, and that the adoption of royal organization and rites involved also the adoption of the language of monarchy in the shape of specific terms, set forms and written texts. In this respect, Israel was no different from other nations. We can speak of a 'court style' which was widely disseminated in the ancient Near East and which helps us to understand many features of Israel's royal psalms, for example, statements about the extent of the king's dominions, which go far beyond anything that could ever actually be realized. Other exaggerated royal predicates in these psalms are also to be explained in the same way. A profusion of royal oracles is known from Mesopotamia and such oracles were probably taken over into Israel's coronation ceremony, as we see especially in Psalms 2 and 110. The distinctively Israelite elements in the royal psalms are those which show the clearest dependence on other psalm types in the Psalter.

Messianic significance

Not one royal psalm originated as a prediction of a future saviour king; all of them originally referred to the king actually reigning at the time. A messianic meaning was given to them only after the disappearance of the Davidic dynasty. In particular, it arose from the contrast between Nathan's promise of an everlasting rule for David's house and the fact that that the dynasty had ceased to be a political reality, the situation reflected in psalm 89.

The royal psalms were admitted to the Psalter when it was collected together after the exile because they were now understood messianically; this is shown by the way in which royal psalms have been added on the fringes of already existing psalm collections.[20]

<hr/>

[20] See C. Westermann, 'Zur Sammlung des Psalters', *Theologische Bücherei 24*, 1964, pp. 336-343.

Psalm 72: A Psalm of Solomon

1   Give the king thy justice, O God,
     and thy righteousness to the royal son!
2   May he judge thy people with righteousness,
     and thy poor with justice!
3   Let the mountains bear prosperity for the people,
        and the hills righteousness!
4   He shall defend the cause of the poor of the
        people,
     he shall give deliverance to the children of the
        needy,
     but crush the oppressor.
5   May he live while the sun endures,
        and as long as the moon, throughout all
        generations.

6   May it be like rain that falls on the mown grass,
     like showers that water the earth!

7   In his days may righteousness flourish, and
        abundance of peace,
     till the moon be no more!

8   He shall have dominion from sea to sea,
     and from the River to the ends of the earth.
9   His foes shall bow down before him,
     and his enemies lick the dust.
10   The kings of Tarshish and the isles shall render him
        tribute,
     the kings of Sheba and Seba bring gifts.
11   All kings shall fall down before him,
     all nations serve him.

12   For he delivers the needy when he calls,
     and the poor, who has no helper.
13   He has pity on the weak and the needy,
     and saves the lives of the needy.

14 From oppression and violence he redeems their
       life,
    and precious is their blood in his sight.
15a [Long may he live, may gold of Sheba be given to
       him!]
15b May prayer be made for him continually, and
       blessings invoked for him all the day!
16 There shall be abundance of grain in the land,
    on the tops of the mountains may it wave;
    may its fruit be like Lebanon,
    its shoots blossom forth.
17 May his name endure for ever, as long as the sun,
    may his fame flourish,
    like the grass of the field!
    In his name shall bless themselves all races of the
       earth,
    all nations call him blessed!

Text

v. 5: *weja'arīk* is to be read with the Septuagint.
v. 6: 'may it', see the comment below.
v. 9: reading *ṣārājw* for *sijjīm*.
v 16: 'there shall be' or 'may there be'. For *jir'aš* read
        ja'asīy, for *mē'īr* read *'amīrājw*.
v. 17: 'may his fame flourish' or 'may his seed have
        issue'.

Structure

The structure of this psalm is unclear; the various elements
and motifs run into one another. Also, only minute traces
remain of the underlying psalm type. But this much is clear:
it is a petition for the reigning king and so of pre- exilic date.
Its setting is the coronation ceremony or some other royal
festival, such as that in Psalm 132. Probably, however, it
found its place in the Psalter because it was interpreted

messianically, as the later changes made to it suggest. To make the explanation easier to follow, we shall not go through the psalm verse by verse but discuss each of the leading motifs in turn.

A petition that the king may govern justly, vv. 1, 2, (3), 4, (7): **vv. 1-4**: The psalm starts by addressing God in a petition for the king, uttered at a religious festival. In it the just government of the king is placed at the beginning and is strongly emphasized, vv. 1-4, 7. The king is to be specially concerned for the poor and needy, vv. 2, 4, 12-14. In royal hymns and rituals from the ancient Near East the just rule of the king and his concern for the weak is repeatedly stressed,[21] but the particular emphasis on the poor and needy here may represent post-exilic changes to the text with the king of the future era of salvation in mind, compare Isaiah 11: 1-11; 32: 1 ff.; Jeremiah 23: 5 f.; Zechariah 9: 9. These changes may have affected vv. 3 and 7 which originally spoke only of abundant blessings (mountains and hills, v. 3, abundance and fertility, v. 7). But even if this is so, it was the Israelite king's supreme duty to rule justly and to protect the weak, as had always been the case throughout the whole ancient Near East. Behind the form of words in v. 1, 'Give the king thy justice, O God' lies the very ancient notion that the legal statutes were actually handed to the king in a cultic ceremony on the occasion of his coronation.[22]

A petition for the king's person, vv. 1, 5, 15, 17: This motif is inseparable from the preceding one and v. 1 is the introduction to both. All over the world we find petitions which primarily ask that the king may enjoy a long life, as here in vv. 5 and 15; we may compare Psalm 89: 36-37 and an inscription of Ashurbanipal.[23] The cry 'Long live the king!' was heard at every royal coronation for thousands of years and still is at the coronation of British monarchs.

[21] See the work referred to in footnote 4.
[22] On the poor in this connection, see H.-J. Kraus, *Psalmen*, Biblischer Kommentar XV, 1958, pp. 82-83.
[23] Translated in J.B. Pritchard, *Ancient Near Eastern Texts Relating to the Old Testament*, 1952, p. 300.

Behind it lies an age-old concept of sacral kingship, that the life of the nation was inextricably bound up with the life of the king. So the lengthy extension of the petition, 'while the sun endures, and as long as the moon', is no extravagant exaggeration: while the king continues to live, so does the nation. The fact that this petition for a long life, as with similar ones elsewhere, says nothing about the king's health, is the result of a different understanding of what is meant by 'life': 'life' in the full sense includes health, freedom from injury and joy in living.

v. 15a: 'Long may he live, may gold of Sheba be given to him': wealth and splendour are the marks of the king and his court, and this is so throughout the whole world. Originally, this wealth and splendour only reflected the blessing bestowed on the country: where there is affluence, there is blessing. How dangerous the wealth of the king and the splendour of the court could become is shown by Solomon's reign, and so the saviour king expected in future is to be poor, Zechariah 9: 9.

v. 17: More important is the belief, which is inseparably connected with kingship, that the king is the one blessed of God. Blessing here includes what we mean by 'good fortune'; a king must enjoy good fortune. The royal state of blessing radiates tremendous power. 'In his name shall bless themselves all races of the earth', that is, by invoking his name they are asking a blessing for themselves; the same is said of Abraham, Genesis 12: 3.[24]

vv. 3, 6, 16: The blessing bestowed on the king brings about the fertility of the land, its crops and fruits – 'May it (the blessing) be like rain that falls on the mown grass, like showers that water the earth', v. 6 Here again is an ancient concept belonging to sacral kingship, that the king, as the bearer of blessing, bestows fertility and prosperity on his

---

[24] See C. Westermann, *Genesis 12-36*, translated by J.J. Scullion, 1986, p. 150.

country: 'May there be abundance of grain in the land, on the tops of the mountains may it wave', v. 16. And it is characteristic that blessing and just government work together: 'Let the mountains bear prosperity for the people and the hills righteousness!', v. 3.

vv. 7, 12-14: This is the central part of the psalm, into which vv. 8-11 have been subsequently inserted. We may ask whether here it is the reigning king who is meant or whether the passage is looking to the king who will come with the era of salvation. The wording of v. 7 suggests that the latter is intended: 'In his days may righteousness flourish, and peace abound, till the moon be no more'. But this could be an older text, referring to the reigning king, and only slightly altered. However, a future reference best suits vv. 12-14, where the whole emphasis falls on the concern of the saviour king for the weak and needy and the language is reminiscent of the post-exilic period. In any event, the passage shows how easily the late development of the idea of a future king of peace could be grafted on to the ancient royal prayers.

vv. 8-11: These verses give the impression of being a later expansion. This is the only place in the psalm which mentions a foreign policy of conquest and domination over other nations and their kings, such as we see in Psalm 2. The section only strengthens the impression that what was stressed in the ancient royal prayers of Israel was the king as the mediator of blessing, as the preserver of peace through the exercise of justice and righteousness and as the protector of the weak and helpless.

But at the same time, the psalm mirrors the expectations current in Israel after the exile, when one part of the nation looked for a king of peace without splendour or political power and another part for a king who would restore Israel to its former political supremacy and bring victory over the neighbouring peoples. This conflict persisted even up to New Testament times.

THE INDIVIDUAL PSALMS OF LAMENT

The individual psalm of lament is the most common psalm type in the Psalter. More than fifty of the 150 Psalms are of this type, Psalms 3-17 (with the exception of 8; 9; 15); 22-28 (except for 24); 35-43 (except for 37); part of 40; 51-64 (with the exception of 60), and many individual passages as well. Outside the Psalter we have Lamentations 3; Jeremiah 11; 15; 17; 18; 20 and many sections in the book of Job; individual motifs typical of this psalm category occur frequently. But this does not mean that the individual psalm of lament should be considered the most important of the various types of psalms. The large number of examples is accounted for by the period when the Psalter was formed as a collection. At this time, the identity of nation and worshipping congregation was dissolved and the division into pious and godless became a decisive factor. The division is mirrored time and time again in the individual laments. This particular situation must always be kept in view when one considers both the large number of individual laments in the Psalter and also their content. For side by side with some of these psalms, which are among the most beautiful and profound in the Psalter and which we can use as our own prayers, as if they had been written with us in view, there are others of which we are forced to ask whether as Christians we really can recite and pray them, because of the imprecations against the psalmist's The individual psalm of lament is the most common psalm decisive an element in a psalm that one has been led to speak of 'revenge psalms', though this name is not wholly justified. The enemies in the psalms of lament are discussed below in the excursus on pp. 297-8.

But there is another and more significant way of viewing the individual psalms of lament. They provide the clearest evidence that the Old Testament knows not only the prayer of God's people on its journey through history but also the personal prayer of the individual which arises from his day-to-day experiences, and that the Old Testament gives full weight to this.

Psalm scholarship has long been dominated by the opinion that Israel's worship consisted primarily of the important Temple festivals, so that 'cult' is virtually identical with 'festal cult'. But this is impossible, if only for the reason that the Temple personnel, priests, Levites, Temple singers and the other Temple servants, would then have been employed only for a few weeks in the year, and this can be ruled out on economic grounds. Rather the Temple was so central to the nation's life that something was always going on there the whole year through; and this is the impression we receive from the New Testament, when we read the story of the twelve-year-old Jesus in the Temple or the parable of the Pharisee and the tax-collector. Included in what went on in the Temple were regular visits by families and individuals, such as the family of Hannah in 1 Samuel 1 or King Hezekiah in Isaiah 38. And because in their private sphere families and individuals live by the blessing which is experienced in the Temple and which flows out from the Temple, the prayer of the individual also has a momentous place in the Psalter. Hence we must suppose that there was once a wide variety of such individual prayers, though only traces of them remain in the Psalter. There were the prayers of a person in sickness, of someone unjustly accused, of someone seeking sanctuary, of a barren woman, 1 Samuel 1, and many others. But such prayers could be uttered not only in the Temple but equally outside it, for example on a sick-bed, in exile and so on. Further, from time to time and under certain conditions – of which we are, however, ignorant – the individual petitioner could receive from a priest the assurance that his prayer would be heard, as happened to Hannah; that is, the priest would give him an 'oracle of weal'. We must not, however, think of this as obligatory, so that the assurance of being heard was always more or less given automatically. The situation remained open, receiving such an oracle was not more than a possibility, and this is what we find in many psalms, as well as in the case of Hezekiah's illness, for Isaiah 38 clearly pictures the assurance given by the prophet as something exceptional. But common to all psalms of lament is a movement from the lament to the relief of the suffering, in which they achieve their fulfilment.[25]

A Note on the Lament

In the course of Christian history the lament has completely, or almost completely, vanished from Christian prayer. Lament is seen as a negative way of speaking, unfitted for a prayer to God. In private prayer and public liturgy only the penitential psalms 6; 32; 51; 38; 102; 130; 143 are picked out as being significant for Christian prayer : that is, those psalms of lament which explicitly lay stress on sin and its forgiveness.

The reasons for this state of affairs go beyond simply the theological. In the middle ages and well into more recent times, most people generally regarded suffering as a consequence of sin and a punishment for sin. As a result of world wars and worldwide communications, the problem of undeserved suffering, suffering for which no-one can be held directly responsible, has moved into the forefront of the human consciousness, to such an extent that it has become something that stirs humanity profoundly. But thereby lament as the speech of suffering has acquired a new meaning for us. Suffering is brought to our attention in all sorts of ways in public life, in the media, in many institutions, in demonstrations, so that attention is again being paid to the Biblical psalms of lament and they are being understood once more in their own right.

But the psalms of lament do not make things easy for us. Their language is in many respects foreign to us, centuries of usage have blunted its edge. Much in them we can no longer understand, much only with difficulty. So it is

---

[25] See in general R. Albertz, *Persönliche Frömmigkeit und offizielle Religion*, Calwer Theologische Monographien 9, 1978.

amazing that so much in them still speaks directly to our condition. A prerequisition for understanding these psalms is that we should first listen to them as a whole and only then try to grasp the meaning of the individual elements in the light of the whole.

Psalm 13: How long?

1   How long, O Lord, wilt thou forget me for ever?
     How long wilt thou hide thy face from me?
2   How long must I bear pain in my soul,
        and have sorrow in my heart day and night?
     How long shall my enemy be exalted over me?

3   Consider and answer me, O Lord my God;
        lighten my eyes,
        lest I sleep the sleep of death;
4   lest my enemy say, 'I have prevailed over him';
     lest my foes rejoice because I am shaken.

5   But I, I have trusted in thy steadfast love;
        my heart shall rejoice in thy salvation.

     I will sing to the Lord,
        because he has dealt bountifully with me.

Text

v. 2   (Heb. 3): the meaning 'pains' for *'ēsōt* can perhaps be supported by the Hebrew of Ecclesiasticus 30: 21, but probably read *'asābōt*, with the same sense. At the end of the verse, on metrical grounds, read 'day and night' with the Septuagint, or *jōm jōm*, 'day by day'.

   v. 3   (Heb. 4): 'the sleep of death', following GKC §117 *r*N, or 'sleep in death', following GKC §117 *s*. For death as sleep, see also Jeremiah 51: 39; Job 3: 13; 14: 12.

v. 4 (Heb. 5): better *jākōlti lō*.

Structure

vv. 1-2: Lament

1: thou   2a:I   2b: the enemy

v. 3: Petition

3a: appeal to God   3b: intervention of God

vv. 3c, 4: Motifs accompanying the petition

3c: I   4: the enemy

v. 5a: Expression of confidence
v. 5b: Promise of praise

On reading the psalm through several times, from the first sentence to the last, one observes a marked change in the course of it. By the end, the situation of the suppliant has altered; he does not stand where he stood at the beginning. The psalm is a lament but the final words have moved away from lament and the psalm closes with an expression of sure and certain confidence in the future. This is characteristic of all psalms of lament, although it is not always as clear as it is here. The one who laments his suffering to God does not remain in his lament. But before this point can be reached, the suffering must express itself, it must be put into words through the lament in which the sufferer 'pours out his soul' before God, Psalm 42: 4. But this is done here with unsurpassed and concentrated brevity: the language of this psalm is extremely dense, especially in the lament of vv. 1-2. That lament displays a threefold structure characteristic of all the psalms of lament.

Excursus: The threefold lament structure. This appears with particular clarity in Psalm 13. What invariably meets us in the psalms is a confrontation between three participants; alongside God and the suppliant, 'the others' are involved, Psalm prayer also has always a communal or social aspect: a man is never alone with God, 'a soul conversing with God'; others, his fellow-men, are there too. Here we see a social relationship, in sharp contrast to any idea of an inner individual piety: living with God cannot be separated from living with others, the two belong together. The threefold structure of the lament mirrors an understanding of man, where the areas with which theology, sociology and psychology are concerned have not yet become autonomous realms but are still aspects of one and the same reality. Man can be seen as man only under all three aspects. In the lament we are made aware of the threat that death poses to man. The threat here is not merely to the isolated individual's own existence; equally threatened is man's life as a member of a community, what is at stake is what he means to others and they to him. At the same time, the meaning of his very existence is threatened, an existence that can only be comprehended as a whole, in its whole course, and hence from outside itself: this comprehension is what the sufferer is seeking when he asks the question 'why?'. Thus lamentation to God or complaint against Him is an aspect of the lament, where we hear the voice of existence threatened by death. Were this aspect lacking, the lament would not truly be that of a human being but rather that of the mythical hero of Hölderlin's poem 'Hyperion's Hymn of Fate'.

The threefold lament structure represents a progression from the lament uttered by any individual who is enduring suffering. In the course of this progression, the laments of many very different individuals were brought together and then united in a comprehensive formula which received its final form in worship. Thus was found a common speech which all could use, in which every individual could recognize again his own suffering. This is why, in the lament form, particular kinds of suffering are rarely, if ever, specified; they are all included under these three aspects which serve for all human suffering.

v. 1: The question 'How long?', which is repeated four

times, twice in this verse, to emphasize the lament to God, binds together the three aspects of the lament. The question is specifically the utterance of one who is experiencing a suffering that seems determined to continue. Here, time itself becomes a destructive force, wearing down a man's ability to hold out and intensifying the suffering to an inhuman level. The very human and natural question 'How long?' is neither distinctively Biblical nor distinctively Israelite. It is frequently met with in Babylonian lamentations but also in prayers of primitive religions and even in the Christian hymn: 'O how long, how long? is the anxious heart's song . . . '[26]

Psalm 13 is uttered in the midst of this apparently ceaseless suffering. But because the question 'How long?' is addressed to God, something already changes. The question does not die away into infinity; there is One who hears it.

In the lament to God, the deity's relationship to the petitioner's suffering is expressed by two verbs which speak of God in very human terms. The verbs 'forget' and 'hide the face' or 'turn away' are not really suitable to God; anyone praising God would be bound to say the opposite and in their denunciation the prophets use these verbs of men, to indict those who have forgotten, or turned away from, God. But the questions 'How long wilt thou forget me?', 'How long wilt thou hide they face from me?' cannot be changed when statements are made about God. Here nothing is really being said about God's forgetfulness or hiddenness. Rather the clauses embody the harsh reality experienced by those who find that God has forgotten them and hidden Himself from them in their suffering. The hiding of God's face does not refer to His essential being but to His activity. The questions show that, for those who asked them, it was not a matter of God in His essential nature, of God as pure being, or of God as 'a concept of divinity'. They could not speak of Him as other than the

[26] The German original is: 'Ach wie lang, wie lange ist dem Herzen bange . . . '

God who acts and whose actions they had met in their own lives.

v. 2a: This is a lament in the 'I' form. The question 'How long?' is still addressed to God but the subject of this 'I' lament is the one who is himself lamenting. The details of the suffering are not given here either, so we do not know whether 'interior' or 'exterior' suffering is intended. For the nearer definition 'in my soul' or 'in my heart' means that pain and sorrow have taken hold of the sufferer's entire being, body and soul.[27] The words are familiar to every sufferer, everyone understands them.

v. 2b: The sentence 'how long shall my enemy be exalted over me?' denotes the lament about enemies; perhaps a half-verse has fallen out here. In the threefold lament structure, 'the others' appear as enemies or those closely linked with them. This is because suffering always isolates, a fact known to all, a fact experienced from the dawn of human history. And in spite of all the changes in human history, a trace or shadow of this primaeval experience remains with us even now: the invalid, the man on trial, the victim of loneliness, anyone conscious of guilt, all feel themselves isolated. When, in the lament, the others are the enemies, it is this experience which lies behind the words.

In this psalm, the enemies feel able to exalt themselves over the suppliant because they view his suffering as his own fault and hence as a punishment. But the sufferer cannot accept this; like Job, he cannot admit that he has deserved his fate, and only God can remove the slur which his enemies cast on him. There is no imprecation against the enemies in this psalm, see p. 297 f. below.

vv. 3-4: These verses form the petition. Here and in what follows, 'petition' is intended to have the same sense as 'plea', that is, not requesting something, but rather

---

[27] See the article on *nēfeš* in *Theologisches Handwörterbuch zum Alten Testament II.*

imploring God in a situation of distress. In other words, petition is really transitive, plea intransitive.

This imploring of God in the psalms, in contrast to the transitive petition, is always a two-stage process, structured by two verbs, the first of which denotes God's turning to the suppliant and the second His intervention to save and deliver; such is also the case in passages where the structure is not so plainly visible. The sufferer's state of distress can only be ameliorated when God again shows Himself gracious, as we see from v. 1. Everything turns on this: 'Consider' – that is, consider the depths I am in – 'and answer me', so that my lament does not die away into the void. When God again has regard to the sufferer and hears him again, all will be well. This is expressed in the words: 'lighten my eyes!', that is, let me once more be glad!, which, properly speaking, do not denote God's saving intervention but rather its consequences. Here, as often in the psalms, we have a passage which serves to indicate how one thing follows from another: when God intervenes, gladness returns, as we find in Psalm 30: 11. In vv. 3b and 4, the petition is enlarged by motifs intended to stir up God to intervene on the sufferer's behalf and setting out the grounds why He should do so. While the petition itself is the equivalent of the complaint against God, the two motifs, 3b and 4, correspond to the 'I' lament and the lament about enemies. The words' that I sleep not in death' understand the sufferer's grief and pain as steps on the road to death; death's mighty scream is already heard in the suffering that seems determined not to end. But his death would mean that his foes had triumphed and this God must prevent.

The motifs in question, which we also meet in many other passages and which are aimed at intensifying the petition, may appear to us naïf, primitive or even irreverent. They are meant quite otherwise. They are one expression of the movement which controls the whole psalm, a movement from the lament to a determination to look ahead in confident trust. That we must take them in this way is shown by what follows.

v. 5a: For now follows the 'but', *wāw* adversative in
Hebrew,[28] that we meet somewhere or somehow in every
psalm of lament, 'But I have trusted in thy steadfast love
. . .'. The 'but' marks a step forward and this is what gives
the clause its meaning. The 'trust in God' mentioned here is
not what we usually understand by the term, a stance or
conviction that one either has or not, and such is certainly
not its meaning in our psalm. Rather, it indicates the step
forward into trust which the suppliant takes in the face of
his suffering and in spite of the persistent force of that
suffering. Only with this 'but' is it possible to understand
what trust really means; only in this movement, this
clinging to God's goodness, which the facts seem to
contradict, can it be seen for what it truly is.

v. 5b: Only by thus clinging to God has the suppliant a
future. Only then does he really come out of his lament and
look forward to the possibility of his lament turning into
praise: 'my heart shall rejoice in thy salvation!'. But this is
more than just anticipation. The suppliant promises that the
salvation he now entreats will determine his future: that
salvation is to resound in the praise he will offer to God, just
as we see in Psalm 30: 1. The deliverance he has experienced
in being freed from his suffering will preserve him
throughout the course of his life.

Psalm 6: O Lord, save my life!

1   O Lord, rebuke me not in thy anger,
     nor chasten me in thy wrath.
2   Be gracious to me, O Lord, for I am languishing;
     O Lord, heal me, for my bones are troubled.
3   My soul also is sorely troubled.
     But thou, O Lord – how long?
4   Turn, O Lord, save my life;
     deliver me for the sake of thy steadfast love.

[28] See C. Westermann, *Praise and Lament in the Psalms*, pp. 70 ff.

5   For in death there is no remembrance of thee;
      in Sheol who can give thee praise?
6   I am weary with my moaning;
      every night I flood my bed with tears;
      I drench my couch with my weeping.
7   My eyes waste away because of grief,
      they grow weak from all that presses upon me.

8   Depart from me, all you workers of evil;
      for the Lord has heard the sound of my weeping.
9   The Lord has heard my supplication; the Lord
      accepts my prayer.
10   All my enemies shall be ashamed and sorely
      troubled;
      they shall turn back, and be put to shame in a
      moment.

Text

v. 7 (Heb. 8): the second line could also be read as: 'I have grown old, *'ātakti*, because of all my foes'.

Structure

Prefatory note: In contrast to the structure of Psalm 13, which can be recognized at a glance, the verses of Psalm 6 seem to follow one another in a disorderly manner, with no organic connection between them. But this is precisely a characteristic of the psalms of lament. They do not follow a set pattern, rather the order and succession of the motifs is quite free and very variable. All they have in common is that the principal motifs are the same and that they all describe a movement, though not always in the same way, which develops from the lament.

The main part of Psalm 6 consists of the petition or plea to God, vv. 1-5. The lament follows in vv. 6-7, while vv. 8-10 denote a change and are characterized by the motif of the certainty of a hearing.

vv. 1-5: The petition is formulated negatively in v. 1, but positively in vv. 2-4. It is followed by a petition motif in v. 5 and linked with numerous other motifs.

v. 1: At the outset the suppliant implores God to take away His anger from him, v. 1; possibly he has aroused God's wrath, which he feels in his suffering, through some error. But this possibility is only hinted at and there is no request for forgiveness, even though Psalm 6 is to be reckoned among the penitential psalms.

vv. 2-4: The positive petition extends from v. 2 to v. 4 but in company with other elements. Into it are inserted a plea for God to change His stance, v. 2, and a plea for His saving intervention, vv. 2, 4, so that the latter is framed by the former – 'Be gracious, O Lord', v. 2 . . . 'for the sake of thy steadfast love', v. 4. The ground for the petition is found with the reference to the speaker's sufferings in the two sentences 2a-2b, 3a. The meaning of the petition is determined by the verbs it employs. Decisive here is the plea for God to be gracious, which frames the remainder, beginning with the verb *ḥānan* which is picked up again by the noun *ḥesed* at the end. Both words are also used between human beings; so Jacob is apprehensive as to whether or not he will find 'grace', *ḥēn*, in Esau's eyes, Genesis 33: 8, or the father takes pity on his children, Psalm 103: 13. Human experience shows what is meant when God turns to men in mercy and all prayer draws its life from this awareness of His true nature. The second key verb is 'heal me', which, when applied to God, is no 'metaphorical expression'; rather that God is healer and saviour[29] belongs to His essential being. The healing which the suppliant begs is for the whole man, as the use of the two parallel nouns 'bones' and 'soul' clearly indicates. We need not necessarily assume from the petition 'O Lord, heal me' that the suppliant is suffering from sickness; this is perhaps suggested by vv. 6-7 but it is not certain. In any case, Psalm 6 would have been used as a prayer by many different sufferers.

[29] In German, Heilender and Heiland.

The petition 'Turn, O Lord!', v. 4, shows that God has turned away from the sufferer; in both v. 4 and v. 2 the petition for God to turn back again is followed by a petition for His saving intervention, here in the words 'save my life' and 'deliver me', verbs frequently used in pleas to God in the psalms. In vv. 2a–2b, 3, the ground of the plea is the suppliant's desperate condition: he is 'sorely troubled' both in soul and body, an expression of anguish in the face of death. In content, these verses are an 'I' lament. To this terror of death, v. 3b opposes the abrupt and logically barely comprehensible cry: 'But thou, O Lord – how long?'. The phrase is one of those in the psalms of lament which have lost their original sharpness and which we can only understand from their earlier history: such worn-down phrases also occur frequently in Mesopotamian psalms. This particular phrase can easily be expanded by the words of Psalm 13: 1: 'How long, O Lord? wilt thou forget me for ever?' or by some corresponding expression. Perhaps the two questions 'why?' and 'how long?' presuppose a more detailed complaint against God; from the history of the lament form we know that the complaint was avoided or pushed into the background at a later period, and hence only a hint of it remains here. But this hint still shows that a complaint against God was a regular part of the lament.

v. 5: This verse represents a motif allied to the petition, the purpose of which is to stir up God to help.[30] On the one hand, when it is said that the dead do not praise God, we see that, for those who once prayed the psalms, all relationship with God was ended by death. We see how profound a change was brought about by the death of Jesus, whose death 'glorified' God. On the other hand, however, these words also tell us that for the Old Testament praising God is something that belongs to human life; there can be no true life without the praise of God. For to praise God is confidently to ascribe all the joy of existence to Him.

[30] See C. Westermann, *Praise and Lament in the Psalms*, pp. 186 ff., where all references are given.

vv. 6-7: Now follows the lament as the ground of the preceding petition, as with vv. 2a.-2b, 3a. Apart from v. 7, it is an 'I' lament. As such, it shows how powerfully the personal suffering of an ancient Israelite can still speak directly to us through all the intervening centuries, even in those aspects of the lament which seek to gather together the sufferings of many individuals in many varied forms. Who has not known those sleepless nights ruined by suffering!

Only in the last line of v. 7, which may be translated as 'because of all my foes', are the suppliant's enemies mentioned, and then again at v. 10. Nor do we learn what is the relationship between the suffering of the one who laments and his enemies. For those who join in praying the psalm, it is enough that suffering isolates and can turn trusted friends into enemies.

vv. 8-10: These verses signify a change, occasioned by the certainty that God has heard and accepted the petition, which is quite unmotivated and incomprehensible from the context of the psalm; we cannot account for the change. How are we to understand this sudden appearance in these final verses of the certainty of a hearing, for which nothing that has gone before has prepared us? The usual explanation is that an oracle of salvation, probably given by a priest, has intervened at this point, and this explanation gains support from the story of Hannah, 1 Samuel 1-2; however, the text here gives no indication of it. Also, it is hardly possible to think of such a priestly oracle of salvation as a regular accompaniment to every lament; it must have been confined to special cases. But even if we cannot explain this sudden change in vv. 8-10, we may tentatively suggest that it is tantamount in some way to that movement from lamenting to being heard, which is a feature of all psalms of lament.

It is also striking that in vv. 8-10 the certainty of a hearing, vv. 8b-9, appears only in connection with the lament about enemies, vv. 8a, 10. We can no longer understand this either; all that these final lines tell us is that the suppliant's oppression at the hands of hostile powers – if that is what is meant – must have overwhelmed him, and that the hearing of his lament brings deliverance from these powers.

Psalm 22: My God, why hast thou forsaken me?

1   My God, my God, why hast thou forsaken me?
    Why art thou so far from my supplication, from the
        words of my groaning?
2   O my Lord, I cry by day, but thou dost not
        answer,
    and by night, I find no rest.
3   Yet thou art holy,
    enthroned on the praises of Israel.

4   In thee our fathers trusted;
    they trusted, and thou didst deliver them.
5   To thee they cried, and were saved;
    in thee they trusted, and were not put to shame.
6   But I am a worm, and no man;
    scorned by men, and despised by the people.
7   All who see me mock at me.
    they make mouths at me, they wag their heads;
8   'He committed his cause to the Lord; let him deliver
        him, let him rescue him,
    if he delights in him!'

9   Yet thou art he who took me from the womb;
    thou didst keep me safe upon my mother's
        breasts.
10   Upon thee was I cast from my birth,
    and since my mother bore me thou hast been my
        God.
11   Be not far from me, for trouble is near
    and there is none to help.

12 Many bulls encompass me,
 strong bulls of Bashan surround me;
13 they open wide their mouths at me,
 like a ravening and roaring lion.
14 I am poured out like water,
 and all my bones are out of joint;
 my heart is like wax,
 it is melted within my breast;
15 my palate is dried up like a potsherd,
 and my tongue cleaves to my jaws;
 thou dost lay me in the dust of death.
16 Yea, dogs are round about me;
 a company of evil-doers encircle me;
 like a lion (?) my hands and feet.
17 They stare and gloat over me,
 they count all my bones;
18 they divide my garments among them,
 and for my raiment they cast lots.

19 But thou, O Lord, be not far off!
 O thou my help (?), hasten to my aid!
20 Deliver my soul from the sword,
 my only one from the power of the dog!
21 Save me from the mouth of the lion,
 my afflicted soul (?) from the horns of the wild
 oxen!

22 I will tell of thy name to my brethren;
 in the midst of the congregation I will praise thee:
23 You who fear the Lord, praise him!
 all you sons of Jacob, glorify him, and stand in awe
 of him, all you sons of Israel!
24 For he has not despised or abhorred
 the affliction of the afflicted;
 and he has not hid his face from him,
 but has heard, when he cried to him.
25 Thy faithfulness is my praise in the great
 congregation;
 my vows I will pay before those who fear him.

26 The poor shall eat and be satisfied;
    those who seek him shall praise the Lord!
    May your hearts live for ever!
27 All the ends of the earth shall remember and turn to
      the Lord;
    and all the families of the nations shall worship
      before him.
28 For dominion belongs to the Lord, and he rules over
      the nations.
29 Only to him shall bow down all who sleep in the
      earth,
    before him shall bow all who go down to the
      dust.
30b Men shall tell of the Lord to the coming
      generation,
31 and proclaim his deliverance to a people yet
      unborn,
    that he has wrought it.

Text

v. 1 (Heb. 2): read 'from my supplication' instead of 'from my help'.

v. 8 (Heb. 9): instead of the original 'commit!' read 'he committed'.

v. 9 (Heb. 10):a *gōḥī* from *gaḥah*, compare Psalm 71: 6, but the meaning is uncertain.

v. 15 (Heb. 16): instead of *ḳōḥī*, 'my strength', read *ḥikki*, 'my palate'.

v. 16a (Heb. 17a): on grounds of metre add 'many'.

v. 16b (Heb. 17b): the meaning is uncertain: perhaps instead of 'like a lion' read *kā'aru*, to mean 'they have pierced'.

v. 17 (Heb. 18): the Massoretic reading 'I count' is very uncertain. Probably the third person plural should be read and 17a and b transposed.

v. 21 (Heb. 22): the Hebrew word rendered 'my afflicted soul' is uncertain.

v. 25 (Heb. 26): instead of *mē'itteka*, 'from thee', read *'amitteka*, 'thy faithfulness'.

v. 27 (Heb. 28): read 'before him' instead of 'before thee'.

vv. 29 ff: here the text is corrupt and uncertain and the meaning of 29b and 30a can no longer be recovered.

v. 29a (Heb. 30a): in place of *'ākelŭ*, 'they have eaten', read *'ak lo*, 'only to him'; instead of *dišnēj*, 'the fat ones', read *ješenēj*, 'the sleepers'.

Structure

The structure of Psalm 22 is so carefully thought out down to the smallest detail that we can confidently assume a late literary reworking of an older psalm. Another peculiarity is that the conclusion not only envisages the theme of the praise of God but in its final part, vv. 22-31, is expanded into a narrative psalm of praise, something which does not occur elsewhere. The whole of Psalm 22 is thus a 'lament that is turned round', in which the praise of God follows on the lament.

The section vv. 1-21 is basically structured on the lament 'why art thou so far?', v. 1, and the plea 'be not far', vv. 11 and 19, which makes a frame for the section vv. 12-18. This section corresponds to that of the psalm of lament: after the call to God, we have the lament or complaint to God, vv. 1-2 and also 3, then the 'I' lament, 6-8, 14-15 and the lament about the enemy, 7-8., 12-13, 16-18, and finally the petition in 11, 19-21.

Another peculiarity which differentiates Psalm 22 from the other individual laments consists in the introduction of a review of God's past saving acts, which otherwise is confined to the communal laments. This is in two parts, intentionally distinguished from one another: God's dealings with His people, 4-5, and His dealings with the supplicant, 9-10.

The second part, vv. 22-31, starts with the utterance of praise; it still represents part of the lament but here it functions as a transition. The ground for it is given in v. 24, which goes with v. 22 (compare Psalm 13: 6): the act of God which brings release for the sufferer. But this conclusion of the lament is expanded in v. 23 by a summons to praise using three imperatives, fitting for the descriptive praise which is carried further in vv. 27-31. Both these features are also found together in Psalm 107.

In addition, there appears in vv. 25-26 an element which belongs neither to vv. 22, 24 nor to 23, 27-31, and this is the redeeming of the promise or vow, an element that concludes the lament, vv. 25-26. In these two verses we can recognize the later formulation of the psalm, in that to the promise made in the hour of need is added the redemption of the promise or vow, which elsewhere occurs as a separate psalm category, for example Psalm 30. Psalm 22 thus embraces the elements of lament and both narrative and descriptive praise, in the sequence lament-psalm of thanksgiving-hymn. In this, it witnesses to the fact that these three elements all belong together; all three are rooted in God's act of compassion for a sufferer, v. 31b. Simply from this all-embracing significance of Psalm 22, as revealed in its structure, we can understand why it has had a special significance for the gospels' portrayal of the passion and death of Jesus.

vv. 1-2: The psalm begins abruptly with the complaint. The suppliant's passionate complaint levels against God the charge that He has forsaken him and the suppliant asks Him why He has done so, v. 1a; he is forced to this conclusion because his tireless supplication, vv. 1b, 2, receives no answer. The fact that his suffering changes not at all convinces him that God does not hear him. An answer from God would mean the reversal of the suffering; the possibility of its being reversed by any other means is here unthinkable. This introduction to the psalm presents an acute paradox, in that the urgent and even twice-repeated address is contrasted with the complaint that follows it. However abrupt he may be with God, the complainant cannot cease from calling on Him as 'his' God; in spite of the complaint, the address shows that a relationship with 'his' God continues to exist. He may reproach God but he cannot break with Him. The complaint cannot be turned into a straightforward statement of fact. Because the suppliant still speaks to Him, He is still his God; he cannot cease from calling on Him.

It is to be noted that, in this opening of Psalm 22, there is a fundamentally different understanding of man's relationship with God from the one that has grown up since the period of the Enlightenment. We describe that relationship as 'belief' and equate the term with religion itself. But in a relationship with God viewed as belief, it is man who is the subject; one either believes in Him or not. In this respect the relationship with God in the psalms is quite other; there God is the subject, He it is who initiates the relationship. So even when a man despairs of God, he can never break free from Him, as we see clearly in Psalm 139.

v. 3: And we see it also in the verse here: the complainant cannot escape from God. Over against his complaint, he sets a 'But thou . . .' (compare Psalm 13: 5). God is silent, at a distance where He cannot be reached, but He is still there, there is nothing apart from Him. Yet the divine holiness is felt as something distant, something alien, by the one who cries to God day and night in vain; it is for him something terrifying, the mysterium tremendum. To God's remoteness belongs also His being enthroned in lofty majesty. But now there follows in v. 3 a remarkable addition not met with elsewhere ' . . . enthroned on the praises (or songs of praise) of Israel', which makes the transition to vv. 4-5. What the phrase tells us is that whenever God is praised or extolled, He is also exalted, and so God is exalted in Israel's songs of praise.

vv. 4-5: God's present remoteness is shown when it is said in vv. 4-5 that He has delivered the people from distress in the past, a theme corresponding to the contrast motif of a review of God's former saving acts in the communal laments. But if all this is far away for the one who now calls on God, yet this contrast motif recalls the fact that God has indeed helped His people: 'in thee they trusted and were not put to shame'. With this, a first step away from the lament has been taken.

vv. 6-8: But the suppliant's own suffering has not yet been relieved, as he now unfolds to God, 'But I . . .'. Vv. 6-8 are a motif from the 'I' lament, but in them there is laid out only the social aspect of the suffering, what the attitude of others means for the sufferer; in other words the scorn that suffering provokes. The others derisively reject him because God has abandoned him without help or pity, and because in their view he is the object of God's just punishment – this is implied by the words 'if he delights in him'.

vv. 9-11: To confront such scorn, the suppliant clings to what remains to him, to what he knows for a certainty. He carries further the review of the past in vv. 4-5 by recounting his own experience of how from his birth God has preserved and protected him. God's concern, shown in what He has done for His people in the past, vv. 4-5, now comes closer, becomes a concern for the suppliant's physical being: God was with him, with him personally, right from his birth, a truth underlined four times in vv. 9-10. There had never been a moment throughout his existence when God was not with him and this is the ground of his confidence. Here we learn what it could mean that humanity is made and created by God. As he recalls what God has done for him from birth, the suppliant finds in his despairing lament a firm foothold that enables him to step from lament to petition, 'Be not far from me!' (compare v. 1b). The entire first part of the psalm leads up to the petition of v. 11, which will be repeated again in v. 19.

vv. 12-18: But before this, the lament is carried on through vv. 12-18; after the lament to God, vv. 1-2, and the unit of the 'I' lament dealing with the mockery of the suffering, vv.6-8, there now follows the lament about the enemies,

vv. 12-13, 16-18, which, however, is linked with the other
unit of the 'I' lament dealing with the suffering itself, vv.
14-15. The verses here throw up a barrier against our
attempts at interpretation. We can easily recognize here
how the 'I' lament and the lament about enemies are linked
together, but not who the enemies are or what they do or
how they are a threat; nor can we discern in what the
lamenter's suffering consists. Here a formal element in the
lament has emerged, probably as the result of a lengthy
development, a language in a code we can no longer break.
Something similar is seen in the Babylonian psalms, where
too the enemies are depicted as wild beasts. It is also possible
that, by the enemies here, not human beings but demonic
powers are intended or were once intended; demons that
cause illness are also known from the New Testament.
However, this is not a satisfactory solution either.

vv. 12-13: Vv. 12-13 portray a state where hostile powers
pose a threat, whoever they are meant to be, as also does v.
16 and perhaps 17. It is noticeable that all the clauses speak
only of the threat. The language is too different from that of
vv. 7-8 to allow us to think that the same 'enemies' are
meant in both passages.

vv. 14-15: While the speaker of the lament laments the
shame of his suffering in vv. 6-8, vv. 14-15 speak of the
suffering itself, which has taken hold of the whole man,
bones, heart and mouth. We cannot recognize what the
suffering is: the expressions used suggest an illness, but this
is not certain. Nor is there any recognizable connection
between the threat from hostile powers, vv. 12, 13, 16, and
the suffering in 14-15. V. 14a seems to mean that the body
has lost its vigour, as does 14b with the reference to its
central organ, the seat of the life force. But it is not said how
the weakening of heart and body has been brought about.
Probably v. 15a implies a fever, which dries up mouth and
throat, and 15b finally states that the speaker is threatened
with death.

vv. 16-18: The threat posed by hostile powers in animal form in vv. 12-13 is continued in v. 16a. The text of 16b is uncertain; the opening phrase, 'like a lion', would be a suitable continuation of 16a but it does not seem to fit with what follows. Instead of 'like a lion', the Septuagint has a verb, *kā'aru*, 'they have pierced', to accompany the succeeding 'my hands and feet', which is then applied in the New Testament to the crucifixion. But what should be read is quite uncertain.

Vv. 17-18 no longer speak of threatening powers in animal form but of men who observe the speaker's suffering; clearly they continue vv. 7-8. These men have no pity for him, they watch his suffering as they would a play, v. 17, and they treat him as one already dead, for the expressions used in v. 18 apparently relate to the death of an outcast. The two clauses of v. 18 are in parallelism, with the latter explaining what is meant by the former, '. . . in that for my raiment they cast lots'.

vv. 19-21: After the end of the lament of vv. 12-18, the petition of v. 11 (compare v. 1b) is resumed. The carefully thought out structure of the psalm appears in the way v. 11 prays for deliverance from distress, referring to vv. 6-8, and v. 19 for deliverance from enemies, referring to vv. 12-13, 16, who are again portrayed as wild beasts in vv. 20-21. Here too the connection between the threat of hostile powers, 20-21, and the suffering described in 14-15, remains hidden from us. We are in the presence of a stereotyped and metaphorical language which we can no longer understand.

vv. 22-31: In the second part of the psalm, the lament changes to the praise of God, which is expanded by the closing words of the lament, vv. 22, 24. This feature is unique in the Psalter and we can see in it the design of a later author, who deliberately sought to express this change from lament to psalm of praise by showing the connection between them. Thereby he gave greater emphasis to a movement toward praising God which was already present in the structure of the psalm of lament, in so far as that psalm type reaches its conclusion in a promise or vow of praise.

vv. 22-24: Hence vv. 22 and 24 form the link between the two parts of the psalm, in that they belong to both.[31]

The promise of praise at the end of a psalm of lament is evidenced not only in the Old Testament but frequently also in Egyptian and Babylonian psalms. It is therefore impossible to maintain that Psalm 22 is made up of two psalms, the second beginning with v. 22. The meaning of the promise of praise as the conclusion of the psalm of lament is that what the psalm describes as happening is to continue for the future. Because the speaker, God and the others are all part of this, the deliverance envisaged at the close also involves those others, as the circle to which the speaker belongs. That circle too must learn of the deliverance: 'I will tell of thy name to my brethren', where the 'name' stands for what God has done. What is meant is the reaction of joy which must announce itself, as with the woman who has lost a coin in the New Testament parable: 'Rejoice with me for . . . !'. So when the parallel line proclaims: 'in the midst of the congregation I will praise thee', it is saying that the praise of God is consummated in what is being related. Here the praise of God is to be understood as a narrative of what God has done (see the excursus on narrative praise below, p. 168). This is elaborated in v. 24, where the story of the one who has experienced God's deliverance is briefly sketched, concentrating on the fact that his plea has been heard. At the same time, all the clauses of v. 24 obviously refer back to the beginning of the psalm, vv. 1-2. If there the suppliant has reproached God for forsaking him, for turning away from him and for being deaf to his cry, here he testifies that he has been heard: He has not despised or abhorred or hidden His face, but has heard when I cried to Him! In these emphatic expressions, we glimpse again the purpose of the author of

[31] For the structure of this type of psalm, see C. Westermann, *Praise and Lament in the Psalms*, pp. 52 ff. and 64-70.

our psalm. He intends to say: 'the desperate man is justified in accusing God, provided that is balanced by an avowal like this'.

Between vv. 22 and 24, which form the final part of the psalm of lament, an imperative summons to praise is inserted, v. 23. Properly speaking, this is a component of the descriptive psalm of praise or the hymn and frequently occurs at its beginning. This imperative call to praise is often extended by clauses in the jussive, 'shall', and such is the case here, where the imperative, v. 23, is succeeded by the jussive, vv. 27 ff. But the insertion of v. 23 between 22 and 24 reveals a deliberate intention on the author's part; what he achieves by it is the grounding of the summons to praise for the worshipping congregation, v. 23, in the narrative of what God has done: 'For he has not . . .', v. 24. This report of what God has done is expanded in vv. 28-29 by the description of God in majesty, and both make up the ground of the call to praise: the author has of set purpose linked together the motifs of both narrative and descriptive praise.

vv. 25-26: The promise of praise, v. 22, is carried out in vv. 25-26; elsewhere the two are always separated. In vv. 25-26, the payment of a vow appears in the setting of a religious festival, which, however, is only very sketchily described. V. 25a is a transition. 'Thy faithfulness' includes all that is recounted in v. 24; now this must be heard by a great assembly, before whom the one who has lived through these experiences will redeem his promise, 25b. The festival includes a sacrificial meal, the shared-offering, to which the needy are also invited, v. 26a; and so the praise of God which the individual utters before the assembly is continued by its members, v. 26b.

vv. 27-31: But, in addition, a motif from the liturgical psalms of praise is picked up and developed in the psalm's closing words. It appears already with the imperative summons to praise of v. 23; beyond the small circle, to whom speaks the one paying his vow, the praise is to go out

through all Israel, 'the sons of Jacob and the sons of Israel'.
But now the circle grows even wider, to embrace 'all the
ends of the earth' and 'all the families of the nations', v. 27.
This can happen because 'dominion belongs to the Lord', v.
28, a clear reminiscence of the psalms celebrating God's
kingly rule, Psalms 93; 95-99. All these psalms, with their
glorifying of God as king of the nations and His royal
dominion over them, find their place in the context of an
universalism which became important with the exile and
the preaching of Second Isaiah. A set formula for the idea of
God's kingly rule, as embracing all nations, and of the
homage they are to pay Him, is not to be seen here. Rather,
the aim is to portray the extension of the praise of God to
ever wider circles. It begins when God hears a sufferer's plea
from the depths of despair. It moves on to his promise to
recount his experience to others and then, from that small
group, the praise of God echoes forth with hidden power
through ever wider circles.

vv. 29-31: But to this spatial extension of the praise to all
nations, a temporal one is finally added: the summons to
praise must make headway both into the past and into the
future. Death sets a limit to praising God, as we are told in
Psalm 6: 5 and many other passages. Only here does v. 29,
greatly daring, look beyond death: now the summons to
praise must also reach 'all who sleep in the earth'. Only in
apocalypses do we meet anything like this. But v. 29 is not a
set formula either; its bold vision only aims to make clear
that the advance of the praise of God knows no bounds
either in time or space, and, as the final sentences, vv. 30b,
31, tell us, this also applies to the future. The coming
generations are to learn of God's marvellous acts, which
must then be proclaimed from parent to child 'to a people
yet unborn'. We see here the chain of tradition, of which
Psalm 22 itself forms part, that is handed down in worship
from one generation to another.

The ground for the extension of the praise of God
throughout all time and space is given in the psalm's brief
final sentence, *kī 'āsāh*, 'that he has wrought it'. This is what

provides the motive force to power the movement of the whole psalm: God has acted. This final sentence shows what is meant by Old Testament theology, how the Old Testament speaks of God. The centre of all the Old Testament's theological discourse is found in a verbal clause: God has acted. That can only be said by one who has actually experienced what God has done, in this case the speaker of Psalm 22. His experience has been shaped by the contrast which determines the progression of the psalm from its first to last verse. Only because he had experienced God's remoteness and God's silence could he experience their reversal; and because he had experienced this reversal, he had to recount it. What he had to recount had to advance ever further, for God has acted. It is of God's actions that Old Testament theology speaks, and in so doing it speaks of the divine-human relationship, past, present and future.[32]

Psalm 51: Have mercy on me, O God!

For the choirmaster. A Psalm of David, when Nathan the prophet came to him, after he had gone in to Bathsheba.

1   Have mercy on me, O God, according to thy
         steadfast love;
      according to thy abundant mercy blot out my
         transgressions.
2   Wash me thoroughly from my iniquity,
      and cleanse me from my sin!
3   For I know my transgressions,
      and my sin is ever before me.
4   Against thee, thee only, have I sinned,
      and done that which is evil in thy sight,
      so that thou art justified in thy sentence,
      and blameless in thy judgement.

---

[32] For the use of Psalm 22 in the New Testament story of the passion of Jesus, see below p. 296.

5   Behold, I was brought forth in iniquity,
     and in sin did my mother conceive me.
6   [Behold, in truth thou delightest in faithfulness
        (?),
     in secret thou dost teach me wisdom.]

7   Purge me with hyssop, and I shall be clean;
     wash me and I shall be whiter than snow.
8   Fill me with joy and gladness;
     let the bones which thou hast broken rejoice.
9   Hide thy face from my sins,
     and blot out all my iniquities.
10   Create in me a clean heart, O God,
     and put a new and right spirit within me.
11   Cast me not away from thy presence,
     and take not thy holy Spirit from me.
12   Restore to me the joy of thy salvation,
     and equip me with a willing spirit.

13   Then I will teach the godless thy ways,
     and sinners will return to thee.
14   Deliver me from bloodguiltiness, O God, Thou
        God of my salvation,
     and my tongue will sing aloud of thy deliverance.

15   O Lord, open thou my lips,
     that my mouth may show forth thy praise.
16   For thou hast no delight in sacrifice;
     were I to give a burnt offering, thou wouldst not be
        pleased.
17   The sacrifice acceptable to God is a broken spirit,
     a broken heart, O God, thou wilt not despise.

18   [Do good to Zion in thy good pleasure;
     rebuild the walls of Jerusalem,
19   then wilt thou delight in right sacrifices,
     in burnt offerings and whole burnt offerings;
     then bulls will be offered on thy altar.]

Text

v. 6 (Heb. 8): the meaning is dubious. Another translation of the first line is: 'thou desirest truth in the inward being'.

v. 8 (Heb. 10): 'fill me', with the Syriac.

v. 13: this verse would fit better after v. 15.

Structure

Psalm 51 is one of the psalms in which a single psalm motif has itself become an independent psalm, in this case the avowal of sin. Here the separation of the motif is probably to be explained as follows: under certain circumstances, the avowal of sin, vv. 3-5, along with the prayer for forgiveness, vv. 1-2, 7-12, became a specifically liturgical service of confession, in which this psalm was included. Thus the psalm was seen as a confession of sin, similar to the practice of the Christian church. The title of the psalm also understands it in this way.

The detailed arrangement is the following:

vv. 1-2 petition for forgiveness
3-4 (5) avowal of sin
5 'conceived in sin', a motif to influence God to forgive.
6 perhaps a supplement to v. 16.
7-12 petition for forgiveness of sin
    7-8 petition for cleansing and a new life of joy
    9-12 petition for the blotting out of iniquities and an inner change
    10 clean heart and new spirit
    11 union with God
    12 joy in God's salvation and a willing spirit
13-17 promise of praise
    14-15 petition for deliverance and promise of praise
    13 passing on of the speaker's own experience
    16-17 sacrifice and praise
18-19 a later appendix: petition for the rebuilding of the walls of Jerusalem

The title, in addition to the liturgical direction 'To the choirmaster', contains a piece of information from the author, 'A Psalm of David' (for this, see the comments on

Psalm 23 below), and details of the situation which gave rise
to the psalm or in which it was first uttered. These details
were added by those who collected the Psalter together.
Psalm 51 cannot belong to David's time, since it certainly
originated in the post-exilic period (see the comments on
vv. 7-12). But the particulars given of the situation, which
refer to 1 Samuel 12, are important for the understanding of
the psalm because they show that those who collected the
psalms viewed it as the reaction to a definite and grave
transgression, for the forgiveness of which the speaker of
the psalm pleads. This is a correct understanding of the
psalm's original meaning.

vv. 1-2: The first sentence is a cry pleading for God's
mercy: 'Have mercy, O God!'. As the motivation for God
to show mercy, it mentions simply His steadfast love,
ḥesed, and abundant mercy, *raḥamim*.[33] The whole psalm is
dominated by this appeal for God's mercy. Behind the cry
'Have mercy!' which begins the psalm, lies the awareness of
the speaker and his ancestors of God's true nature; thus He
can be appealed to, however severe the guilt. Various
expressions are employed to describe the speaker's guilt:
pešaʿ, 'transgression' or 'rebellion', *ʿāwōn*, 'iniquity', *ḥattāʾt*,
'sin'. Originally they referred to precise and well-defined
actions, clearly distinguished from one another. Thus we
are also to understand their origins as different, and
consequently the offences they denote as being originally
more or less serious. They were to begin with secular terms
referring to human relationships; only subsequently were
they adopted to describe man's behaviour towards God.
The Old Testament has no general, all-embracing term for
sin against God; it knows of no theological concept for sin.
But from Psalm 51 we can see how such a concept has
gradually emerged: in its petition for forgiveness the
individual terms mentioned earlier have lost their particular
concrete meaning and are used more or less synonymously.

[33] For these expressions, see especially Psalm 103 and the relevant
articles in *Theologisches Handwörterbuch zum Alten Testament*.

They have become expressions all of which mean sin against God and so there arises a general concept of sin.

The same applies to the verbs that describe the wiping out of sin: in v. 1 *māḥah*, 'blot out', also in v. 9, in v. 2 *kibbēs*, 'wash' and its parallel *ṭāhār*, 'cleanse', also v. 7. All these verbs understand sin as something that defiles and besmirches a man, so forgiveness effects a cleansing. In the background lies the old idea of cultic impurity, found in the laws concerned with purity and cleansing, of which a man must rid himself before can appear before God. This idea is even more evident in v. 7, where the words, 'Purge me with hyssop' – a herb to which the power of cleansing was ascribed – 'and I shall be clean' allude to a cultic rite of cleansing. But in all these expressions the original sense of physical impurity has faded and all the verbs refer only to the removal of sin. They too embody a general concept of sin; they are all subordinated under a concept of personal forgiveness, as the parallelism in v. 1 shows.

vv. 3–4: The petition for forgiveness takes it for granted that an offence has been committed; an avowal of sin does not need to be made explicit in a petition for forgiveness and most such petitions lack it. Where it occurs it calls attention to some special feature, as is the case here: vv. 3 and 4 are deliberately associated with one another, the former describing what the suppliant's confession means for himself personally, the latter what it means for his relationship with God. V. 3 says that he knows his transgression, that it is always before him, that is, it so determines his existence that he can no longer go on living in this way; while v. 4 adds that his relationship with God is fundamentally affected by it. Both verses taken together show that the suppliant is deadly serious about the offence he has committed. The words of 4a, 'Against thee, thee only, have I sinned', do not mean, as H. Gunkel thought, that the offence was only against God and not against men, rather they mean: 'all that now matters is that I have sinned against thee'. This meaning is supported by the succeeding parallel line, 'and done that which is evil in thy sight', an

expression which includes offences against men and,
indeed, elsewhere is always used with reference to such
offences, for example Genesis 39: 9. For in the Old
Testament trespasses against men are viewed from the start
as trespasses against God.[34] The confession of vv. 3-4
relates then to a definite offence on the part of the one who
asks for forgiveness, a deed he has committed, 'done that
which is evil in thy sight', as in the two similar passages
Genesis 39: 9 and 2 Samuel 12: 13. The sinful act is before
him, v. 3, and it is what determines him to beg God's
forgiveness. V. 4b is therefore to be understood as follows:
'(I admit) that thou, O God, art justified in acting as thou
dost'. God's sentence of punishment, which the speaker's
confession endorses, could be an illness, but it could also
consist in the consciousness of guilt which torments him
and with which he can no longer live; both are viewed in the
Old Testament as very near to each other. In any case, he
acknowledges that the divine punishment is justified.

v. 5: This is a motif belonging to the petition, which aims to
move God to intervene or rather, in this case, to forgive.
The suppliant wants to say: 'Thou knowest how easily a
man is inclined to offend, how easily tempted to sin!' Here
the motif is expressed in intense and exaggerated language.
The clause needs to be understood from its function; it is not
a statement that can be loosed from its actual context to
stand alone. It may well be alluding to the legal impurity
incurred in procreation and giving birth, but this is not the
important thing. The verse seeks to influence God to
forgive; in no way is it speaking of a state of corruption in
which the human being is confined from birth. That would
contradict the whole Old Testament understanding of man,
and, in our psalm too, it is undoubtedly assumed that God
in His mercy can forgive the sin and thereby really blot it
out. But above all 'sin' in the Old Testament, including all
the terms listed earlier, is something that is done, never a

[34] See the title of this psalm and H.-J. Kraus, *Psalmen*, p. 386,
referring to 2 Samuel 12: 13.

permanent state; sin as a term for a state of existence is foreign to the Old Testament.

v. 6: The text is difficult here; difficult also is to grasp how the verse functions in its context. It gives the impression of being a foreign body here and probably v. 7 originally followed directly on v. 5. V. 6 is then a marginal note later incorporated into the text, as is indicated by the introductory 'Behold!', *hēn*, which seems harsh after the 'Behold!' of v. 5, with which it apparently has no organic connection. This marginal note fits badly with v. 5 but would suit well after v. 16: 'For thou hast no delight in', *kāfēṣ*, v. 16a . . . 'thou desirest', *kāfēṣ*, v. 6a. The beginning of v. 6 should then be translated, 'Behold, in truth thou delightest in . . . '. But the following word, *battūḥot*, defies explanation. With a change of the final consonant, we may conjecture *bittāḥōn*, 'faithfulness', but this does not fit well with the second line 'in secret thou dost teach me wisdom'. So v. 6 remains obscure; all we can say is that it is not in its original place here.

vv. 7-12: The petition for the forgiveness of sin, with which the psalm began, vv. 1-2, is now developed further, vv. 7-12. But, going beyond vv. 1-2, vv. 7-12 not only ask that the sin be removed but also that the whole man be changed. V. 7 repeats the petition for cleansing (see the comments on vv. 1-2) but adds a statement about what its result will be, 'and I shall be clean'. And v. 8 develops this positive aspect in a petition for a renewed life of joy, a petition that the one stricken by God may again be happy (see the comments on v. 4). Within this petition, v. 8, as often in the psalms, depicts the consequences of God's intervention to help and save. It is taken for granted that a life that is saved must be a happy life, as in v. 12 'the joy of thy salvation'. In vv. 9-12 we find the same succession of negative and positive petitions that we have met earlier, v. 9 corresponding to 7 and vv. 10-12 to 8. In v. 9 the petition for the blotting out of sin is equivalent to a wish that God will overlook the sufferer's sins, lest they have a damaging effect. But while v. 9 in the main recapitulates what was said earlier, in vv. 10–12 the whole emphasis falls on the positive petition, a petition that, by forgiving him, God may make possible a new and changed life for the suppliant. The section vv. 10–12 is *one* petition in different words and this petition represents the centre of the psalm. In this petition, the speaker asks for more than just the blotting out of his sins, as we see from the two parallel verbs in v. 10, 'create-renew'. He asks for a renewal of the whole man, for 'heart' and 'spirit' signify the centre of man's being, and he sees the renewal as a new creation. The use of the word 'create' in this context is remarkably bold and is met with only here. The verb *bārā'*, 'create', is only used of God, as in Genesis 1, and it can also indicate a divine creative act, understood as marking a fundamental change. The speaker asks for a 'clean heart' (compare the verbs of cleansing discussed earlier) and a 'right spirit', that is, a firmly fixed spirit. What the request means is seen in the next verse, 11: the clean heart and the right spirit are endangered when fellowship with God is destroyed (compare v. 4); so the speaker asks that he may always be one with God. The two lines of the verse reveal a well thought out correspondence; 'Cast me not away from thy presence' is a reminiscence of the liturgical blessing 'The Lord make his face to shine upon you'. The shining face of God means His benevolent, shielding protection, and 'take not thy holy Spirit from me' points to the danger of violating the Holy. The speaker knows that only through uninterrupted communion with the gracious and holy God is true renewal possible. V. 12 describes a life so renewed, it is a life which rejoices in the experience of God's help and which is ready and willing to be 'upheld' by that experience.

This blossoming of the petition for forgiveness in vv. 10–12, which forms the heart of the psalm, clearly shows the influence of the prophets of the exilic period. The speaker of the psalm uses the word 'create' and Second Isaiah promises a new creation for the nation in exile, Isaiah 43: 19; Ezekiel's promise of cleansing includes the gift of a new heart and a new spirit, Ezekiel 36: 25–27, and compare also Jeremiah 31: 31–33; 24: 7; 32: 39. Echoes of these promises are clearly to be heard in this psalm and they occur as frequently in no other.

vv 13–17: The promise of praise attached to the petition closes the psalm. The verse order is clearer if v. 13 is placed after v. 15. The transition from vv. 10–12 to 13–17 is then made by an address, 'O God!', that is recognizable as a new element; it is another concise and transitional petition for forgiveness: 'Deliver me from bloodguiltiness' (in Hebrew 'from bloods', the plural). The meaning is the same as in Psalm 30: 9, that is, deliverance from the death that could be the result of the speaker's guilt. To this supplication there is attached the promise, which is formulated in v. 14b as a quite natural reaction to the speaker's having been heard: he must express his joy by singing aloud! The fact that in v. 15 the petition is continued, 'O Lord, open thou my lips', really implies the same: it is being freed from guilt which will open his lips to praise God, 'that my mouth may show forth thy praise'. From these words it is plain that, in the psalms, praising God is a completely human and natural reaction to the experience of being set free, an experience that is a feature of every human life.

In v. 13 the promise is taken a stage further. The speaker does not only relate his experiences; in addition he wishes to help the sinner to get back on the right road. This extension of the promise, in this form found only here, is very appropriate to a confession of sin, for the one who implores forgiveness is himself a sinner. As one who has known forgiveness, he is able to help others find the path to repentance. Correspondingly, in certain individual psalms of praise, especially Psalms 32 and 34, we find just such a progression from praising God to giving instruction.

vv. 16–17: These following verses no longer form part of the prayer in the true sense but are a reflection added on to the promise of praise, vv. 13–15. The reason is that earlier the vow included both praise and sacrifice, as we see in Psalm 66: 13–20, where the payment of a vow, vv. 13–14,

consists in bringing a sacrifice, v. 15, and in praising God,
vv. 16-20; compare also Psalm 54: 6. With the destruction
of the Temple the sacrificial cult ceased for a lengthy period,
and the cessation also found justification from the influence
of the prophetic critique of sacrifice, to the effect that God
takes no pleasure in sacrifice, thus Psalms 50: 12 ff.; 69: 30 f.;
40: 6-10. But while in such passages sacrifice and praise are
opposed to one another, here 'a broken spirit, a broken and
contrite heart' is described, in a metaphorical sense, as 'the
sacrifice acceptable to God', which corresponds to the
avowal of sin (compare Isaiah 57: 15; 66: 2). We must not
take this as meaning that a man must first be broken before
he can be acceptable to God. Rather the 'breaking' is
directly linked with the subject matter of the psalm; it is the
hostile stance against the divine will which has to be
broken. The sacrifice consists in abandoning that
sacrilegious attitude which sets itself against God. What
God highly regards is the admission of guilt.

vv. 18-19: As all commentators agree, these verses are a
postscript. In them we find a different and a positive
attitude to animal sacrifices, which views the fact that, for
the moment, they cannot be offered as a grievous loss.
Hence v. 18 is a request to God to rebuild the walls of
Jerusalem, so that under their protection the sacrificial cult
can again be carried out as before.

   The special significance of Psalm 51 is that it witnesses to
the way in which the promises of the exilic prophets were
adopted and taken over into personal piety and individual
prayer, and so lived on in post-exilic times to become an
important link between the Old and the New Testaments.
The prophetic recognition that a complete new beginning
and entire renewal can only come about when guilt is
forgiven conditions this psalm's understanding of the
individual and his relationship to God.

   Its significance lies also in this: the change brought about
by forgiveness which we see here is to be understood as a
change to a new and joyful life, in a new and right spirit,
through a renewed fellowship with God. It is not seen as

consisting in a perpetual awareness of sin or an attitude of submissive penitence.

Psalm 77: I think of God

1   I cry aloud to God, aloud to God,
       that he may hear me!
2   In the day of my trouble I seek the Lord;
       in the night my hand is stretched out without
           wearying;
       my soul refuses to be comforted.
3   I think of God, and I moan;
       I meditate, and my spirit faints.
4   Thou dost hold my eyelids from closing;
       I am so troubled that I cannot speak.
5   I consider the days of old,
       I remember the years long ago.
6   I commune with my heart in the night;
       I meditate, my spirit searches.
7   Will the Lord spurn for ever,
       and never again be favourable?
8   Has his steadfast love for ever ceased?
       Is his truth at an end for all time?
9   Has God forgotten to be gracious?
       Has he in anger shut up his compassion?
10   And I said, 'Has it grown weak,
       has the right hand of the Most Hand changed?'
11   I will call to mind the deeds of the Lord;
       yea, I will remember thy wonders of old.
12   I will meditate on all thy work,
       and muse on thy deeds.
13   Thy way, O God, is holy.
       What god is great like the Lord?
14   Thou art a God who workest wonders,
       who hast manifested thy might among the
           peoples.
15   Thou didst with a mighty arm redeem thy

people,
the sons of Jacob and Joseph.

16 When the waters saw thee, O God, when the waters
        saw thee, they were afraid,
    yea, the deep trembled.
17 The clouds poured out water; the skies gave forth
        thunder;
    thy arrows flashed on every side.
18 Thy thunder rolled and crashed; thy lightnings
        lighted up the world;
    the earth trembled and shook.
19 Thy way was through the sea,
    thy path through the great waters;
    yet thy footprints were unseen.
20 Thou didst lead thy people like a flock
    by the hand of Moses and Aaron.

Text

vv. 5/6 (Heb. 6/7): the first word of v. 6 (Heb. 7) 'I
remember' should go with v. 5.

v. 8b (Heb. 9): reading *gemōrāh 'amittō* with the apparatus
of BHK.

v. 10 (Heb. 11): reading *šānetāh* and *ḥāletāh* with the
apparatus of BHK, following H. Gunkel.

v. 15 (Heb. 16): perhaps read 'with thy arm', with the
Versions.

v. 18 (Heb. 19): instead of *bagalgal* read perhaps
kagalgal.

Structure

This psalm diverges so markedly from the individual
laments that it can barely be reckoned among them. Yet the
introduction in vv. 1-4 marks it as belonging to this
category and the psalm shows how it was possible to

modify the regular lament form. Vv. 1-4 are the unchanged
introduction to an individual lament. Vv. 7-10 are also a
lament, but one that is changed through the introductory
vv. 5-6, which make it into a meditation or reflection. Over
against this meditation in lament form, vv. 11-15, along
with 20, are another meditation, a 'calling to mind' of God's
former deeds, which has somewhat the same function as the
declaration of confidence in the lament. However, this
calling to mind no longer relates to the fate of the suppliant
of vv. 1-4 but to that of his people. The recalling of God's
past deeds for His people is expanded in vv. 16-19 by a
divine 'epiphany': God draws near to help His people. The
transition from prayer to meditation or reflection shows
that the psalm belongs to a late period when prayer and
pious reflection could be linked together in various ways
(compare, for instance, Psalms 32; 34; 39 and also 73).

vv. 1-4: In these opening verses, the speaker, with words
that overwhelm him, places himself in the long line of
sufferers who have lamented their distress to God in earlier
generations. Vv. 1-2 bring out the intensity of this prayer of
lament: he cries aloud, day and night, body and soul, but he
finds no comfort (the same expression in Genesis 37: 35;
Jeremiah 31: 15; Job 6: 10), until God hears him, v 1b.
   In v. 3 the lament moves over to meditation: 'I think of
God . . . ', which in both lines is linked with moaning or
faintness of spirit. It is a meditation overshadowed by
sleeplessness and trouble of mind, v. 4.

vv. 5-10: The connection between lament, vv. 7-10, and
meditation, vv. 5-6, is further developed in what follows.
We are to conclude from vv. 1-4 that the subject matter is
personal suffering, as elsewhere in the individual laments.
But vv. 5-6, which continue v. 3, introduce a sorrowful
meditation, vv. 7-10, of which the subject is God's dealing
with His people. It is directed to the distant past, which
presents an inexplicable contrast for the suppliant. Hence
here one thing is already clear: for the speaker of the psalm
the suffering of his people takes the place of his personal

suffering. It is for the former that his grief is meant, as is the questioning and reflection to which his pain and incomprehension give rise.

vv. 7-10: For behind vv. 7-9 there obviously lies the unit of the communal lament 'the complaint against God', which we have in such passages as Psalms 74: 1, 11; 60: 1; 44: 9 ff., 23-24; 80: 4; 89: 46; Isaiah 64: 6; 40: 27; Lamentations 5: 20. And behind the complaint there always lies the anxious question: Has God abandoned us, His people? This is the question which stirs the speaker of Psalm 77, on which he reflects and which gives him no peace. This is the question being asked in the textually uncertain v. 10: 'Has it grown weak (reading *ḥāletāh*), has the right hand (the activity) of the Most High changed?' This question is forced on the speaker by the contrast between the inconsolable present and God's mighty acts for His people in the past.

vv. 11-15: So he calls to mind these acts of God, they get a new lease of life before his eyes, he realizes them in the present. Vv. 11-12 show the new direction that his meditation takes. In vv. 1-2, his thoughts had incessantly circled round present misery, and hence round the question whether God is still His people's God, vv. 7-10. But now he resolves to think back to the days when God miraculously showed Himself as Israel's helper: 'I will remember thy wonders of old'. We should note the change from the third to the second person; the meditation on God goes over at once to an address, a prayer, to Him. V. 12, picking up again the verbs of vv. 3, 5, 6, indicates the change that now occurs in the speaker's thought: as he reflects on God's earlier deeds, his meditation changes to astonished praise.

vv. 13-15: Here we reach the centre of the psalm. The language is unmistakeably that of the psalm of praise, both in its descriptive, vv. 13, 14a, and its narrative form, vv. 14b, 15, 20 – 'thou art . . . thou didst'.

For the understanding of the psalm, it is important to observe that the author does not achieve his turning back to

God through a contrast between past (*then* didst thou show thy goodness to us) and present, but rather his thought builds a bridge between them: God remains the same as He always was! Vv. 13a and b, 14a laud God's majesty, a regular element in the descriptive psalm of praise or hymn, for example, Psalm 113: 3-6. God's majesty has in no way altered. To His majesty belongs His holiness (compare Isaiah 6). By the singular expression, literally 'O God in the holy place (or in holiness) is thy way', the author means that for us God's activity, 'thy way', is not plainly to be seen. But that He is the God who works wonders, 14, is grounded precisely in His majesty: vv. 14b, 15, 20 state that He has worked wonders and can still do so today, compare Exodus 15: 11. But they mention only the one miracle of God at the beginning of Israel's national life, when He delivered His people from direst distress through His infinite might, v. 15, in the face of the Egyptian world power, v. 14b. This part of the psalm shows that the 'historical Credo' was a living reality for Israel. An Israelite, many centuries later, still remembers; what had happened was never forgotten. And in this individual's psalm the remembering also functions to magnify God in the gloomy present.[35] This remembering, which we meet in many passages, can be expressed in quite different words. When Israel is described here as 'the sons of Jacob and Joseph' this is only one of many possibilities: compare Psalm 78: 67-68; Amos 5: 6, 15; Ezekiel 37: 16; Zechariah 10: 6. The historical reminiscence often includes, along with the deliverance at the Sea, a mention of the wilderness wanderings, compare Psalms 74: 13-14; 78: 52-53; the latter also occurs here in v. 20, which originally followed v. 15, though now vv. 16-19, which are recognizable as an originally independent unit, have been inserted in between.

vv. 16-19: This relatively independent unit, which stands out from what precedes it by the different metre 3:3, develops the theme of God's drawing near to save His

---

[35] See C. Westermann, 'Vergegenwärtigung der Geschichte in den Psalmen', *Theologische Bücherei 24*, 1964, pp. 306-335.

people. It belongs to a group of closely related texts, epiphanies or epiphany descriptions, the common feature of which is a description of God's intervention to deliver His people. The function of all of them is to portray the miraculous and overwhelming power of this intervention.[36] They all have the same three elements: God's going forth and/or His subsequent journey, accompanying cosmic tremors and, as the goal of God's coming, His intervention to defeat or to deliver (this third unit in many cases only follows from the context). The epiphany description rests on a mythological motif, as is shown by a series of Babylonian and Egyptian texts.[37] The epiphany is to be distinguished from the theophany, the classic text for which is Exodus 19, for the context of the latter is always the cult, of the former always history.

Verses 16 and 19 clearly refer to the deliverance at the Sea but the description is very different from that of Exodus 14-15, in that it is linked with the traditional elements of the epiphany. 'The waters saw thee..,', as with Psalm 114: 3-5 in a similar context, that is, when God appears to help those who in their need appeal to Him; compare Psalm 18: 6. God draws near in power and majesty, He makes the sea tremble and shake. Here God's power is portrayed in operation; it reaches into the whole cosmos. In vv. 17 f., God's power in the cosmos displays itself by storms of thunder and lightning, a frequent motif in many religions,[38] and this answers to human experience, which recognizes the working of a supernatural power in storms and tempests. In 18b the divine power is further displayed in an earthquake.

The final v. 19 of this section resumes the beginning of v. 16. Here God's coming is expressly named, 'thy way',

[36] The relevant passages are Judges 5: 4-5; Psalm 18: 7-15; Habakkuk 3: 3-15; Psalms 68: 7-8, 33; 97: 2-5; 114; Isaiah 63: 1-6. Modifications are found in Psalms 29; 50: 2-4; Deuteronomy 33; Isaiah 30: 27-33; 59: 15b-20; Micah 1: 3-4; Nahum 1: 3b-6.

[37] For the details, see C. Westermann, *Praise and Lament in the Psalms*, pp. 93-101.

[38] For example, see the comments on these verses in H. Gunkel, *Die Psalmen*, 1926.

where v. 13a is also resumed; what is meant is the Exodus event. Now, however, the author adds in v. 19b a phrase which does not belong to the epiphany description but which continues and concludes the praise of God introduced in vv. 13–14a: 'yet thy footprints (referring to God's journey) were unseen'. It is the mark of God's holiness, of His inscrutable 'way', that no recognizable footprints are left behind. In considering this amazing statement, we must keep in view the whole context of the psalm, for it has arisen from the meditation there on God's deeds and is a result of that reflection on God's marvellous acts. Twice before in the psalm we hear of these marvellous acts, v. 11: 'I will remember thy wonders of old', and v. 14: 'Thou art a God who workest wonders'. So this psalm in particular shows us what the Old Testament understands by 'wonders'. What is meant here is God's marvellous deeds for His people, especially His acts of deliverance, and the change they brought about. It is the shock of amazement felt by those who experience these acts of God that causes them to be recognized as a 'wonder'. A wonder can only be experienced, not established objectively, and v. 19 expressly demonstrates this. Wonders happen when God and man come face to face and part of the experience of a wonder is a silent amazement before the work of the divine majesty, v. 13 f. This amazement always has something of incomprehension in it; a wonder understood is a wonder no longer. Hence a wonder is never explicable from its ascertainable phenomena, v. 19. When we try so to understand it, we fail to appreciate what the Bible understands by a wonder. The insertion here itself indicates that the phenomena accompanying a wonder may be of very different kinds. When a wonder is experienced as God's work, all we can say of it is that a 'wonderful' or 'marvellous' change has occurred; as Psalm 118: 23 puts it: 'This is the Lord's doing; it is marvellous in our eyes'. So the praise of God is the appropriate setting in which to speak of wonders.

A final word: I have given this psalm the heading, 'I think of God'. In this psalm, an Old Testament man of prayer

speaks of the thoughts that move him when he thinks of
God. 'I think of God, and I moan', v. 3 – the thought of God
arises from the lament: he thinks always in deep sorrow of
the wretched fate of his people. He asks whether God has
abandoned His people. Then his thoughts return to the
past, he thinks of God's wonderful saving acts which the
people once experienced. In place of lament, there appears
restrained praise of God, vv. 13-14. Nothing has changed in
respect of God's majestic work, but His ways remain
hidden, v. 19. 'Thinking of God' can take very different
forms; in the Old Testament it is always the case – as in this
psalm, where it is indeed clearly expressed – that to think of
God is to think of the God who acts and thus to think of a
reality. A fundamental change occurred in the history of the
Christian church when thinking of God became a reflection
on an eternal divine being. Thus such thought became
speculative, divorced from reality. Today we must ask
which is truer to the Bible – this speculative thought about
God or thinking of Him as real and active.

Psalm 102: A prayer of one afflicted, when he is faint

A prayer of one afflicted, when he is faint and pours out his
complaint before the Lord.

1   Hear my prayer, O Lord;
     let my cry come to thee!
2   Do not hide thy face from me in the day of my
        distress!
     Incline thy ear to me; in the day when I call
     answer me speedily!

3   For my days pass away like smoke,
     and my bones burn like a furnace.
4   My heart is scorched like grass and withered;
     I am too weak to eat my bread.
5   I am worn out because of my loud groaning;
     my skin cleaves to my bones.

6   I am like a jackdaw of the wilderness,
     like an owl of the waste places;
7   I lie awake and sigh like a lonely bird on the
          housetop.
8   All the day my enemies taunt me,
     those who deride me use my name for a curse.
9   For I eat ashes like bread,
     and mingle tears with my drink,
10   because of thy indignation and anger;
     for thou hast taken me up and thrown me away.
11   My days decline like a shadow;
     I wither away like grass.
12   But thou, O Lord, art enthroned for ever;
     thy name endures to all generations.

13   Thou wilt arise and have pity on Zion;
     it is time to favour her; the appointed time has
          come.
14   For thy servants hold her stones dear,
     and have pity on her dust.
     (v. 15 transposed to follow v. 22)
16   For the Lord will build up Zion, he will appear in his
          glory;
17   he will regard the prayer of the destitute,
     and will not despise their supplication.
18   Let this be recorded for a generation to come,
     so that a people yet unborn
     may praise the Lord!
19   For he looks down from his holy height,
     from heaven he looks down on the earth,
20   to hear the groans of the prisoners,
     to set free those who were doomed to die;
21   that men may declare in Zion the name of the
          Lord,
     and in Jerusalem his praise,
22   when peoples gather together,
     and kingdoms, to worship the Lord.
15   The nations will fear the name of the Lord,
     and all the kings of the earth thy glory.

23 He has broken my strength in midcourse; he has
     shortened my days.
24 'O my God', I say, 'take me not hence
     in the midst of my days,
         thou whose years endure throughout all
             generations!'
25 Of old thou didst lay the foundation of the earth,
     and the heavens are the work of thy hands.
26 They will perish, but thou dost endure;
     they will all wear out like a garment.
     Thou changest them like raiment, and they pass
         away;
27 but thou art the same,
     and thy years have no end.
28 The children of thy servants shall dwell secure;
     their posterity shall be established before thee.

Text

v. 2 (Heb. 3): perhaps in v. 2b (Heb. 3b) a verb 'take heed'
has fallen out.

v. 4 (Heb. 5): for *šakaḥti*, 'I forget', read *kāšaḥti*.

v. 5 (Heb. 6): after the opening words perhaps *jāba'ti*, 'I
am worn out', has fallen out.

v. 7 (Heb. 8): reading *wā'ehjah* instead of *wā'enheh*.

v.15 (Heb. 16): this verse should be transposed to follow
v. 22 (Heb. 23).

Structure

Psalm 102 is a an individual lament, as its title also shows,
but it has received several expansions. Proper to the
individual lament are vv. 1-12 and 23-24, together with vv.
17 and 18-20 within the first expansion. One expansion, vv.
13-22, is concerned with Zion's future destiny, and a
second, vv. 25-27, with the Creator's everlastingness. The
following discussion will show how these different sections

relate to one another.

Arrangement:

The title indicates that the text follows the pattern of an individual lament.

> vv. 1-2 Introductory cry for help, petition for God to turn back again; the petition for God to intervene only occurs in v. 24
> 3-11 Lament
>> 3-7 'I' lament, also vv. 9, 11, 23
>> 8 lament about enemies
>> 10 complaint against God
> 12 complaint, as v. 10, 'But thou, O Lord . . . '
> 13-17 God will have pity on Zion (certainty of a hearing)
>> 13 the time of favour has come
>> 14 the reason: mourning over Zion
>> (15 must be transposed to follow v. 22)
>> 16 God appears to build up Zion
>> 17 He hears the prayer of the destitute
> 18-22 (15) promise to praise God
>> 18 God's work for a coming generation to be recorded
>> 19-20 God looks down in mercy from His height into the depths
>> 21 in Jerusalem men are to declare the Lord's name
>> 22, 15 before the nations going on pilgrimage to Zion
> 23-24a continuation of the lament of vv. 10-11, and petition
> 24b-27 the Creator's everlastingness
>> 24b God endures throughout all generations
>> 25 He has made heaven and earth
>> 26-27 they will perish, but God endures
> 28 the children of thy servants shall dwell secure

Psalm 102 is the only psalm of lament so described in its title. The first word, *tephillāh* (prayer), is properly the plea, as is the same word in v. 1, but it later acquires the more general meaning of 'prayer'. It is the 'plea of one afflicted' (the Hebrew preposition *le* denotes the genitive here). The description of the type of text is followed by the *Sitz im Leben*, 'when he is faint'. Here it is made clear that the psalms of lament do not originally form part of regular acts of worship but presuppose the situation of one afflicted by grave suffering. The psalms of lament belong to real life.

vv. 1-2: The psalm begins with a cry for help, a petition for God to turn to him again. All the clauses of vv. 1-2 give expression to this petition in various ways. In many psalms of lament, an introductory petition precedes the lament, though normally the petition follows the lament. The reason for the variation is that the cry for help was once an independent unit and it is found as such in narratives. The psalm of lament can be seen as a development from this cry for help.

vv. 3-11: Now follows the lament, divided into 'I' lament, vv. 3-7, 9-11, lament about enemies, v. 8, and complaint against God, v. 10, with the main weight concentrated on the 'I' lament. It gives a description of bodily suffering, so we may think of an illness, although it is not possible to diagnose its nature. The description is very different from the way we would speak of our illnesses. It does not aim realistically to enumerate and describe the symptoms, but rather to express what the condition of sickness means for the human condition and how gravely it restricts and diminishes human life. That this is so is shown by the comparisons. They are not picture language which aims to make the description more vivid, but their object is to strengthen and intensify the meaning of the sickness for the sufferer's life. Such is the significance of burning like a furnace and being withered and scorched like grass, which means the same thing as the loss of vigour described, without employing a comparison, in vv. 4b-5. The lament over life's transitoriness, 'my days pass away like smoke' and 'my days decline like a shadow,' which in v. 3 and v. 11 frame the lament section, expresses the suppliant's sense of the approach of death; death's power is at work in his sickness.

A common feature in the lament is the disruption or destruction of life's supportive rhythm, eating and drinking, vv. 4b, 9, and sleeping, v. 7, compare Psalm 80: 5. Exceptional, however, is the comparison here with birds: 'jackdaw of the wilderness', 'owl of the waste places', 'a lonely bird on the housetop', vv. 6-7. Suffering brings loneliness and the man stricken with a severe illness feels himself to be an outcast.

While the whole weight falls on the 'I' lament, the lament about enemies, v.8. sounds, by contrast, like a stock formula. The complaint against God, v. 10, also consists of only a single verse but its tone is very harsh: the suppliant, who now appears as plaintiff, can only see behind his suffering the God who in His wrath has rejected him (for the expression 'taken up and thrown away', compare Job 27: 21; 30: 22). But as compared with the 'I' lament, the complaint too sounds somewhat formal.

v. 12: This clause comes in abruptly and it is possible that the verse order here has been disturbed. V. 11 belongs to the 'I' lament and would better follow v. 7. V. 12 would be more comprehensible as a contrast to v. 10 and as following on from it. V. 12 begins with the 'but thou . . .', the *wāw* adversative, which here serves to indicate the contrast between God enthroned in majesty and the suppliant's awareness of being rejected by Him. Although, like the almost identical sentence in Psalm 22: 3, it is closely connected to the complaint against God, it nevertheless signifies a change. For it is a word of praise to God that the suppliant speaks here: that God is enthroned in eternal majesty means not only that He turns away in wrath but also that He can turn back to the suppliant again.

vv. 13–22: These verses follow as the first expansion. Up to now, all the verses 1–12 belong to the individual lament, as the psalm is also described in the title.[39]

Otherwise than in Psalm 77, where the reference to the fate of the speaker's people is integrated organically into the individual lament, what we have here is a later mechanical addition. But the author's intention was the same in each case, to bind together the lament of the individual sufferer with the searing pain he feels for the fate of Zion. Also, this later addition indicates a situation after the destruction of Jerusalem, where the suffering occasioned by the ruined city was so significant that it had to find expression along with the individual's suffering. We find a similar linking of the motif of the rebuilding of Zion with an individual

[39] As was seen correctly by F. Delitzsch, opposing attempts to interpret vv. 1–12 as a communal lament.

lament in Psalm 69, where the appended verses 35-36 have the same content as Psalm 102: 16 and 28. V. 17 is clearly recognizable as the link verse. What is more, this added section has in view the structure of the psalm of lament; in the section vv. 13-22, the first part, vv. 13-17, corresponds to the element 'the certainty of a hearing', and the second, vv. 18-22, to the vow of praise, although both elements are very considerably altered.

vv. 13-17: Contrary to the view of many commentators, this part does not have the form of a prophetic announcement but of the psalm unit 'the certainty of a hearing'. The only difference is that it speaks of the fate of Jerusalem instead of personal distress. In the impressive wording of v. 14, the grieving and wistful expectation of Jerusalem's rebuilding corresponds to the expectation that God will take pity on the ruined city. All who have experienced their city's destruction understand such phrases as 'hold her stones dear' and 'have pity on her dust'; the act of destruction is inherent in the dust or rubble. In its present position, v. 15 makes no sense and should be read after v. 22. Vv. 16-17 repeat the 'certainty of a hearing' theme in the way that v. 16 continues v. 13a: God will have pity on Zion and build her up again. V. 17 may refer back to the mourning for the ruined city in v. 14, but it is so formulated as to be identical in its wording with the 'certainty of a hearing' of the individual lament, and hence could be the continuation of vv. 1-12. By means of v. 17 the addition 13-17 is linked with the preceding lament.

vv. 18-22, 15: This section occupies the position of the vow of praise. Vv. 18- 20 are so closely connected with v. 17 that they too could represent the end of an individual lament, as is shown by their closeness to Psalm 22: 22-31, where vv. 30-31 are almost identical with v. 18 here. Instead of being recited, the events to which the psalm bears witness are to be written down, as in Psalm 139: 16, showing how in the later period oral transmission was supplanted by written. But the purpose remains the same: the praise of God is to extend to generations to come. There follows in vv. 19-20 a typical example of the language used in praising God (compare, for example, Psalm 113): God is praised in His majestic glory, from which He looks down into the depths to hear the groans of the prisoners and to set them free. Only at vv. 21-22, with the addition of v. 15, is the supplement dealing with Zion's rebuilding continued; vv. 21 f. could be attached directly to vv. 13-14, 16. Here the praise of God is concerned with the rebuilding of Jerusalem, in Jerusalem is to be recounted what God has done for His city. But this is to take place before the nations assembled in Jerusalem; in v. 22 the author of the supplement is alluding to the pilgrimage of the nations to Zion prophesied in Isaiah 2 and Micah 4. But the way in which this has been adapted to the psalm shows how a prophetic announcement could be taken up into the liturgical worship of the late period.

vv. 23-28: V. 22, along with 15, reads like a conclusion. It is difficult to grasp the purpose of vv. 23-28 in their context. V. 23, and the following petition in v. 24a, is an abrupt continuation of the 'I' lament. Since in both verses it is a question of an imminent premature death, vv. 23-24a could be linked with v. 11, and v. 24b belongs closely with v. 12: God's everlastingness is contrasted with the suppliant's own premature death, vv. 12 and 24a. The theme of God's everlastingness is expanded in vv. 25-27: here we can recognize a second expansion, from the fact that v. 27 recurs to 24b. This second addition is probably to be understood as setting God's creative activity, v. 25, alongside His activity in history, vv. 13-16, 21-22; in the psalm of praise both develop the theme of the praise of God's majesty (for example, Psalm 33). Here the creation motif, 25, emphasizes God's everlastingness, 26-27. With the lament for human transitoriness, vv. 23-24, God's everlastingness, vv. 24b-27, is contrasted in such a way as to set earth and heaven together with an individual human being on the finite side of the divide: 'they will all wear out like a garment'. By this, the individual being in his suffering and anguish in the face of imminent death is taken out of his isolation, vv. 6-7, and his existence, even as it draws near to death, gains a meaning from the mighty unity of creation which in its transitoriness remains over against its Creator. 'But thou dost endure' – by this, even the one approaching his end can know that he is secure.

v. 28: The final verse belongs to the first expansion, dealing with Zion, as is shown by the similar words, following on a clause corresponding to v. 16 of this psalm, in Psalm 69: 34-35. The placing of this statement about the secure dwelling of Zion's posterity at the end after vv. 25-27 has the effect of associating the continuation of life through succeeding generations with God's enduring presence. Even for finite humanity, there remains at the frontier of transitoriness the possibility of 'dwelling securely', of 'being established'.

Psalm 130: Out of the depths

1   Out of the depths I cry to thee, O Lord!
2   Lord, hear my voice!
    Let thy ears be attentive to the voice of my
        supplications!
3   If thou, O Lord, shouldst mark iniquities,
    Lord, who could stand?

4   But there is forgiveness with thee, that thou mayest
        be feared.
5   From the heart I hope in thee, O Lord,
    and on his word I wait.
6   My soul waits for the Lord
    more than watchmen for the morning.

7   O Israel, hope in the Lord!
    For with the Lord there is steadfast love,
    and with him is plenteous redemption.

8   And he will redeem Israel from all his iniquities.

Text

v. 5: the third word *qiwwetāh* is to be transferred to the beginning of v. 6.

v. 6: the second 'watchmen for the morning' is to be omitted as a doublet.

Structure

Arrangement:
  vv. 1-2 petition for a hearing
  3-4 motivation for the petition
  5-7 avowal of trust
    5-6 hope for forgiveness
    7b certainty of a hearing
7a-8 an addition: forgiveness for Israel

Psalm 130 is among those psalms where one element of the psalm of lament has become a separate psalm in its own right, in this case the petition for forgiveness (compare Psalm 51 where, however, the stress falls on the confession of sin). The psalm as a whole is a petition for forgiveness and the lament element is only hinted at in vv. 1-2. As vv. 3-4 also belong to the petition, the entire psalm consists only of the petition for forgiveness, 1-4, and an expression of hope that it will be granted, 5-7. Also, it is to be observed that, like Psalm 51, the context of this psalm is an act of worship concerned with the forgiveness of sin. The two clauses, vv. 7a and 8, in which Israel's sins are the object of the forgiveness, are a later addition.

vv. 1-2: 'Out of the depths' – the word means 'depths of water' and is an expression of distress, as, for example, in Psalm 69: 2 and 14: 'I sink in deep mire, where there is no foothold; I have come into deep waters', and so similarly Isaiah 51: 10; Ezekiel 27: 34.[40] Thus a real distress, affecting the whole man, is in view and not merely 'distress because

---

[40] Compare Luther's hymn, translated by Catherine Winkworth: 'Out of the depths I cry to Thee'.

of sin'. The cry to God in distress is a cry in deadly peril; the anxious hope, vv. 5-6, is hope in the face of a threat of death.

In this respect, Psalm 130 is no different from all the other individual psalms of lament. But one must emphasize the point, because this psalm has been so widely interpreted as though it referred only to distress caused by sin and as though in vv. 1-2 a man tortured by the awareness of sin were calling on God. But such an abstract awareness of sin is as unknown to the Old Testament as is a general, abstract term for sin itself (see the comment on Psalm 51 above). Rather, a man's offence against God affects his whole being in his relationship with God, his body and soul and his life in community with others. The sin against God has its impact on his whole existence as a human being. The suppliant in Psalm 130 cries out to God from the depths into which his entire being has sunk. But he knows that he himself is responsible for the distress in which he finds himself and so everything for him depends on God forgiving him. This is why, unlike Psalm 51, there is here no explicit confession of sin. The one who cries to God has no doubt that he is guilty, for he has long admitted this. All that matters to him is that God should forgive him. Here is the reason why the petition in v. 2 for God to turn to him again is so strongly emphasized.

vv. 3-4: We can now understand the two motivations of vv. 3-4 which seek to influence God to turn to the suppliant again. One has men in view, v. 3, the other God, v. 4. Were God to 'mark' all his iniquities and punish them accordingly, no man could stand before God; for man is fallible and his inclination is to sin. But God is merciful, 'there is forgiveness with thee', an expression that occurs only here in the Psalter; we meet it elsewhere in Ecclesiasticus 5: 6: 'His mercies are great', in Nehemiah 9: 17: 'But thou art a God ready to forgive, gracious and merciful . . .', and in Daniel 9: 9: 'To the Lord our God belong mercy and forgiveness'. These two last passages, which are very similar to v. 4, show that Psalm 130 is a late composition. Like

Psalm 103, the verse praises the God who shows mercy. Here it is stated as clearly as possible that God's mercy is the one thing which the man threatened by the deadly consequences of his sin can hold on to.

V. 4 continues with the words 'that thou mayest be feared'. The connection of thought is not immediately clear, because for us the word 'fear' has of itself a negative sound. But the case is different here. 'Fear of God' implies a positive relationship to Him; he who fears God is safe with God. So what is meant here is this: it is simply the certainty that God is merciful, that His 'property is always to forgive', on which a relationship with Him (the fear of God) can be founded, a relationship which means finding security in Him. Awe in the presence of God is awe in the presence of the God of mercy.

vv. 5-6: Corresponding to the structure of the psalm of lament, the petition of vv. 1-2 is succeeded by the declaration of confidence. Vv. 5-6 are a locus classicus for what the Bible means by hope and hoping. The word hope in the Bible does not mean a vision of the future, though this is how it is commonly and wrongly interpreted. Nor does it mean 'what one hopes for oneself', what one imagines or dreams for oneself. Rather, hope and hoping is an action, setting one's expectation on something,[41], whereby what one hopes for results from the situation in which one hopes. When here God Himself is introduced as the object of hope, in a formula specially characteristic of the language of the psalms, 'I hope in thee', it tells us that everything to be hoped for is entirely comprehended in the One who alone can bring deliverance from distress. Deliverance is the decisive act of the Deliverer. The expression of hope is accompanied by a comparison: '. . . more than watchmen for the morning'. Its purpose is not to add vividness to the 'hoping in God': it cannot do so, because this hope is no vision but an action, and because hoping cannot be described in picture language. Rather, the comparison

---

[41] See C. Westermann, 'Das Hoffen im Alten Testament', *Theologische Bücherei 24*, 964, pp. 219-265.

intensifies what is being compared, the hoping in God gains stronger and more powerful expression by means of the comparison, which is particularly felicitous in this case. For those who hear the psalm know, from their own experience, those night watches, when men exposed to danger and with responsibility for others watch all the night through and long for morning to come. V. 5a is followed by a line in synonymous parallelism: 'and on his word I wait'. By this can only be meant God's word of pardon, the word that bestows forgiveness. If this psalm belongs to an act of worship, the reference would be to the words of forgiveness pronounced by a priest. But in any case we are to understand that a divine deliverance out of the depths is only possible through God's word of forgiveness.

v. 7b: This verse originally followed directly on v. 6 (7a is lacking in the Septuagint); it provides the ground for the hope and thus moves forward the praise of the merciful God in v. 4 ('with him is' in 7b = 'is with thee' in v. 4). 'Steadfast love' and 'redemption' (only elsewhere at Psalm 111: 9; Isaiah 50: 2 and perhaps Exodus 8: 19) are here in parallel; God's steadfast love, *hesed*, brings about 'plenteous redemption', compare Psalm 103.

If for the moment we read the psalm without vv. 7a and 8, the consistency of its structure becomes clearer. It begins with the words 'out of the depths' and ends with the word 'redemption'; the middle v. 4 corresponds to the final verse 7b, both praising God's mercifulness.

vv. 7a–8: Here we have two appendices, or even just one, which the psalm acquired later. For there can be no doubt that Psalm 130 is the prayer of an individual and the praise of v. 7b is its original conclusion. Apart from the fact that v. 7a is absent from the Septuagint, the same words appear as an added appendix also at Psalm 131: 3, and this too is a psalm of an individual. V. 8 expresses the certainty that God will redeem Israel from all its iniquities. A verbally identical verse has been added as an appendix at Psalm 25: 22, another individual psalm. As this is an alphabetic psalm, the final verse of which, 21, begins with *tāw*, the last letter of the Hebrew alphabet, it is obvious that v. 22 must be a later addition. The reason why 7a and 8 were added to Psalm 130, just as in Psalm 131, is easily recognizable. Psalms 120–134 form an originally independent collection. All of them have the same title 'A Song of Ascents' or song of pilgrimage. Since pilgrimage songs are really songs of a group or community, when individual psalms were admitted to the collection, they received this kind of appendix in order to give them a community reference.

There was also a theological reason for such additions. As we have already seen with respect to Psalms 77 and 102, in the period after the exile Israel's sad fate, which the prophets viewed as a judgment on the guilty nation, became highly significant for individual piety as well and so was linked, in a variety of ways, with the individual prayers. This is also the case with the appendices to Psalm 130.

Luther's hymn 'Out of the depths I cry to thee' shows that in this psalm particularly the Reformers found again their own understanding of sin and grace. When Luther renders vv. 4 and 7b: 'Though great our sins and sore our wounds . . . His helping mercy hath no bounds',[42] he gives the same weight to the praise of God's grace that the psalm does. Psalm 130 is one of those psalms which speak of God's mercy, goodness and purpose to forgive in such a way as to give us an immediate impression of what these things meant for those who prayed the psalms. Hence it is a gross distortion of the truth, when, as still happens, Old and New Testament are set in opposition and the former is said to speak of God's wrath, the latter of His mercy. The petition in Psalm 130, and in many other psalms, for God to turn again in mercy makes it absolutely clear that for those who prayed the psalms the most important attribute of God's nature was His abundant and inexhaustible compassion. Alongside, Psalm 130 tells us something of what the Old Testament understands by sin. To a great extent, the particular effect the psalm makes on us depends on the

[42]; Translated by Catherine Winkworth. The original is: 'Ob bei uns ist der Sünde viel, bei Gott ist viel mehr Gnade'.

movement which controls it from beginning to end. 'Out
of the depths' is its beginning, 'with him is plenteous
redemption' its end; in the middle stands the verse which
brings out the agitated tension between beginning and end:
'My soul waits for the Lord more than watchmen for the
morning'. His sin has brought the speaker down to the
depths from which his urgent plea rises. But his hope sets in
motion his emergence from the depths, which is made
possible by the certainty that God's mercy is stronger than
the power of sin. Here sin is in no way the decisive element
in human existence, even though the speaker knows that he
is fallible and always inclined to sin. Rather, sin is part of the
human story which moves from the heights to the depths
and back to the heights again; and the decisive element in
the story is what happens between a man and his God.

INDIVIDUAL PSALMS OF TRUST

Psalm 4: In peace I will both lie down and sleep

1   Answer me when I call, O God of my right!
     Thou hast given me room when I was in distress.
     Be gracious to me, and hear my prayer.
2   O men, how long shall my honour suffer shame?
     How long will you love vain words, and seek after
         lies?
3   But know that the Lord has shown me marvellous
         grace;
     the Lord hears when I call to him.
4   Be angry, but sin not;
     let your heart be bitter on your beds, but be
         silent.
5   Offer right sacrifices, and put your trust in the
         Lord.
6   There are many who say, 'O that we might see
         some good!
     Lift up the light of thy countenance on us, O
         Lord!'
7   Thou hast put more joy in my heart
     than others have when their grain and wine
         abound.
8   In peace I will both lie down and sleep;
     for thou alone, O Lord, makest me dwell in
         safety.

Text

v. 4   (Heb. 5): on grounds of parallelism, instead of
       'imrū, 'say', or 'commune', *hāmērū*, from *mrr*, 'be
       bitter', is to be read.

Structure

The psalm begins as an individual lament and then becomes a psalm of trust, that is, the motif of trust is dominant.

The structure is very loose and the motifs are only partly discernible. V. 1 is an introductory petition. The lament is indicated in vv. 2-5 but it is considerably altered by the address to the speaker's enemies. Vv. 6-8 consist of the declaration of confidence but it has a quite free and meditative form here. In the psalm as a whole reflection and meditation play a large part. Exegesis must seek to trace the course of the meditation, but this is only possible to a limited degree. It is not necessary, therefore, for everyone to understand it in exactly the same way. The essential point is that a single reading cannot unlock the psalm's meaning for us. We must read it over and over again and repeatedly think through the problem of how the motifs and sections are connected with one another.

v. 1: The psalm begins like a psalm of lament, with the introductory petition for a hearing. The plea for an answer in the first and third lines betrays the speaker's anguish that God could remain dumb, his anguish at losing contact with Him: this is a common feature in laments, for example Psalm 22. In his anguish, the speaker holds on to what he has earlier experienced; this is expressed in the second line, in between the two petitionary lines which surround it. He recalls that God had once aided him when he was in distress, had 'given him room', given him freedom to breathe.

vv. 2-5: Now the lament should follow and it does, but it is restricted to the lament about enemies (though the 'I' lament is observable in 6a) and greatly altered by the address to the enemies threatening the speaker. Hence the lament style only remains in v. 2. In this verse, the speaker accuses his foes: it is deliberate lying, when they speak of him or behave towards him so as to bring shame on him among his community. In the sentence 'how long shall my honour suffer shame?', we must understand that in the Old

INDIVIDUAL PSALMS OF TRUST 125

Testament 'honour' and 'shame' do not signify two extremes; honour is not a distinction, which separates or singles out some from others (for example, official position or freeman status) but rather the normal respect and recognition by the community.

vv. 3-5: In these verses which follow, the speaker no longer complains about the enemies; rather, he seeks to bring about a change in their behaviour, to prevail on them to consider what they are doing. This is something that occurs only rarely, almost never, in fact, in psalms of lament. It is a consequence of that change from lament to trust which is determinative for this psalm. The confident trust in God which fills the speaker also affects his attitude towards his opponents. He seeks to prevail on them by drawing three matters to their attention: he holds up to them his close fellowship with God, v. 3, he points out that God has heard him (see also v. 1b), and that so He has shown him marvellous grace – can it be right for them to set themselves against God? His experience of God gives support to the man overcome by enemies but it can mean something for them as well.

v. 4: This verse is entirely foreign to the style of the psalm of lament: it only makes sense as part of the address to the opponents. The speaker comes to meet them, he puts himself in their position and admits that their agitation and bitterness are understandable. Unfortunately we cannot gather from the psalm why this should be so, but we all know how our heart can grow bitter at night on our bed over some injustice we have experienced and how we then become ever more and more bitter. So the speaker warns his opponents: Do not give vent to your rage!

v. 5: The speaker now goes on to offer a suggestion which can help them: 'Offer right sacrifices', by which he means not just cultically correct sacrifices but, in line with Psalm 51: 17, 'the sacrifice acceptable to God', that is, giving up pressing their claims and no longer seeking to get their own way without thought for others. Abandoning such egotistical self-concern is for the speaker equivalent to trusting in God, 'and put your trust in the Lord'.

v. 6: The address to the opponents ends with v. 5. While there is a close connection between vv. 3-5, vv. 6a and 6b each stand out on their own. One cannot see any connecting link either between vv. 3-5 and 6 or between 6a and 6b. To resolve the question, we must begin from the structure of the psalm of lament. The lament about enemies, v. 2, expanded in 3-5, is often followed by the 'I' lament. The latter is presupposed by v. 6 in the words 'there are many who say', but it is now set in the meditative context of vv. 3-5.

With the opening words, 'there are many who say', the speaker merges with his opponents. They meet together in the cry of the unfortunate: 'O that we might see some good!', which, in the clauses of the 'I' lament, is raised in many different ways in the psalms of lament. It forms part of human existence now as then. But to this lament the speaker opposes his own experience and from it again addresses his opponents: when he turned to God (compare v. 1), his misfortune was turned round, 'lift up the light of thy countenance on us, O Lord!', which echoes the liturgical blessing: 'The Lord make his face to shine upon you!'

vv. 7-8: In what way this turning to God is in fact the turning round of his misfortunes is revealed by the two final verses. In clear and matter-of-fact language, the speaker tells us what trust in God means for him. He summons his opponents to trust likewise, v. 5, he acknowledges before them what he himself has discovered by so trusting, v. 3. In trusting, man's needs are supplied, v. 7, and his safety assured, v. 8, now as then, always and everywhere. The speaker acknowledges that food and drink have ceased to be his greatest concern: 'Thou hast put more joy in my heart'. He will no longer be upset by worrying about 'grain and wine'. He needs them like everyone else and is confident that God will provide him with what is necessary; but what is 'more joy' for him is to be in contact with God and to receive the gifts from His hand. And the same holds good for his safety. For trusting in God is not something more or less played out in life's back room or in the sphere of 'religion': such trust is at the very heart of life or it is nowhere. So what it means can be expressed in a very down-to-earth everyday sentence: 'In peace I will both lie down and sleep'. The one who says this can sleep in peace and quiet in spite of all possible dangers; for he remembers the deadly peril in the midst of which he uttered these words and then went peacefully to sleep, 'for thou alone, O Lord, makest me dwell in safety'.

The two verses 7 and 8 where, at the end of Psalm 4, trust in God finds expression, correspond to two comparisons that, in a whole range of psalm passages, also give expression to it. God is my rock, my fortress, my refuge – that is one of them. God is my portion, my lot – that is the other. As the relevant passages show, these two comparisons, which also link vv. 7-8 together, have arisen from the myriad experiences of many generations. They show what God means for those who have prayed and still pray the psalms.

Psalm 23: The Lord is my shepherd

1   The Lord is my shepherd, I shall not want;
2   he makes me lie down in green pastures.
     He leads me beside still waters;
3   he stills my longing.
     He leads me in right paths for his name's sake.
4   Even though I must go through a dark valley,
     I fear no evil, for thou art with me,
     thy rod and thy staff give me confidence.
5   Thou preparest a table before me in the presence of
         my enemies;
     thou anointest my head with oil, my cup
         overflows.

6   Surely goodness and mercy shall follow me all the
      days of my life;
      and I shall dwell in the house of the Lord as long as I
      live.

Text

v. 2: literally, 'waters of rest' (plural); the accent marking
      the end of the verse in the Hebrew text is to be
      transposed to follow the second Hebrew word of v.
      3.
v. 4: the Septuagint adds 'in the midst'. For 'rod and
      staff', L. Köhler translates 'club and support'.
v. 6: instead of *wešabti*, 'I turn back', *wejāšabti* is to be
      read.

Structure

Psalm 23 does not display the structure of any of the general
psalm types. Rather, in it a motif of the individual lament,
the avowal of trust, has been expanded into a psalm. All six
verses belong to the motif of the avowal of trust.

Vv. 1-3 are dominated by the comparison of God with the
shepherd and in them the avowal of trust, 'thou art my
shepherd', is developed along the lines of the two functions
of the shepherd: he leads his flock, v. 3, and he provides it
with water and pasturage, vv. 1-2. The central v. 4
expresses the certainty that Yahweh is with the speaker and
protects him in danger; in the third line the comparison of
God with the shepherd appears again. V. 5 links the first
part of the psalm, 1-3, with the second, 4, by its statement
of the psalmist's further certainty that God will make
provision against enemy threats, and this has the effect of
heightening what is said about the divine provision of the
necessities of life on the occasion of a joyful feast. v. 6 closes
with the expression of the speaker's certainty that his

fellowship with God will last as long as he lives.

A note should be added on the background of the expression 'The Lord is my shepherd'. The history of this expression is in two stages:

A. The comparison of kings or gods with the shepherd is already met with in Sumerian texts:

> 'King of the city that flourishes like a cow,
> a good shepherd thou art!'
> 'O shepherd, thou knowest how to protect the black-headed people
> (= men).
> Ewe and lamb seeking (nourishment),
> come for it to thee;
> how to lead goat and kid with thy staff for all time,
> thou knowest,
> Ningizzada (an underworld deity) thou knowest how to lead with thy
> staff for all time'.[43]

These parallels prove that a very ancient comparison underlies Psalm 23. At the period when it emerged, the existence of the group depended on the leader, as the flock on the shepherd. Such was the case with the nomadic groups and so it remained when the concept was taken over into the settled Sumerian culture.

B. The second stage is represented by the transfer, as seen in Psalm 23, of the comparison to the individual's relationship with God. In the Old Testament the older use of the comparison to refer to the relationship of God to His people is also retained, Psalm 80; Isaiah 64. This is only to be expected, for only in this context can the comparison have arisen. Its transfer to the individual's relationship with God indicates a change towards a greater prominence for the individual, such as we see elsewhere in later Old Testament writings, particularly Ezekiel. Therefore we can certainly conclude that Psalm 23 is a late composition.

vv. 1-3: The declaration of confidence could have been adequately expressed by a single sentence: 'Yahweh is my shepherd, in him I trust', or 'in thee I trust'. The author of

---

[43] Texts in A. Falkenstein, *Sumerische Götterlieder, II Teil*, 1960, pp. 58 f., 82.

the psalm lingers over the comparison and develops it: what the shepherd means for the flock God means for me. He provides me with food and drink, he leads me in the right path. All this that is said in the comparison with the shepherd is a reflective expansion of a psalm motif; in incisive yet inviting words, it carries further the thought of what God means for the speaker here. It can only be understood from the structure of the individual lament that lies behind it. As the speaker, in the face of his distress and anguish, professes his trust in God's help, so, by the reflective expansion, the psalmist seeks to highlight this profession, to reinforce and emphasize it, and, in so doing, to strengthen his own confident certainty and that of his fellow men – 'I shall not want'.

v. 4: The background of the psalm of lament emerges more clearly in this central verse. Here we see that the psalm is no idyll; trust proves its worth in deadly danger, 'I fear no evil, for thou art with me'. The comparison is abandoned in v. 4a and the psalmist speaks of real experiences. Only in the last line, 'thy rod and thy staff give me confidence', does the comparison reappear. 'Rod and staff' perhaps represents a double description of the shepherd's crook: L. Köhler's translation 'club and support' would be better. The reason given for the confidence, 'for thou art with me', *ki 'attāh 'immādi*, may reflect the formal motif of God's promise to 'be with' the patriarchs, as that appear in Genesis 26: 3 and elsewhere.

v. 5: This verse does not just add the picture of the good host to that of the good shepherd (one commentary gives to our psalm the title 'Yahweh, good shepherd and good host').[44] It is in direct speech, as in part is v. 4. It links protection, v. 4, with provision, vv. 1-2, and also heightens the latter: thou lettest me celebrate a feast without hindrance from my foes! – so sure is the psalmist of God's support, which guarantees him a joyful feast in spite of all that besets

---

[44] In German, 'der gute Hirt und Wirt'.

him. The phrase 'in the presence of my enemies' reveals again the background of the psalm of lament, for here too we have the three subjects of the individual lament, God, the supplicant and the enemies.

v. 6: The psalm closes on a note of certainty: the fellowship with God which the speaker's trust has won will remain as long as he lives. We must not take this as implying persistent optimism. The speaker here knows that he must still often walk through a dark valley, but he also knows that no exposure to danger can separate him from God. This final verse does not mean that from now on he will always dwell in the Temple; rather, it echoes a similarly formulated vow of praise like the one in Psalm 17: 15 or in the Psalm of Hezekiah, Isaiah 38: 20: 'As for me, I shall behold thy face in righteousness; when I awake, I shall be satisfied with beholding thy form'. Here as there, what is meant is continual fellowship with God.

A final word: The twenty-third Psalm, the best known of all the psalms, is often viewed as an idyll, as a cheerful, ideal picture of a quite unreal relationship with God. That it is not and that it never was. One only has to read the extremely realistic description of a shepherd's work in Genesis 31: 38-41 for the gentle countenance of a smiling, friendly shepherd to vanish at once. Above all, the intention of the text is not to paint a picture, the picture of the good shepherd. It does not aim for a picture either of a shepherd or a 'little lamb'. What it does is to place two actions side by side: the provision a shepherd makes for his flock and the provision God makes for the one who trusts Him. It is this trust, this 'declaration of confidence', which above all makes it possible to compare God to a shepherd; it is this trust which the comparison enshrines and develops. But this trust rests on real life experiences, in which suffering, anguish and doubt all play a part. In and from them trust has grown, in the dark valleys, in deadly threat.

But Psalm 23 still has something more to say. It begins with the basic sentence: 'The Lord is my shepherd', *yhwh rō'ī*. The question whether there is a God is not posed here and cannot be posed here. What the psalm says is this: when a man in all that he experiences in life seizes hold of trust – whether he is worrying about his daily bread or asking after the right path or feeling himself in deadly peril – when he trusts that he will be upheld, that there is someone who takes care of him, then in and through that trust he has achieved fellowship with God and he can say 'God is my shepherd'. Thereby his life gains a meaning which it did not have before, and a context which it did not have before. The question whether there is a God receives its answer from real life experience, not from theoretical discussion.

Psalm 73: I am continually with thee

1 Truly God is good to the upright,
  to those who are pure in heart.

2 But as for me, my feet had almost stumbled,
  my steps had well nigh slipped.

3 For I was envious of the arrogant,
  when I saw the prosperity of the wicked.

4 For they have no pangs;
  their bodies are sound and sleek.

5 They are not in trouble as other men are;
  they are not stricken like other men.

6 Therefore pride is their necklace;
  violence covers them as a garment.

7 Their eyes swell out with fatness,
  their hearts overflow with follies.

8 They scoff and speak with malice;
  loftily they speak falsehood.

9 They set their mouths against the heavens,
  and their tongue struts through the earth.

10 Therefore . . .

11 And they say, 'How can God know?
  Is there knowledge in the Most High?'

12 Behold, these are the wicked;
  always at ease they increase in power.

22 But I – stupid and ignorant,
   I was like a beast toward thee.
21 For my heart was embittered and pain cut through
   my reins.
13 All in vain have I kept my heart clean
   and washed my hands in innocence.
14 For all the day long I have been stricken,
   and chastened every morning,
15 When I enumerated these things, I thought:
   'Thou betrayest the generation of thy children'.
16 And when I sought how to understand this,
   it was weariness to my eyes,

17 until I came into the sanctuary of God;
   then I perceived their end.
18 Truly thou hast set them in slippery places;
   thou makest them to stumble in deception.
19 How they are destroyed in a moment,
   and swept away utterly by terrors!
20 They are like a dream, vanishing when one
   awakes,
   on awaking you dismiss its phantoms.

23 But I am continually with thee;
   thou dost hold my right hand.
24 Thou dost guide me with thy counsel,
   and finally thou wilt receive me in honour.
25 Whom have I in heaven but thee?
   And there is nothing upon earth that I desire besides
   thee.
26 My flesh and my heat may fail,
   but God is my portion for ever.

27 For lo, those who are far from thee shall perish;
   thou dost put an end to those who are false to
   thee.
28 But for me it is good to draw near thee;
   in the Lord I set my trust,
   that I may tell of all thy works.

Text

The text of Psalm 73 is very poorly preserved. V. 10 is virtually beyond restoration and there are textual errors in most of the verses. But that is no way surprising in view of the method by which these texts have been transmitted. In considering Psalm 73, the poor state of the text gives particular significance to the point, made earlier in the Introduction, that a psalm can only be understood as a whole, and as a unity. Because the structure of Psalm 73 is easily recognizable, the general sense of the psalm can be understood with certainty, in spite of the text's bad condition.

v. 1: *lejisrāēl*, 'for Israel', should be divided into two words, while retaining the consonants, to read *lejāšār 'ēl*, 'to the upright, God'. The reason for the emendation is the parallelism and also the fact that the psalm is not dealing with Israel but with an individual. The emendation is accepted by BHK, BHS and most commentators.

v. 2: in the case of the two verbs, read the Qerē rather than the Ketīb, following BHK and BHS.

v. 4: the fourth word in the Hebrew is to be divided into two, *lāmō tām*, the word *tām* belonging to the second line.

v. 8: by transposing two consonants, read *'qš* for *'šq*.

v. 10: the text is incomprehensible.

v. 13: v. 12 is clearly the end of the section comprising the description of the wicked. But v. 13 does not suggest a fresh beginning, which requires 'But I . . .'. The text becomes comprehensible when vv. 22 and 21, which do not fit their present position, are inserted here.

v. 22: read 'beast' in the singular, in place of the Hebrew 'beasts'.

v. 14: read the passive *wehūkaḥti*, 'chastened'.

v. 15: *'amarti*, 'I thought', is to be removed to the beginning of the second line.

v. 18: 'their feet' would be better than 'them'.

v. 20: instead of '*adōnāj*, which makes no sense here, read *ējennū*, 'they are not (any more), 'they vanish'; *bā'īr* here for *behā'īr*, 'on awakening'.

v. 25: at the end of the first line, supply 'but thee'.

v. 26: omit as an addition 'rock of my heart' on grounds of metre.

v. 28: instead of 'near to God' read 'near to thee'. At the end, a line has fallen out.

Structure

After the introductory v. 1, the psalm is controlled by an image that marks off v. 2 and v. 17:

v. 2 I had almost stumbled . . .

v. 17   until I went into the sanctuary of God . . .
The section vv. 3-16 gives the reason why the psalmist had almost stumbled; this section is divided into the meditation on, and description of, the wicked, vv. 3-12, and the psalmist's thought of himself, vv. 22, 21, 13-16.

The section vv. 18-26, introduced by the turning-point of v. 17, is divided in the same way: vv. 18-20 describe the fate of the wicked, vv. 23-26 the psalmist's own fate. The closing vv. 27-28 repeat the same contrast.

This structure is clear and simple but it is not that of any of the psalm types. Admittedly, behind Psalm 73 the individual lament is plainly visible, but from it only the lament unit, with all its three elements, and the unit 'declaration of confidence' appear. Actually, what is significant for the psalm's structure is the change from lament to declaration of confidence, compare Psalm 4; and hence Psalm 73 can be described as a psalm of trust. But in contrast to Psalm 23, the avowal of trust motif is here not expanded to form an entire psalm. The point is rather that the progression from lament to declaration of confidence is pictured exclusively in terms of the contrast between the godless and the pious. This contrast governs the whole psalm and takes in fact the form of a meditation – the psalmist reflects on the contrast. Only at the end in vv.

23-28, when God is directly addressed, does reflection turn into prayer. We shall have something more to say about this conjunction of reflection and prayer at the end of the exposition.

v. 1: The opening verse closely resembles the 'praise of God' unit; it presents at the very beginning the result of the conflict of which the psalm speaks. The question in the psalm is whether in fact God is 'truly good' to the pious, something about which the psalmist was to become very doubtful, vv. 2-16. But he came to recognize that it was so and he reaches this conclusion in vv. 27-28, which corroborate and justify the opening sentence of v. 1.

v. 2: But what this opening sentence says is not self-evident. The psalmist, as he himself says ('But as for me . . . '), had almost come to the opposite conclusion and he is conscious that this would have been a stumbling, a false step, for it would have separated him from God.

The reasons why he had almost stumbled he gives in vv. 3-16, where he meditates on the wicked he sees before him, and in vv. 22, 21, 13-16, where by contrast he considers and reflects on himself.

vv. 3-12: The description of the wicked in these verses differs substantially from the lament about enemies in the psalms of lament. There is no direct involvement of the suppliant here, no indication that the enemies have attacked the speaker or that he himself has had to suffer at their hands. Nor does what is said here arise from a situation where the wicked are threatening him, unlike Psalm 22: 16: 'a company of evildoers encircle me'. Rather, he surveys them and his consideration leads to a dispute. So instead of lament, we have the language of observation and meditation, as the speaker reflects on God's dealings with them.

The pattern of this meditative description is as follows: vv. 3b-5, the prosperity or good fortune of the wicked; vv. 6-8, their behaviour towards others; vv. 9-11, their behaviour towards God. V. 12 is the conclusion.

vv. 3b–5: As he laments his own wretched state, vv. 22, 21, 13–16, the speaker sees alongside him the godless, plump and portly and enjoying their prosperity. He cannot bear the contrast between the laughing sinner and the suffering pious: the wicked blaspheme God and yet things go so well with them that they seem immune from ordinary human suffering, 'they are not in trouble as other men are'.

vv. 6–8: This undisturbed prosperity determines their attitude towards their fellow men. They are arrogant, they do not shrink from acts of violence, they speak 'loftily' and their words are full of malice and falsehood. It is noteworthy that between the verses referring respectively to the actions, v. 6 and the words, v. 8, of the wicked, their physical well-being is again emphasized, v. 7 (compare 4b). Here we can observe a great change from the former outlook of Israel. To be prosperous and well-fed earlier indicated that one was enjoying the divine blessing; now all that is despised as a mark of the wicked and godless! We see here the other side of what is meant when the pious are described as poor and wretched.

vv. 9–11: V. 9 plainly reproduces a proverbial expression, meaning something like: 'their slanderous tongue stops at nothing'.[45] The following verse, beginning with 'Therefore', is no longer understandable; it would have drawn a conclusion from v. 9. V. 11 again cites the words of the wicked and reflects the style of the psalms of lament. They say: 'How can God know?', which can only refer to the deeds and words of the wicked: God knows nothing of these and so neither can He punish them. They can do what they want. The wicked – and this is the basis of the judgment of the pious on them – deny that they have any responsibility towards God. This is not 'atheism' in our sense of the term; it is not a theoretical but a practical denial of God, emancipation from His will and commandments.

---

[45] So A. Weiser, *The Psalms*, 1962, p. 510.

v. 12: This verse is the conclusion of the description of the wicked in which the ground of the dispute, v. 3, is again stated – the good fortune of the wicked, who increase in power and riches. And the dispute goes really deep, when one thinks of the book of Deuteronomy, where invariably obedience is the absolute prerequisite for receiving blessing. How can God give blessing to those who renounce Him? So must we understand the words: 'I had almost stumbled'.

vv. 22, 21: With the opening words 'But I . . . ', the speaker's gaze moves from the wicked to his own condition, 'stupid (as in Psalm 49: 10) and ignorant'. Because he could no longer understand how God was acting, his relationship with God was destroyed. It was no longer the relationship of one created by God in His image, after His likeness: 'I was like a beast toward thee' – without understanding and thus without speech or hearing, so deeply embittered was he, so grievous his pain, v. 21. Yet even in the depths of alienation, even though 'stupid as a beast', the psalmist was still face to face with God.

vv. 13-14: As he reflects on the contrast between his own life and that of the wicked, he reaches the conclusion that his piety is meaningless, 'all in vain have I kept my heart clean'. The second line of v. 13 plays on the rite of handwashing in the context of a declaration of innocence, compare Psalm 26: 6. While this is a component of the psalm of lament, the motif intended to influence God to intervene (for example, Psalm 17: 3-5), here the psalmist reflects on what he himself has done and asks himself whether it made any sense, whether it was not 'all in vain'. His innocence, his clean heart has in no way altered the fact that all the day long he is stricken and chastened. V. 14 corresponds word for word to the 'I' lament of the psalms of lament. When in vv. 15-16 there follows the complaint against God, though in a different form, we see how this reflective meditation in Psalm 73 also is conditioned by the structure of the lament.

vv. 15-16: Two of the verbs here speak explicitly of meditation: 'When I enumerated these things (or 'brought them before my eyes'), I thought (I reached the conclusion)'. They are both verbs of speaking,[46], which here are to be translated by verbs of thinking, for, in Hebrew, thought has not yet been divorced from speech; so both *sippēr*, 'recount', and *'āmar*, 'say', can indicate a thought process, since all thought is speech. His meditation leads the psalmist to the conclusion that 'thou betrayest the generation of thy children', they are left in the lurch. With this, the meditation opens up the possibility that from questioning and passionate complaint against God a cool and objective ascertainment of the true situation can arise. And the speaker knows that such an ascertainment would involve his own case, v. 2. V. 16 tells us why he cannot ascertain the truth: he cannot understand it. He must keep seeking painfully, 'it was weariness to my eyes'. But it is through the very painfulness that he keeps hold on God.

vv. 17-20: Because the psalmist, even in his grief at not any longer being able to understand God, still holds on to Him, he can move from the situation of v. 2. He does not remain in painful weariness, a change occurs. If the whole psalm is seen as autobiographical, a confession in narrative form, then two sections are clearly recognizable in the narrative. The first is introduced by the 'I had almost stumbled' of v. 2 and vv. 3-16 recount how this has come about, with particular emphasis on the danger of abandoning God in vv. 15 f. In the midst of this supreme danger comes the change of v. 17, introduced by the words: 'until I went into the sanctuary of God', where the pilgrimage to the sanctuary is to be understood as a turning to God, in the sense that it has in the psalm of lament. It is the turning to God of a sufferer who implores God to turn back to him, and who can find what he seeks in the sanctuary. We should think of the oracle of weal, the assurance that God has heard which

---

[46] Compare the RSV translation of v. 15: 'If I had said, "I will speak thus"'.

Hannah received on her pilgrimage to the temple, 1 Samuel 1 f. But here, in place of a promise of deliverance, the whole reflective psalm has become the answer which the speaker discovers through his agonizing attempt to understand.

The answer, vv. 17b-20, consists of the perception he gains of the end of the wicked: they are utterly ruined, vv. 18-20. This a conventional and frequently recurring theme, above all in the speeches of the friends in the book of Job.[47] It is the wicked who will stumble, contrast v. 2. When they are said to stumble 'in deception', v. 18, there is a reference back to v. 11; they are deceived precisely in thinking that God does not notice their wicked deeds. Their terrifying end, v. 19, points up the arrogant security from which they are torn. The comparison with the dream that vanishes on waking, v. 20, means that ultimately there is no future for their deeds and words. In contrast to its function in the friends' speeches in Job, the use of this theme here lays the whole weight on the fact that, by setting themselves against God, v. 11, the wicked bring abysmal destruction on themselves, v. 27. That such is the meaning is shown by the contrast in vv. 23-26.

vv. 23-26: With the 'but I' at the beginning of v. 23, the psalmist contrasts his destiny with that of the godless in vv. 18-20. In that he is now convinced that there is nothing behind the apparent good fortune of the wicked, at the same time he is certain of good fortune for himself, in which he will share in spite of his wretchedness, v. 14. When Luther and several English versions render: 'Nevertheless I am continually with thee', that 'nevertheless' is applicable to the entire psalm. However, we must translate here 'But I . . . ', because vv. 23-26 stand in opposition to the fate of the wicked in vv. 18-20, even if the transposition of vv. 22, 21 is not accepted. The psalmist had almost stumbled, v. 2, but now he is certain that nothing can any more separate

[47] See Job 4: 7-11; 5: 2-7; 8: 8-19; 11: 20; 15: 17-35; 18: 5-21; 20: 4-25 and C. Westermann, *Der Aufbau des Buches Hiob*, second edition, 1977, pp. 92-96.

him from God. 'But I am continually with thee', he can say, although nothing in his situation, v. 14, has changed. In the following verses, which give the reasons for his certainty, it is important to observe that in all of them God is the subject: v. 23 'thou . . . ', v. 24, 'thou . . . thou', v. 25 'but thee . . .', v. 26 'God'. In these verses 23-26 the psalm flows into a declaration of confidence and, since these verses represent the goal and climax of the psalm, it can therefore be recognized as a psalm of confidence or trust. But the verses are so deeply moving that the avowal of trust passes over into praise of God; indeed at this point one cannot distinguish between them. This psalm has been called 'Faith's "nevertheless"', but that title does not understand these verses as they are interpreted here. It is not an individual's faith that is celebrated here but what God does for him.

vv. 23-24: These two verses belong closely together; together they form an extended parallelism. Vv. 23b and 24 make up a more restricted parallelism, 'thou dost hold . . . thou dost guide' – they are almost identical in meaning. Both verses speak of the certainty of being with God, and this being with God is expressed, as in the patriarchal narratives, in terms of God's hand and God's counsel. The verses thus use traditional language to express this certainty and together they represent one of the loveliest avowals of trust in the whole Bible. Vv. 23a and 24b, which again go together, make a frame round the whole two verses, and represent an amplification or expansion of the two middle lines. It is an expansion, however, which goes beyond the traditional declaration of confidence and is conditioned by what has preceded it in the psalm. The certainty of fellowship with God has become so overwhelming for the psalmist, after all that he has undergone, that he must add this: it will always exist, it will know no end. That is what he is saying in the words of v. 23a: 'But I am continually with thee', and from this it follows that this fellowship cannot be destroyed even by death: 'finally thou wilt receive me in honour'. There is no question of the belief in resurrection being already anticipated here in the Old Testament.[48] All that is said is that the psalmist's fellowship with God cannot be destroyed even by death. Such certainty does not need any particular concept of a life beyond.

vv. 25-26: Like vv. 23-24, these verses together form an extended parallelism. They are structured by the two pairs of terms heaven and earth, v. 25, and flesh and heart, v. 26. Here, as frequently in Hebrew, a whole is described by two terms, like the two poles of a magnetic field. Heaven and earth stand for the entire creation, flesh and heart for the whole man. The two pairs of terms taken together span all that God has made, both the creation of the universe and the creation of man.

In these two verses the psalmist speaks again of his fellowship with God. Alongside God or apart from God, neither heaven nor earth nor even his own unhappy plight can have any meaning for him. That here fellowship with God and the whole of existence are set over against one another is decisive for our understanding of Psalm 73: for to be with God is then neither an escape from the real life of this world into a life beyond nor an escape from bodily existence into an other-worldly 'life of the soul'. Here not only the world but heaven too is rejected in so far as it is something alongside or apart from God. To be in heaven is neither more nor less than to be with God. The contrast 'this world – the other world' is as such rejected and its place taken by the contrast 'with God – without God'.

But similarly the contrast between body and soul is not absolute either, v. 26. The clause, as Luther renders it, 'though both body and soul fail me', is not an extravagant way of speaking, but it is to be taken literally. Body and soul are in the same position when it comes to being with God; the soul is no closer to Him than the body. Fellowship

---

[48] For a detailed discussion, see C. Barth, *Die Erettung vom Tode in den individuellen Klage- und Dankliedern des Altern Testaments*, 1947, pp. 161 f.

with God is for the whole man; it cannot be destroyed by the failure either of body or soul.

vv. 27-28: Again these two verses, which close the psalm, belong closely together. Many psalms of lament end with the 'double wish or request' for destruction of the enemies and deliverance for the supplant, for example Psalm 55: 23, and vv. 27-28 follow this pattern. When these concluding verses begin 'For lo . . . ', the intention is to confirm the certainty at which the psalmist has arrived. V. 27 summarizes what was said about the fate of the wicked in vv. 18-20, while v. 28 once more reaffirms the declaration of confidence of vv. 23-26.

The two verses are governed by two contrasting verbs: 'those who are far from thee' is balanced in v. 28 by: 'But for me it is good to draw near thee', which gives the sense more accurately than, for example, the Prayer Book's: 'it is good for me to hold me fast by God' (compare Isaiah 58: 2 where the same word is used; also Psalms 65: 4; 119: 169). What is indicated is a movement, behind which there is the idea of an actual pilgrimage to the Temple. It is clear, therefore, that this clause points back to v. 17: the same correspondence between 'to come' and 'to draw near' is to be seen in Psalm 119: 169, 170, where, as also in v. 17, drawing near to God brings perception or understanding. What has caused the change of v. 17 is also to be seen in v. 28. One cannot be with God, be in fellowship with Him, without thus drawing near to Him.

The last clause of Psalm 73 also corresponds to the conclusion of the psalm of lament: 'that I may tell of all thy works'. The clause comes in rather abruptly and perhaps a synonymous half-line has dropped out. But it must not be regarded as an addition, though many commentators so take it. The psalmist wants to go on to tell others about the certainty he has gained, and of this the psalm is a witness.

In conclusion, Psalm 73 is particularly significant in that it is not only speech to God but also goes over into speech *about* God, meditating on His being and His work. For this reason it is considered by many commentators to be a

Wisdom psalm. But this does not seem correct; meditative speech about God and His work is not of itself indicative of a background in Wisdom, and the psalm as a whole is too strongly influenced by the structure of the individual lament for this to be likely. The psalm is to be viewed as a perfect example of how speaking *to* God, vv. 23-28, can become speaking *about* God, of how prayer becomes theology (understanding theology as discourse about God).

If this is so, there is an even more important conclusion for all theology to be drawn from Psalm 73. In it, speaking to God comes before speaking about God. The starting-point for theology, as discourse about God, is not the intellectual question: 'What can we say about God?', 'What sense does it make to speak of God?'. Much more does theology begin by speaking *to* God and so here in Psalm 73 reflection on God develops from speaking to Him. In this psalm, what is in question is existence in relation to God, the quest for God in the hopelessness of existence pushed to its limits. Theology grows not from thought but from life.

Excursus to Psalm 73: The Wicked and the Pious and the period to which the Psalms belong.

When we read a number of psalms one after the other, rather than, as here, in an anthology, we are apt to be somewhat taken aback. Very often the pious and the wicked or godless are so opposed to one another that the psalmist takes it for granted that he is to be reckoned with the pious, while the wicked are always the others, God's enemies and his, and he asks and prays only for their ruin and annihilation. How can we pray these psalms where the psalmist seems so self-righteous, as he contrasts himself with the wicked and wishes them nothing but ill?

In this matter, the psalms are children of their time and only to be understood as such. To understand them, we must first look back to the communal laments. They take it for granted that, as God's people, nation and church are identical. When God arises to fight for His people, He can only do so by intervening against their enemies. But this identity of nation and church has now come to an end, once and for all.

Similar considerations apply to some of the individual psalms of lament, but there is an important difference here. As a result of the collapse of the state and the destruction of the Temple in 587 B.C., there came about a division in Israel between the 'pious', who felt an attachment to worship, to the Law and to the regulations governing devout conduct, and the others who no longer adhered to these things – 'the fool says in his heart, "There is no God"'. The separation between the two tendencies was not motivated by the self-righteousness of the pious but by the necessary struggle for survival of a group, loyal to God and His word, in the face of overwhelming opposition. Even though we can no longer use the words in question in our own prayer, we must still try to understand how they came to be uttered in the circumstances of their time.

But there is yet a further consideration. For the pious, the hardest thing was their having to recognize that God did not invariably reward the pious and punish the godless. And what particularly troubled them was God's blessing the wicked and allowing them to prosper. This is what is being said at the beginning of Psalm 73: 'I had almost stumbled'. Some took refuge in asking or praying God to annihilate the wicked (on this, see p. 297 f. below). They barricaded themselves inside a doctrine of retribution, according to which God *had to* punish the wicked and bless the pious; this was the position of Job's friends. Others, like the author of Job or of Psalm 73, realized that this doctrine did not correspond to reality, and from this arose a completely different, and a wholly new, attitude: one must hold fast to God and continue to trust Him even when one no longer understands what He is doing.

So when we recognize that the psalms are of their own time and that much in them can only be understood as belonging to the period in which they originated, we must also be aware that they do not all say the same thing and that a movement of ideas was in train, a movement also visible in Psalm 73, where a change comes about in the suppliant himself.

Psalm 27: 1-6: The Lord is my light and my salvation

1   The Lord is my light and my salvation;
    whom shall I fear?
    The Lord is the refuge of my life;
    of whom shall I be afraid?

2   When evildoers assail me, to swallow me up,
    my adversaries and foes, they shall stumble
    and fall.

3   Though a host encamp against me,
    my heart shall not fear;
    though war arise against me,
    yet I will be confident.

4   One thing have I asked of the Lord, that I will seek
       after;
    that I may dwell in the house of the Lord all the days
       of my life,
    to behold the favour of the Lord,
    and to inquire in his temple.

5   For he will hide me in his shelter in the day of
       trouble;
    he will conceal me under the cover of his tent,
    he will set me high upon a rock.

6   And now I can lift up my head above my enemies
       round about me;
    and I will offer in his tent sacrifices with shouts of
       joy;
    I will sing and make melody to the Lord.

Text

Psalm 27: 1-6 represents an independent and self-contained psalm, with 6b as its conclusion. V. 7 begins a different psalm, an individual lament.

v. 4: Hebrew distinguishes between the intransitive 'to implore' (in distress) and the transitive 'to ask' (for something). The latter, *šā'āl*, is used here. Since the second line of v. 4 is identical with Psalm 23: 6, many commentators regard it as an addition, which is possible but not necessary.

Structure

Psalm 27: 1-6 is a psalm of trust: the motif of the declaration of confidence is expanded into a whole psalm, while in v. 6b a vow of praise is added to form the conclusion. The avowal of trust comprises vv. 1-6a, v. 6a being the transition to the conclusion. After the expression of trust in vv. 1 and 5, it is structured by what is said about the enemies, vv. 2-3, along with the petition for the continuance of fellowship with God, v.4.

v. 1: The two halves have the same arrangement; in the Hebrew, there are not two half-lines, but two whole lines, in parallelism. The lines do not make quite the same effect in English as in Hebrew, where in each case we have an address. Literally the Hebrew is:

> Yahweh, my light and my salvation, whom then . . . ?
> Yahweh, refuge of my life, whom then . . . ?

Hence, in Hebrew, the psalm is closer to a prayer, and the double address accentuates the parallelism. While lines two and four of the translation mean the same, 'fear' – 'be afraid', lines one and three depict two different situations in which the psalmist avows his reliance on God. By 'my light and my salvation' is implied a night attack under cover of darkness, by 'refuge of my life' the deadly danger from some superior force.

It is unsatisfactory to understand these descriptions of God, which are expanded in v. 5 and characterize the 'declaration of confidence' motif, as metaphors or metaphorical language. They are comparisons, and the meaning of such comparisons could in fact be expressed by verbs, that is, they speak of something that God does for the

one who employs them. They have all sprung from actual
experiences where God's activity has been demonstrated.

vv. 2-3: The two succeeding verses describe situations in
which the psalmist has experienced the divine activity and
will be able to do so in the future. He directs his thoughts to
the enemies of the pious who are oppressing him. He is
aware that he can accomplish nothing against them. But
there is One stronger than they and He is on his side. Vv. 3a
and 3b further heighten the peril, but even the greatest
danger cannot shake his confident trust. The two clauses of
v. 3 have much the same form as vv. 1a and 1b, they are
virtually an echo of them. Only by frequently reading the
psalm aloud does one observe this structural refinement,
worked out as it is to the final detail. Here we see the vivid
spoken language of the psalms. So form and content
become fully identified and fear gives way to a growing
trust as one recites the psalm after the psalmist himself.

v. 4: In the words: 'One thing have I asked from Yahweh',
the emphasis on '(only) one thing' is inexplicable from the
context of vv. 1-3. The explanation lies in the fact that the
theme of trust, which Psalm 27: 1-6 develops, is properly a
unit of the psalm of lament. In that type of psalm, the
lament, intimated, though in a different form, in vv. 2-3
here, is equivalent to the petition for deliverance which
often follows a petition directed against the enemies. The
psalmist here asks for neither, not even that God may
preserve him from all prospective dangers. Only one thing
does he ask and long for: that he may remain in fellowship
with God.

For the words ' . . . that I may dwell in the house of the
Lord', it is sufficient to refer to the comment on Psalm 23: 6
above. What this abiding fellowship with God means is
explained by two clauses in an extended parallelism, that is,
they must be understood together. The first clause, 'to
behold the favour of the Lord' (the same expression as in
Psalm 90: 17), alludes to the continuing experience of God's
gracious work. 'To behold' has here the sense of 'to know'

or 'to experience', more particularly to experience what is described at length in Psalm 103. The second clause, 'to inquire (or ponder over)' in his temple, alludes to the meditation on what has been experienced, in which the experience is pondered over and kept in mind; we may compare the extended meditation that is Psalm 77. So the psalmist asks this one thing, that his fellowship with God may remain constant both in life, that is, in life's experiences, and in thought. The fact that now only this request matters for him means that his confident trust silences any request he might have been tempted to utter for his enemies' downfall. Such a request is found in none of the psalms of trust.

v. 5: The 'For' at the beginning refers back from the petition to vv. 2-3: 'yet I will be confident, for . . . '. As vv. 2-3 develop what is said in v. 1, v. 5 is linked with v. 1 as well as with 2-3, so that it can be read directly after v. 1 or after 2-3. But this means that the avowal of trust in vv. 1 and 5 could represent the unaltered unit of an individual psalm of lament and is to be seen as the kernel of the whole psalm of trust which is Psalm 27: 1-6. In fact, one finds parallels to the individual clauses of v. 5 in the motif of trust which occurs in many psalms.

The three comparisons provide the ground for the trust experienced in v. 1. In the majority of passages where they occur the terms 'refuge' (*mā'oz*),[49] 'shelter', 'tent cover'[50] and 'rock',[51] as well as fortress, castle, shield and others, are all equated with God, who, for instance, is frequently called 'my rock'. This equation is made clear here by reference to God's actions – 'he will hide me', 'he will conceal me', 'he will set me' – so that it becomes clear that, when God is compared to a rock, fortress or shield, the language is not just metaphorical but the comparison results

[49] As well as v. 1 here, see also Psalms 31: 2; 28: 8; 37: 39; 43: 2; 62: 8.

[50] See also Psalms 31: 20; 32: 7; 61: 4; 91: 1; 119: 114.

[51] See also Psalms 18: 2, 31, 46; 19: 14; 28: 1; 62: 2, 7 and in some fifteen other places in the Psalter.

from experience and is validated by experience. Out of the many comparisons which could be adduced, only those have been mentioned which are attested at an early period; one can think too of narratives in the patriarchal history, such as Genesis 18 and 19.

v. 6: In the final verse of the psalm, v. 6a again mentions the enemies of vv. 2-3, but again there is no petition directed against them. It is enough for the psalmist that he no longer needs to fear them.

The conclusion is a vow of praise such as usually rounds off a psalm of lament, which includes the motif of trust, much as in Psalm 22: 25-26. We are to think of the sacrifices mentioned here as being offered by a small circle gathered in the Temple forecourt to celebrate a divine act of deliverance. The occasion is not just to rejoice in a single act of deliverance but to celebrate the gaining of an unshakeable confidence. It shows how avowal of trust turns into praise of God and thus passes over into worship.

Psalm 62: For God my soul waits in silence

1   For God my soul waits in silence;
     from him alone comes my salvation.
2   He only is my rock and my salvation,
     my fortress; I shall not be moved.
     How long will you set upon a man
     to shatter him, all of you,
     like a leaning wall, a tottering fence?
4   They plan falsehoods, they seek to seduce him.
     They bless him with their mouths,
     but inwardly they curse.

5   For God my soul waits in silence,
     for my hope is from him alone.
     He only is my rock and my salvation,
     my fortress; I shall not be shaken.

7 On God rests my deliverance and my honour;
  my mighty rock, my refuge is God.

8 Trust in him at all times, O my people;
  pour out your heart before him! God is a refuge for
  us.

9 The children of men are but a breath, a delusion;
  in the balances they go up; they are together lighter
  than a breath.

10 Put no confidence in extortion,
   set no vain hopes on robbery;
   if riches increase, set not your heart on them.

11 Once God has spoken; twice have I heard this:
   that power belongs to God;
   and that to thee, O Lord, belongs steadfast love.

12 For thou dost requite a man according to his
   work.

Text

v. 2 (Heb. 3): the final word *rabbāh*, 'greatly', is difficult
     grammar and, since it is lacking in the parallel v. 6,
     it should also be omitted here.

v. 3 (Heb. 4): vv. 3b and 4a are very poorly preserved;
     all translations and textual emendations can only be
     guesswork. The doubtful verb at the beginning of
     v. 3b (Heb. 4b) should be read, following H.
     Gunkel, as *tārūṣū* from rūṣ, 'run upon' or 'set upon',
     compare Psalm 59: 4 (Heb. 5). The two last words
     of v. 3 (Heb. 4) should be read as *gedērāh deḥūjāh*,
     'tottering fence'.

v. 4 (Heb. 5): for the second word is to be read *maššū'ōt*,
     'falsehoods', with the apparatus of BHS, compare
     Lamentations 2: 14. The next words are usually
     translated 'to thrust him down from his eminence',
     but this is both grammatically and contextually
     implausible.

Structure

The psalm is divided into two sections. Vv. 1-7 are determined by the avowal of trust and the remainder is a summons to trust. The avowal of trust forms a frame for the first section, with vv. 1-2 and 5-7, where vv. 5-6 are almost identical in wording with vv. 1-2. Within the frame, v. 3 is an address to the enemies or the wicked, which passes into a description of the wicked, v. 4. The second section, vv. 8-12, begins in v. 8 with a summons to trust which has its ground in the brief expression of trust at the close of the verse. The ground of trust is developed in vv. 9-10 from two points of view, the transitoriness of man, v. 9, and the worthlessness of power and riches, v. 10. The psalm ends with praise of God, vv. 11-12a; v. 12b is probably an addition.

vv. 1-2: The psalm is dominated by the word 'silence' in vv. 1 and 5. The way these verses are formulated, 'my soul waits for God in silence', means that silence is reached when one turns to God. It is a silence directed to God, and, as vv. 1b and 2 tell us, is given and guaranteed by Him. It is not the silence of contemplative piety but the silence after storm, the quietness trustingly entered by the one who has escaped. This is possible because help comes from God alone, it is to be expected from Him alone and it is completely to be relied on. The word 'alone' or 'only' is placed in the Hebrew at the beginning of the first line of vv. 1 and 5; '*only* for God . . . '. This is done on grounds of style; the word is given emphasis by its position at the beginning of vv. 1, 2, 5 and 6 but, as far as the content is concerned, its place in v.2 is with the second half of the verse, as v. 6 indicates. Psalm 62 stresses particularly the aspect of silence which trusting brings and the emphatic 'only', so frequently repeated, adds to the thought: there is a silence, a calm, which cannot be attained by any available human means or by any possible insurance against danger. An individual who has learned this is the one who speaks in Psalm 62. He speaks of his experience by simply acknowledging the salvation he has received from God, v. 1b, and he strengthens what he has to say by means of the comparisons, which are well-known to his hearers as being part of the vocabulary of prayer. Every one of these comparisons with a rock, a fortress or a refuge tells its own story and is founded on actual experience. From them the speaker gradually gains trust that 'I shall not be moved'. This calm trust is not something of which a man could convince himself just by thinking about it: it can only begin and develop when threatened and vulnerable humanity turns to God.

vv. 3-4: The experience of the author of Psalm 62 developed from his own particular situation to reflect the time at which he was living. He is set upon, shattered and seduced by men with whom he must live in the same community – this follows from v. 4 – and thereby becomes their impotent victim, 'like a tottering fence'. We do not know what the circumstances were and we cannot reconstruct them. Probably they are those of the post-exilic period, when Israel had lost its independence and was no more than a province of a great empire, and when the determining factor in its common life was the sharp opposition between those who remained loyal to the old faith and their opponents, the wicked or godless.

In the light of this situation, v. 4 emphasizes that the speaker of the psalm can no longer trust his fellow men. He is the victim of their deceitful and secret attacks, so that he is near to collapse.

vv. 5-7: But precisely in this condition, trust in God grows within him. He holds fast to the One, and only to Him, on whom he can rely absolutely: 'For God my soul waits in silence'. Hence it makes good sense that the opening avowal of trust, vv. 1-2, should once more be resumed after the account of his enemies, vv. 3-4. This balancing of vv. 1 and 5 is no mere literary device, but is inherent in the whole course of the psalm. But further, because he has achieved trust and peace in his silent waiting 'for God', the psalmist no longer needs to respond to his opponents' maledictions, as 'inwardly they curse', 4b, with the request to God to annihilate them. Indeed, when he addresses them with the words 'How long will you set upon a man?', 3a, this implies that he has not given up on them and that they are included in the summons to trust of vv. 8-12. V. 5 is identical with v. 1, except for the substitution of 'hope' for 'salvation' in the second line. While salvation refers more to past experiences, hope looks rather to the future. V. 6a is word-for-word the same as 2a; both verses add, in the second line, as a parallel to 'rock', the word 'fortress', which frequently occurs in the declaration of confidence motif, for example, Psalms 9: 9, 18: 2, 46: 7, 48: 3, 59: 9, 16 f.; 94: 22: 144: 2. The word suggests stability and security and so indicates the speaker's certainty that he himself will remain stable and secure, 'I shall not be shaken'. This stability embraces both the bodily and the spiritual side of humanity.

These comparisons with a stable place of refuge, 'my mighty rock', are the reason for the preposition 'on' which begins v. 7: the speaker's deliverance and honour rest on a sure foundation. Deliverance, *jēša'*, here means well-being in the widest sense and honour is the respect he enjoys among his fellow men with whom he lives.

vv. 8-12: A summons to trust, addressed to the circle to which he belongs ('my people'), follows the avowal of confidence. How are we to take this summons? It is not an admonition to his hearers to trust in God, for the psalmist does not speak with this kind of authority. Rather, on the basis of his own experience, he wants to encourage them to trust. The psalm has shown that trust, which the psalmist here acknowledges to be the ground of his being, springs from human experience. It cannot be learnt as one learns a lesson, confident trust is never the result of a thought-process. Precisely for this reason, it is vitally important for a community that knowledge of the experience from which trust has sprung should be widely disseminated, and this is what happens in the summons to trust[52] when it is

[52] For this summons, see Psalms 4: 5; 37: 3, 5; 115: 9-11; Isaiah 26: 4; Proverbs 3: 5.

continued in 8b with the words 'pour out your heart before him!'. To trust is to take it for granted that one can confide in God all one's deepest emotions, even to complaining to him of all one's sufferings, and this is just what we read of in the title of a psalm of lament, Psalm 102. The words of v. 8 are an expression of confidence but now uttered on behalf of the community, 'God is a refuge for us', compare Psalm 46.

v. 9: V. 8 is expanded by vv. 9-10, which require further consideration; they demonstrate how carefully up to this point the psalm has been constructed. In traditional language, compare Psalms 39; 49, the psalmist speaks of human transitoriness. As men vanish 'like a breath', the only stable thing is the confident trust which binds them to the One who endures, the Everlasting God.

v. 10: This verse is a negative expansion of v. 9. The brute force of the powerful, 10a, or the wealth of the rich do not ensure stability. Because of human transitoriness, neither can be relied on, to neither should one lose one's heart. Here the psalmist is obviously thinking of his enemies, vv. 3-4, with their superior wealth and power, and here too he does not give up on them but is still speaking to them.

vv. 11-12a: Just as a vow or expression of praise concludes many psalms of lament, the same is the case with this psalm of trust, as it is also with Psalms 73; 27: 1-6; 90: avowal of trust passes over into praise of God. The praise theme is introduced, with particular emphasis, using the style of a numerical proverb, in v. 11a. The psalmist wants to make it clear that this saying, which his hearers would also be familiar with, has become for him an authentic word of God, as the result of the experience from which his trust in God has sprung. In descriptive psalms of praise, such as Psalms 33 and 113, the terms power and grace, majesty and mercy, denote the two poles of God's whole being, and by means of them the one who avows his trust in God is able to open out his psalm: I trust this God in all that He is, in all that He does. But, in this connection, we notice a subtle variation in the way the praise of God is formulated: the line that speaks of the divine grace takes the form of a direct address: 'To thee, O Lord, belongs steadfast love'. In Psalm 103 too, grace outweighs all else.

v. 12b: What we have just been discussing sounds like a powerful and deliberate ending to the psalm. What follows, 'for thou dost requite a man according to his work', seems rather abrupt at this point. Perhaps it is the addition of a reader for whom divine retribution was the most important thing.

Psalm 90: A thousand years are but as yesterday

1   Lord, thou hast been our refuge in all generations.
2   Before the mountains were brought forth, or ever
         thou hadst formed the earth and the world,
     from everlasting to everlasting thou art God.
4   For a thousand years in thy sight are but as
         yesterday,
     or as a watch in the night.
3   Thou turnest man back to the dust,
     and sayest, 'Come again, O children of men!'
5   Thou dost sow them year after year,
     they are like the growing grass:
6   in the morning it flourishes and is renewed;
     in the evening it fades and withers.

7   For we are consumed by thy anger;
     by thy wrath we are overwhelmed.
8   Thou hast set our iniquities before thee,
     our secret sins in the light of thy countenance.
9   For all our days pass way under thy wrath,
     our years come to an end like a sigh.

10   The years of our life are threescore and ten,
     or even by reason of strength fourscore;
     yet they are mostly toil and trouble;
     they are soon gone, and we fly away.
11   But who knows the power of thy anger,
     and who is afraid before thy wrath?
12   So teach us to number our days
     that we may get a heart of wisdom.

13   Return, O Lord, at the last, have pity on thy
        servants!
14   Satisfy us in the morning with thy steadfast love,
     that we may rejoice and be glad all our days.
15   Make us glad as many days as thou hast afflicted
        us,
     and as many years as we have seen evil.
16   Let thy work be manifest to thy servants,
     and thy glorious power to their children.
17   Let the favour of the Lord our God be upon us, and
        establish thou the work of our hands upon us,
     yea, the work of our hands establish thou it.

Text

v. 2:   the verb *teḥōlal* means 'to be born', 'brought forth'.
        tēbēl is another common word in the psalms for 'the
        earth'.
v. 4:   after 'but as yesterday' the Hebrew text adds 'when
        it is past'. The text is uncertain and the words could
        follow after 'watch in the night'.
v. 5:   the text of the first line is dubious: most
        commentators read 'year after year' instead of
        'year', after which an incomprehensible word
        follows here. V. 5b is repeated at v. 6a in the
        Hebrew text, instead of which we should prefer the
        text which is translated here.
v. 9:   the Authorized Version translates 'We bring our
        years to an end as a tale that is told', and Luther has

something similar. But the word *hegeh* means 'sigh', as at Ezekiel 2: 10, and because of the parallelism the third person plural is to be read.

v. 10: literally, 'the days of our years in them'; the 'in them', *bāhem*, is unclear. The first word of the third line of the translation, *wrhbm* in the Hebrew, is often translated by 'strength', 'pride' or 'span', all of which are possible: the word is a *hapax* and probably *rubbam*, from *rbb*, is to be read, 'mostly'.

v. 13: the opening words are literally: 'Return, Yahweh, how long!'. The phrase 'how long', *'ad mataj*, is a stock expression of the psalms of lament but, in the course of a long period of time, its meaning changed to 'at the last', understood as a plea, as in the Book of Common Prayer.

Structure

It is difficult to assign Psalm 90 to any of the psalm types. It is possible to count it among the psalms of trust, since the opening declaration of confidence, vv. 1-2, determines the whole. But its base is really a communal lament, as can be recognized from the plural speech which pervades it and from the petitioning clauses of vv. 13, 15, 16, among which the communal lament is still clearly visible in v. 15. Inserted into this framework, however, is a lament for transitoriness, vv. 3-12, which is concerned not with the nation's fate but with the fate of men in general, as in Psalms 39 and 49. The lament for transitoriness goes back to a motif of the individual lament, where the purpose of the references to the inevitability of death or to the shortness of life overshadowed by death is to influence God to intervene and save in present distress. This motif can still be clearly recognized behind vv. 13-16.

The psalm is divided into the avowal of trust, vv. 1-2, the lament for transitoriness, transformed into a prayerful address, vv. 3-12, and the petition resulting from the two preceding sections, vv. 13-17.

vv. 1-4: The language of Psalm 90 has a monumental character and any discussion of the psalm must begin by calling attention to it. Whoever fails to catch this special quality of the language from the words themselves will certainly not be able to do so by reading any explanation of them.

vv. 1, 2, 4: The Psalm begins with the declaration of confidence. The note of confidence dominates the whole and is composed from two very different units. The first, v. 1, is a word of confidence which looks back over the nation's history, recalling the motif of the review of God's past saving acts, as in the communal lament of Psalm 80, but here more broadly expressed by a reference to the entire national history, 'in all generations'. The memory of 'the mighty acts of God' was preserved in a long line of tradition and was the ground for every generation's trust in this God who had delivered His people from so many dangers. But in v. 2 God's activity is given a wider horizon: Israel's God is the Creator of the world, v, 2, and the Creator of humanity, vv. 3, 5. He, the Creator, was there before the world began, and by this statement the author of the psalm wants to say that the Creator holds the world in His hands. The Creator does not share the transitoriness of men and all things: 'from everlasting to everlasting thou art God'. And to emphasize this even more strongly, from the multiplicity of creation he picks out the mountains, the 'primaeval mountains' of which other psalms speak, which make the strongest impression of stability and permanence. But 'the everlastingness of God' is too abstract an expression adequately to convey what the author wants to say. God's everlastingness is something much more real that has been imprinted on the minds of the psalm's hearers in many generations as going on from time immemorial: 'For a thousand years in thy sight are but as yesterday, or as a watch in the night'. Here a subtle distinction is made between a day, which ends after twenty-four hours for one and all alike, and a watch in the night, which someone must see through quite alone – it may be only a short time, but it

can feel like an eternity. The word 'for' at the beginning of
v. 4 refers back to v. 2, so it is better to take v. 4 before v.
3.

vv. 3, 5, 6: The One who has made the world is also the
Creator of mankind. But while, when the creation of the
world is spoken of, God's everlastingness is highlighted and
the praise of the everlasting God in vv. 2 and 4 strengthens
the confidence in Him expressed in v. 1, when the author
comes to speak of the creation of mankind, he by contrast
strongly emphasizes human finitude: when the everlasting
God created man He set limits to him. Hence vv. 3 and 5 f.,
which have the same content, form a chiastic parallelism:

    v. 3: dying – being born
    v. 5: being born – dying

This structuring of vv. 3 and 5 gives an impressive picture
of the rhythm of birth and death; we may compare
Ecclesiastes 3: 2: 'a time to be born, a time to die'. The
connection between v. 3 and v. 5 f. can only be grasped if 5
f. is taken immediately after 3 and v. 4 before v. 3.

Otherwise than in the lament for transitoriness, man's
rapid vanishing away is contrasted here with his 'coming
again', vv. 3b, 5, 6a. Also in contrast to the lament for
transitoriness, the inevitability of death is not simply stated
as fact, but death, just as much as birth, is reverently
acknowledged as God's work, and can invoke the trusting
response 'Thou art God'. The reason for this departure
from the pattern of the lament for transitoriness is that the
middle section of the psalm also, vv. 3, 5-12, is determined
by the declaration of confidence.

v. 3: The first line of this verse repeats Genesis 3: 19, and
Genesis 3 is also presupposed in vv. 7-8: the author turns a
Biblical passage that he knows well into a prayer. The
second line of the verse is usually interpreted as a further
description of death. But in view of the chiastic parallelism
of vv. 3 and 5, it is certain that birth is meant here, just as it is
in v. 5. The word 'again', šūbū, 'come back', does not imply

that life will be restored to those who have died, v. 3a; rather, it says to them 'human life will go on!'

vv. 5-6: The same thing is said once again by means of a comparison. This comparison occurs frequently in the lament for transitoriness. Man is compared with the grass, or with a flower, that springs up and flourishes in the morning but has already faded by the evening. The comparison brings out the fact that birth and death are not to be perceived as mere data; it conveys the impression of an arch that is constitutive of human existence as a whole, and that is particularly significant for the Old Testament understanding of man. There human life is not a straight line with a beginning and an end, but an arch that goes both up and down. Human life here is not an abstract thing, but has concrete reference to this arch of existence which describes the path from early childhood to old age. But, at its beginning, the comparison also has reference to the declaration of confidence: '*Thou* dost sow them'. Human existence in all its limitation and finitude is founded on the creative work of the everlasting God, and thus can found its trust on its very transitoriness: even as the individual life dissolves and vanishes, the new generation is born.

vv. 7-9: These following verses see the frailty of human life as the result of divine action; it finds its significance in the light of what God does. Vv. 7-9 make up a self-contained unit: our transitoriness is the outcome of God's anger, 7, his reaction to our iniquities, 8. V. 9 repeats v. 7 in different words. It is obvious that behind these verses lies the primaeval story of man's expulsion from the garden of Eden in Genesis 3. Both here and there man is depicted as finite and thus fallible. Here, as there, what is in question is the fallibility of the whole human race and not just the sinfulness of the people of God. And in the background of both these verses and Genesis 3 lies the awareness, which all men have, of the necessary connection between guilt and punishment. Under this universal horizon, the author of Psalm 90 sees sin and death as interconnected, but an intellectual calculation of the relation between sin and death is not possible for him. This is the point of v. 8: what is meant in that verse is not sin as we see it, but sin in the light of God's countenance. The issue of the relation between sin and death, which for us is unverifiable and incalculable, is shifted to where it ought to be, into the light of Gods's countenance. But then it is easy to understand that this countenance does not display only anger. When, in this connection, the author stresses 'our secret sins', he again has in mind Genesis 3 and God's question: 'Adam, where are you?', a question which haunts anyone who cannot cope with his failings by himself.

V. 9 refers back to v. 7 but with a fresh nuance. The operation of the divine wrath is not confined to the hour of a man's death, so that one might say that death as punishment for sin would be an isolated event, occurring at a particular point. Rather, death makes up life *as a whole*, it is 'all our days' and years that end with death, our life is *Sein zum Tode*, in Martin Heidegger's words.

vv. 10-12: This theme is clarified in the following verses 10-12 in a way at once surprising and profound. The years of our life, v. 9, are now numbered in figures, just as they are in real life. And it also corresponds to reality when it is said of the span of these years that 'they are mostly toil and trouble', which again reminds of of Genesis 3. It is to be observed that vv. 9-12 develop only one aspect of God's activity; we have a deliberately one- sided way of speaking, with the serious purpose of making us conscious of the frailty of human life. In no way does the author intend to say that life consists only of toil and trouble; rather, his object is to fend off all self- deception and all false idealism. So he adverts again to the downward slope of life's path which no-one can avoid: 'they are soon gone, and we fly away'.

The section vv. 3-12, which speaks of human transitoriness, ends with a petition which makes clear what is intended by all that has gone before. The rationale of the petition of v. 12 is v. 11: men do not take seriously the *Sein zum Tode*, they push it out to the fringes of life. Who considers that beyond the frontiers of humanity stands the Creator? The verbs 'know' or 'consider' and the resulting 'fear', which is to be understood in the sense of our word 'awe', express the truth that this knowledge is lacking in the case of the majority of mankind. They repress this knowledge and so are no match for what befalls them. Hence the petition of v. 12, which Luther thus translates: 'Teach us to remember that must die so that we may become wise'. It is the one who consciously faces death who gets a heart of wisdom. The ways in which wisdom then operates in life can be very diverse. Attention should be drawn, however, to just one thing which arises from the first eleven chapters of Genesis and is frequently echoed in Psalm 90. Genesis 3 is one of those stories about guilt and punishment in Genesis 1-11,[53] the majority of which deal with man's infringement of the limits set for him. Man wants to be as God, what be builds must reach up to heaven. A wise heart is the prize of the one who knows his own limits, because he is aware of the limitations of human existence.

vv. 13-17: After the lengthy interlude of vv. 3-12, in the closing verses 13-17 the structure of the psalm of lament is resumed. On the lament, which in vv. 3-12 is altered to become a lament for transitoriness, there follows the petition of vv. 13-16 which is altered correspondingly. V. 13 could take its place in a psalm of lament without any change: it represents the petition, in a situation of distress, for God to turn again to His people. The petition 'Return, O Lord' presupposes the complaint that God has turned away from them, the petition 'Have pity on thy servants', that He has turned from them in anger. This plea for deliverance from distress is continued in vv. 15-16, where a petition for God's intervention succeeds the petition for His return. V. 15 shows clearly the situation from which the people's lament arises: it is the result of a long period of suffering, affliction and oppression.

[53] The stories are Genesis 3; 4; 6: 1-4; 6-9; 9: 20-27; 11: 1-10.

The petition for restoration in v. 15 has the same parallelism 'days – years' that we have previously met in v. 9 (but it also occurs at vv. 4, 5, 6, indeed it runs as a leit-motif through the entire psalm). By repeating this parallelism, the author deliberately links the plea in distress from the communal lament with the motif of human transitoriness. He uses the description of a time of great distress for a nation, or his own nation, as an example of what he has earlier said in vv. 7, 9, 10 about the 'toil and trouble' of human life in the face of its death. This subtle change of reference, of which we are given no more than a hint, can only be appreciated by someone who is soaked in the psalms. To the nation of Israel this example spoke loudly and clearly.

v. 16: The petition of v. 15 'Make us glad' is developed in v. 16: 'let thy work and thy glorious power be manifest'. Their rejoicing that things are now going better for them, that they can breathe freely again, is really a rejoicing for what God has done. This is a particularly beautiful, because unintended, example of how for those praying the psalm joy in itself could mean the same as joy in the work of God.

In the final section, vv. 13-17, as in the declaration of confidence at the beginning of the psalm, vv. 1, 2, 4, a unit of the psalm of lament can be recognized behind every clause, and hence vv. 3-12 appear all the more clearly as an expansion. Both parts of vv. 13 and 15-16 correspond to the petition, v. 14 corresponds to the vow of praise and v. 17 to the final wish or request.

v. 14: This verse is better taken after v. 15, for the petition in the first line picks up v. 15 f. The phrase 'satisfy us with thy steadfast love' presupposes that, where God's grace prevails, there is abundance, and the words 'in the morning' look back to the picture of the arch of human life in v. 6. Then the whole of life, literally 'all our days', will be dominated by the praise of God, that is, by joy. This clause appears to contradict vv. 3-12, and especially v. 10, with its mention of 'toil and trouble'. But for the author of the psalm and for those who heard and sang it, there is no contradiction. They well know that weeping and laughter, mourning and dancing each have their time, Ecclesiastes 3: 4. The author is saying that joy and the praise of God can exist in the face of human transitoriness, suffering and misery, wherever there remains confident trust in the everlasting God, vv. 1-2.

v. 17: In many psalms of lament the final wish or request is a two-sided one, corresponding to the blessing and the curse, as for example, Psalm 73: 27-28. We do not meet the enemies in Psalm 90, and the final wish seeks only a blessing. In contrast to the plea for deliverance, v. 13, the closing wish is for stability, that God may continue to look favourably on His people and that through His blessing He may 'establish the work of our hands', v. 17b. Translations of v. 10b, such as those of the Authorized Version, which speak of 'labour and sorrow', may give the impression that in this verse we find Psalm 90's doctrine of work. But this is incorrect because neither of the Hebrew terms means 'work'. What Psalm 90 really has to say about work is found in its closing wish. God's good will towards us is revealed in His requirement that men should work, and this corresponds to the task laid on men at Genesis 2: 15. The final wish of the psalm of linked with the petition that ends the middle section vv. 3-12. With the wisdom gained by accepting human transitoriness, one can await the divine requirement of daily work. So in this psalm the majestically divine and the everyday human come together: trust in the everlasting God, who, since human life is finite, was at its beginning and will be at its end, reaches down into daily work that finds its meaning in the command of the Creator.

INDIVIDUAL NARRATIVE PSALMS OF PRAISE OR PSALMS OF THANKSGIVING

Psalm 30: Thou hast drawn me up from the depths

1   I will extol thee, O Lord,
    for thou hast drawn me up from the depths,
    and hast not let my foes rejoice over me.

2   O Lord my God, I cried to thee for help,
    and thou hast healed me.

3   O Lord, thou hast brought up my soul from Sheol,
    restored me to life
    from among those gone down to the Pit.

4   Sing praises to the Lord, O you his saints,
    and give thanks to his holy name!

5   For his anger is but for a moment,
    and his favour is for a lifetime.
    Weeping may tarry for the night,
    but joy comes with the morning.

6   But I thought in my prosperity, 'I shall never be moved'.

7   By thy favour, O Lord, thou hadst established me on rock;
    thou didst hide thy face, I was dismayed.

8   To thee, O Lord, I cried, to my God I made supplication:

9   'What profit is there in my death,
    if I go down to the Pit?
    Will the dust praise thee? Will it tell of thy faithfulness?

10   Hear, O Lord, and be gracious to me!
    O Lord, be thou my helper!'

11   Thou hast turned for me my mourning into
        dancing;
        thou hast loosed my sackcloth and girded me with
        gladness,
12   that my soul may sing to thee and not be silent.
        O Lord my God, I will praise thee for ever.

Text

v. 7   (Heb. 8): read *leharerē 'ōz*, 'on strong mountains',
        with the apparatus of BHK.
v. 9   (Heb. 10): literally, 'in my blood'.
v. 10: this verse would go better before v. 9.
v. 12 (Heb. 13): instead of *kābōd*, read *kebēdi*, 'my
        inward parts', as in Psalm 7: 5 (Heb. 6).

Structure

The structure shows that this psalm is an individual
narrative psalm of praise. It begins with a resolve to praise
God, which has its grounds in the succeeding extended
narrative. The conclusion, v. 12b, returns again to the
opening but adds here, 'for ever'.

The ground of the praise, vv. 1b–12a, is a narrative of the
deliverance which the psalmist has experienced: at the
beginning, this is briefly summarized, 'thou hast drawn me
up . . . ', and developed in vv. 2–12a. In vv. 2–3, the
psalmist, recalling that he was in danger of death, tells of his
cry for help and the deliverance he then experienced. In vv.
4–5, he summons his hearers to join their voices to his
praise. Vv. 6–12 carry on the narrative: in vv. 6–7a we have
his previous prosperity, in v. 7b its collapse, in vv. 8– 10 his
supplication from the depths, and in vv. 11–12a once again
the narrative of his deliverance, as in vv. 1b–3.

vv. 1–3: The structure of this psalm is so clear and its
language so simple that an exposition of it hardly seems

necessary. However, much of it is foreign to our way of speaking and thinking and can only be understood in the context of the entire Psalter.

Excursus: Thanksgiving and Praise: This and the following psalms are usually described as thanksgiving psalms and the Hebrew verb *hōdāh*, v. 12b, translated as 'give thanks', as here in RV and RSV. This description and translation can be retained to the extent that they have supplanted in our language the older sense of 'praise' for the word. But if one wants to understand both the psalm category and the verb in their original meaning, one must be clear that a change has here taken place. For the verb *hōdāh* does not mean 'to give thanks' but 'to praise'. To prove this, it is only necessary to observe that it is never used when human beings are described as thanking one another. A verb corresponding exactly to our 'to thank' is unknown in Hebrew. But Hebrew is not unique in this; no early language has a word for 'thank', as can easily be demonstrated. In all languages known to us, the word in question is derived from some other verb (in English from 'think') and only subsequently comes to mean 'thank'. The reason for this is a development connected with the comparatively late emergence of the individual from society. This too can be demonstrated beyond doubt: a small child can voice his pain and pleasure on his own (corresponding to the adult's lament and shout of joy), but he has first to be taught to say 'thank you'.

But praise differs from thanksgiving above all in being spontaneous; it can never become a duty, something one has to do. When one praises, it is a sign that one is happy; praise is never mandatory, thanksgiving always is. The difference is seen in the way each concept is given verbal expression. Thanksgiving often occurs in a sentence where the one giving thanks is the subject, 'I thank thee, that . . .', spontaneous praise in a sentence where God is the subject, 'thou hast . . . thou art'. Another difference is that thanksgiving can be a private act where one expresses one's gratitude, and so it is often stressed that the really important thing then is the inner feeling of thankfulness. By contrast, it is characteristic of praise to be given voice and that before other people, as we see in Psalm 30.[54]

v. 1: With the first clause 'I will extol thee, Yahweh', the opening of the narrative psalm of praise picks up the promise of praise which comes at the end of many psalms of lament. There praise is uttered in the context of the petition for deliverance from distress, here it is triggered off by a deliverance already experienced. The clause here forms a connecting link between the psalm of lament and the psalm of praise. The verb 'extol' (from *rūm*, 'to be high') is a synonym for 'praise' or 'laud'. It expresses a particular element in the praise of God: when God is praised, He is exalted. But the exaltation of God can be understood in different ways, so that the single concept of exaltation can be filled out by a whole series of honorific divine predicates. This is commonly the case with Babylonian psalms in particular, which frequently consist almost entirely of such divine predicates; in much the same way, a god is extolled by mentioning the size and splendour of his image, his throne, his house or temple. Such a static representation of divine majesty by means of words or the plastic arts was unknown to Israel, which understood God's exaltation quite differently. There, God is exalted as the wonderful saviour and deliverer, as the one who shows mercy; hence, in the psalms we are considering, He is exalted by means of the speaker's narration of what he has experienced. God's loftiness or greatness are never viewed in the Bible as attributes of His essential divine being; they are always seen in His actions. Thus the Bible, both Old and New Testament, mainly consists of a story of what God does and has done.

The ground of the praise is given in the words 'thou hast drawn me up': the verb has this sense only here, in the Qal it means 'to draw water from a well'. Now the speaker's

---

[54] The detailed reasons for the distinction here are given in C. Westermann, *Praise and Lament in the Psalms*, pp. 25-30.

enemies can no longer harm him. In the lament, as we have seen, the enemies play a large part. In the psalms of praise after deliverance, we meet them but seldom, and then only incidentally. What we saw in the case of the psalms of trust, we also see here: the enemies have lost all significance once the threat they pose is averted.

vv. 2-3: In the brief development of the deliverance narrative, introduced by a fresh address: 'Yahweh, my God', the psalmist, in a short phrase, looks back on his suffering: 'I cried to thee'. Then follows the account of what God has done for him; this is given great emphasis by three clauses which all mean much the same. The whole story of his distress can be concentrated in the one sentence: 'I cried to thee', because in the plea to God his suffering and lament reached their goal, as the structure of the psalms of lament has shown us, and because in this plea, and in this plea alone, lay the possibility of an escape and a future for him.

The next three clauses relate how God has freed him from distress: 'thou hast healed me'; it does not necessarily follow from these words that the distress was a case of sickness. Here, being healed is to be understood as a typical experience of deliverance, as it still is today all over the world. 'Thou hast brought me up from Sheol (the realm of death)' does not imply an awakening from death, as we would understand it. Rather, the psalmist speaks, in a parabolic way, of death's might which reaches to the very core of a man's life. In deadly danger, in the threat of a deadly accident, but also in the fear of dying, death itself is at work. God has snatched the psalmist from the power of death, as the last line of v. 3 again says unequivocally; while others did not escape death, He has restored him to life.

vv. 4-5: After recounting how God has delivered him, the psalmist now summons others to join him in praising God for what He has done. The summons thus assumes that people are listening to his story, that it was told, and will continue to be told, among members of a group. We should think of a small circle celebrating a praise offering, as is also the case in Psalm 22: 22-26, where the verse sequence is the same as here. The summons requesting the hearers to participate is in the form of an imperative call to praise, the usual introduction to the descriptive psalm of praise. The ground of the summons in v. 5 also corresponds to that type of psalm: what has been up to this point the story of an individual's experience is now recounted so as to be relevant for all. The change which the one experienced all can experience, because this answers to the nature of God. The four lines of v. 5 have something important to say for all that the Old Testament understands by God, something which resulted from the experience of a single sufferer but which he can now hand on as applying to all, and this is that God's grace far exceeds his wrath. But it is noteworthy that this is not made as a bald statement but is expressed by two concrete pairs of opposite extremes, which serve to convey the experience: a moment – a lifetime, for the night – with the morning. Co-ordinated with the first pair is the pair God's anger – God's favour and, with the second, weeping – joy as they affect mankind. We have to reflect at length on these meaningful parallels, in order to trace what is being said about God, as the thought moves sentence by sentence and motif by motif to a connected whole.

vv. 6-10: Now the narrative proceeds further to the earlier history of the speaker. His fall into the depths was preceded by a time of false security. The opening 'but' stands over against what has gone before: I had thought I would never need such a deliverance! It was a time of secure prosperity which easily generated the feeling, 'nothing can happen to me!' A feeling of security imperceptibly supplanted trust in God. Only now, after he has plumbed the depths, has he understood that 'by thy favour thou hadst established me on rock'. Clearly the language of the psalms of trust is echoed here. The psalmist had thought that he no longer needed to trust. Then came his fall, as described in the two short lines of v. 7b: 'thou . . . I . . . '. The first clause, 'thou didst hide thy face', corresponds to the clause in the

blessing: 'let thy face shine on me!'. Both clauses take it for
granted that humanity must always stand face to face with
God.

V. 8 repeats v. 2a, only rather more fully. In addition, the
psalmist's prayer in distress is quoted and it makes better
sense to read v. 10 before v. 9. He pleads for God to turn to
him and intervene to help him in the same words as are used
in many psalms of lament. In v. 9, the plea is supported by a
reason why God should intervene which strikes us as naïf:
What profit for thee, God, is there in my death? Can the
dead still praise thee? The same reasoning is met with in
Psalms 6: 5; 88: 10-12; 115: 17; 119: 175; Isaiah 38: 18 f.;
Ecclesiasticus 17: 27 f. What characterizes death in these
passages is that the departed can no longer praise God;
praising God is for real life in all its fulness, as it is put in
Hezekiah's psalm: 'The living, the living, he praises thee!',
Isaiah 38: 19. It is an element in human existence. We can
only understand this outlook when we realize that for
ancient Israel praising God was an expression of the joy of
living and so a life without joy could not be complete life.
For the Old Testament, all true, deep, glowing joy is joy
directed to God because everything that awakened joy came
from Him. This was a fundamental postulate in Israel's
thinking, resting on the final verse in the creation story,
'and behold, it was very good', Genesis 1: 31. The creature's
praise of God is anchored in the goodness of all that God has
made.

v. 11: Following the narrative of distress and the plea in
distress, vv. 6- 10, the narrative of deliverance is resumed
again (after vv. 1 and 3), a narrative which functions as the
leitmotif of the entire psalm. This third narrative differs
from those preceding it in that it views the act of deliverance
as indistinguishable from its consequence: God has once
more made him glad. But here again the idea is embodied in
concrete actions. God has turned the psalmist's mourning
into dancing, that is, a dance to accompany singing,
compare Psalms 149: 3; 150: 4; Jeremiah 31: 13. His whole
body shares in his rejoicing, body and soul are swept along

by joy. And God rejoices with him, loosing his mourning dress and girding him with gladness! So even wearing festal clothing is part of the rejoicing, indeed it marks the consummation of the whole story that began with the alleviation of his distress and ends when he is clothed in festal array!

v. 12: The joyful song which God Himself has put in his mouth, v. 11, is never to fall silent, for he can never forget what God has done for him, compare Psalm 103: 1. So the psalm flows again into the promise of praise with which it began, v. 1, but now that promise is to be 'for ever'. His whole future life will reverberate with the joy God awakened in him when He delivered him from the threat of death. He will never forget the good things God has done for him.

Psalm 31: 7-8, 19-24: How abundant is thy goodness!

7   I will rejoice and be glad for thy steadfast love,
       because thou hast seen my affliction,
       thou hast taken heed of my adversities,
8   and hast not delivered me into the hands of the
          enemy;
       thou hast set my feet in a broad place.
19   O how abundant is thy goodness,
       which thou hast laid up for those who fear thee,
       and wrought for those who trust in thee , before the
          whole world!
20   In the covert of thy presence thou hidest them
       from the calumnies of men;
       thou holdest them safe under thy shelter from the
          strife of tongues.
21   Praised be the Lord, for he has wondrously dealt
          with me,
       and shown his steadfast love to me when I was
          beset.

22　I had thought in my alarm,
　　'I am driven far from thy sight.'
　　But thou didst hear my supplications,
　　when I cried to thee for help.

23　Love the Lord, all you his saints!
　　The Lord preserves the faithful,
　　but abundantly requites him who acts haughtily.

24　Be strong, and let your heart take courage,
　　all you who wait for the Lord!

Text

v. 20　(Heb. 21): instead of *mērūkkesēj*, which is of uncertain meaning and otherwise unattested, read *mērekilēj*, 'calumnies', to correspond to the parallelism.

v. 21 (Heb. 22): the Massoretic text adds: 'as in a besieged city' in the second line.

Structure

Psalm 31 is made up of several psalms that once existed independently. Vv. 1-6 could be a psalm of trust; it enshrines in v. 5 one of the words from the cross: 'into thy hands I commit my spirit'. V. 9 is clearly recognizable as the beginning of an individual lament which extends to v. 18 and of which the conclusion is probably missing. Vv. 7-8 and 19-24 comprise a complete and self-contained individual psalm of praise. This psalm commences in vv. 7-8 with the resolve to praise God, that is, to redeem the promise of praise, together with a short narrative giving the reason for the praise. The praise itself follows in vv. 19-22. In vv. 19-20, it takes the form of a description of God's goodness in general, in vv. 21-22 of a narrative, linked with vv. 7-8, of what the psalmist has himself experienced. In

the final section, vv. 23- 24, he summons those he addresses
to join in his praise.

vv. 7-8: Two verbs are used to give effect to the resolve to
praise God. The first, 'rejoice', *gîl*, primarily indicates in
Hebrew the rejoicing on the occasion of a festival. It
presupposes such a joyful occasion and the common
purpose to express their joy of a group assembled to
celebrate the festival. Such joyful festivals, however,
presuppose a state of security in which people can gather to
celebrate them; this state of security, where the joyful
festivals find their place, is called in Hebrew *šālôm*. The
second verb, 'be glad', here means: I will express my joy, I
will rejoice with and before others, so that they may rejoice
with me. In the Old Testament, secular and religious joy are
not sharply distinguished from one another. Because joy is
part of human existence, it is never divorced from God, for
God has created men as beings who are able to rejoice.

The rejoicing here is 'for thy steadfast love'. A divine
quality is not meant here, rather the words provide the
reason why the psalmist experienced the awakening of joy,
as he recounts in what follows. One can only speak of God's
goodness by experiencing it. The psalmist rejoices because
God has seen his affliction, because One was there to take
heed of his adversity. Such words express a basic experience
known to all men alike, whatever their religion or ideology,
whatever or whomever they believe in. The psalmist was in
affliction and adversity and he has been set free, 'thou hast
set my feet in a broad place'. When he now wants to give
voice before others to his joy at this deliverance, he can only
do so because he sees it as meaningful and relevant. And the
meaning is that when he was afflicted, there was One who
saw him, when he was in adversity, there was One who
took heed of him. Such is the reason for his joy.

vv. 19-20: The arrangement of the section concerned with
the praise of God, v. 19-22, shows that, where an individual
speaks of such an experience, the small group must itself
expand this to include its own experience. God's steadfast

love, which had regard and paid heed to the psalmist in his affliction, is there for all. This is the message of vv. 19-20. They begin with a cry of wonderment: 'O how abundant is thy goodness!'. Such cries of wonderment occur time and again in psalms of praise. Wonderment is something that belongs to childhood, and in their cries of wonderment the psalms have retained this childlike aspect of our relationship with God. The opening cry is telling us that, if a man would fully fathom the meaning of divine goodness, he can never tie it down to an abstract concept. When wonderment ends up as conceptual theological knowledge, then it is no longer God's goodness which is being spoken of. When, by means of such knowledge, we seek to have God's goodness at our disposal, we have no longer any idea of what it really is. Such is the meaning of the second half of v. 19a: 'which thou hast laid up for those who fear thee'. God's goodness is not available for one and all but is laid up for those who receive it with reverent awe; for 'fear' in this verse is what we call 'awe'. And such awe is inseparable from wonderment. But v. 19 adds a third consideration: God's goodness is shown to those who trust Him or, more exactly, to those who take refuge in Him. God's goodness is not something that can be found anywhere; it is known only when we throw ourselves on God, v. 22b, and He responds. But this turning to God does not take place in any realm of introspection but 'before the whole world', as part of our real daily life.

V. 20 goes on to speak of this real life. It deals with only a single slice of reality; God can show His goodness in many ways but always as part of the real life we know. A verse from the book of Proverbs is relevant to the slice of life mentioned here, 'Death and life are in the power of the tongue'. Perhaps the particular demonstration of God's goodness in this verse has been picked out to show how helpless we are when exposed to injurious words, when we are the victims of 'character assassination'.

vv. 21-22: Here the psalmist develops the story of his own experience, of which he has already spoken in vv. 7-8. To understand the opening clause: 'Praised be the Lord, for he has wondrously dealt with me', it is necessary to bear in mind that shouts of praise in precisely this form are frequently met with in narrative accounts. Thus, for example, at Genesis 24: 27 we find: 'Praised be Yahweh . . . who has not forsaken his steadfast love and his faithfulness toward my master'; note also Genesis 14: 20; 1 Samuel 25: 32 f., 39; Exodus 18: 10; 1 Kings 1: 48; 5: 7; 10: 9. These shouts of praise are the immediate reaction of those who have been helped in a wonderful manner: they occupy the middle ground between the actual experience and the psalm based on it and are themselves virtually miniature psalms of praise. Hence the opening words of v. 21, which come in the middle of the psalm, will already have been spoken by the psalmist in the situation which gave rise to the psalm. Then the shout 'Praised be Yahweh' resulted from a definite and unique event, but now in this psalm, which is recited on behalf of many people, the grounds for it are correspondingly more general.

The situation of the original utterance of praise is further unfolded in v. 22 by the psalmist's account of what had gone before. He had gone through the depths of despair and anguish, but then he had discovered that fellowship with God still remained: 'thou didst hear my supplications'. That he can claim that God has dealt wondrously with him, v. 21, is the result of his experiencing the transformation of his profound despair.

vv. 23-24: The praise of God, uttered by the one who has lived through all this, is now to broaden out; his joy is to awaken a corresponding joy in others. This is the force of the imperatives in vv. 23 and 24. At the end of Psalm 31, two psalm types are brought together: the same imperative summons to praise that ends the narrative psalm of praise now opens the descriptive psalm of praise, the congregation's 'hymnic' praise of God. Instead of the imperative: 'Love!', a word for 'praise' could equally well stand here, as it frequently does elsewhere. The verb 'love' does not mean having a feeling or an emotion; rather, it means turning or returning to God, it is the joyful affirmative response which is made to God when He is praised.

The ground for the invitation in v. 23a is given in the two-member clause 23b. In the first part, the particular experience of which the psalmist has spoken is given permanent expression, when narrative praise passes over into descriptive praise: 'The Lord preserves the faithful'. The second part announces the divine retribution on him who 'has acted haughtily'. There is One, the Most High, and there is no need to call in distress on any other.

In the final verse 24, the imperative of v. 23 is carried on by the imperative 'Be strong', but the latter has a different function: you *will become* strong and your heart *can* take courage if you wait hopefully for the Lord. This closing sentence really gets its meaning from the whole course of the psalm. Present festal joy will be succeeded by everyday life with its fresh perils and it is in ordinary life that the certainty gained from joy will prove itself.

Psalm 40: 1-11: He heard my cry

1 I waited longingly for the Lord;
he inclined to me and heard my cry.
2 He drew me up from the horrible pit,
out of the miry bog,
and set my feet upon a rock,
making my steps secure.
3 He put a new song in my mouth, a song of praise to
our God.
Many will see and stand in awe,
and put their trust in the Lord.

4 Blessed is the man who makes the Lord his trust,
who does not turn to idols, to those who speak
lies.
5 Many are thy wondrous deeds, O Lord my God,

which thou hast done for us,
and thy thoughts which are towards us;
none can compare with thee!
Were I to proclaim and tell them,
they would be more than can be numbered.

6 Sacrifice and grain offerings thou dost not delight
in;
[ears thou hast dug for me.]
burnt offering and sin offering thou hast not
required,
7 then would I have said, 'Lo, I come;
in the roll of the book it is written of me'.
8 I delight to do thy will, O my God;
thy instruction is within my heart.
9 I tell the glad news of deliverance in the great
congregation;
lo, I do not restrain my lips, as thou knowest, O
Lord.
10 I do not hide thy saving help within my heart,
I speak of thy faithfulness and thy salvation;
I do not conceal thy steadfast love and thy
faithfulness from the great congregation.
11 Do not thou, O Lord, withhold thy mercy from
me,
let thy steadfast love and thy faithfulness ever
preserve me!

Text

v. 4 (Heb. 5): the word *rehabim*, here rendered 'idols',
is the plural of *rahab*, 'chaos monster', see for
example Job 9: 13. The following expression *sātēj
kāzāb*, only elsewhere in the Hebrew of
Ecclesiasticus 51: 2, is literally 'those who turn
aside to lies'.
v. 5 (Heb. 6): 'none can compare with thee' is literally
'there is no comparison with thee'.

vv. 6-7 (Heb. 7-8): these verses are difficult. The phrase
'ears thou hast dug for me' is odd, it occurs only
here and does not suit the context. Gunkel and
others have attempted to reconstruct a different
text: 'If thou hadst desired sacrifices and grain-
offerings, I would not have shut my ears; if thou
hadst commanded burnt offerings and sin
offerings, then I would have said: "Lo, I bring
them".'

Structure

Psalm 40 too is made up of two psalms. The psalm of praise
ends with v. 11, while vv. 12-18 are a psalm of lament or
part of one, as is proved by the fact that we meet these verses
again in the independent Psalm 70: 1-5: the 'For' of v. 12 of
Psalm 40 relates to the introductory petition, which in
Psalm 70 is placed at the beginning but in Psalm 40: 12-17 is
added at the end as 17b.

An introduction corresponding to Psalm 31: 7a is lacking
in this psalm, which begins straightaway with the narrative
comprising vv. 1-3; this is in two parts, a narrative of
distress, v. 1a, and a narrative of deliverance, vv. 1b- 3. V. 4
is a meditative reflection on the narrative and it is possible
that it is a marginal note.

From the narrative of vv. 1-3, there develops the praise of
God, struck up in v. 3a and again in v. 5. Vv. 9-11 are the
direct continuation of v. 5, the psalmist resolves to proclaim
God's praise. Over against the praise of God as a reaction to
His wondrous deeds, v. 5, vv. 6-8 float another possibility,
that of returning thanks by means of sacrificial offerings.
But this possibility is rejected, for God does not desire such
offerings. The final v. 11 is an expression of certainty that
God's goodness will continue for the psalmist.

vv. 1-3: The psalm begins with a report of the psalmist's
own experience. It is obviously a stylized report or, more
precisely, a narrative shortened to become a report. As

many examples show, this report follows an already well-established pattern, where it is divided into the account of the distress, v. 1a, and that of the deliverance, vv. 1b–3a. The first part is severely abbreviated; nothing is said of the distress itself, though it is indicated in v. 2a. Only the psalmist's patient hope in God is mentioned, with the accompanying appeal to Him which v. 1b presupposes. Translated literally, the beginning of v. 1a reads: 'Hopefully I hoped (the infinitive absolute) in Yahweh' – the repetition intensifies the verb.

The report of the deliverance in vv. 1b–3a strings together the individual events of the work of deliverance, as traditionally prescribed, in a closely- packed succession. Corresponding to the plea in distress, it has two parts, God's inclining to the speaker, v. 1b, and His intervention, v. 2, the latter in turn comprising two divine actions. In v. 3a we have again the reaction to God's act of the one who has been delivered, while v. 3b shows the further effect of that act on those who become aware of it.

vv. 1b–2: A definite and very concrete experience of sinking into a miry pit (compare Joseph and Jeremiah) and of being preserved from death becomes here a parable of experiences of deliverance of many different kinds.

The speaker wants his hearers to share his experience, in such a way that they can participate in it and rediscover their own experiences in it. He does not use abstract generalized language but speaks by way of a comparison. This has the advantage of presenting a whole train of events for the attention of his hearers. They are not just to picture what has occurred, they are actually to be there and so to share in the events that these can also become part of their own story. The comparisons employed all set out a typical situation or a typical succession of events which can embrace many different specific individual experiences. An example will make the point clear: the succession of events pictured in v. 2 could easily be the experiences of a drug addict; the change from sinking into the mire to standing on firm ground would fit exactly. This example is intended to show how the change from distress to deliverance represents a typical human experience which has not basically altered for thousands of years.

v. 3a: As he looks back, the one who has been delivered becomes conscious of the cry of joy, the shout of praise 'Thanks be to God!' after the alleviation of his distress, as a link in the chain of events which comprise the saving acts of God: 'He has put . . .'. So natural, so spontaneous is this reaction to God's act! Here we see a way of speaking of God and man which is characteristic of the psalms. Whoever has had the psalmist's experience can do nothing else but react in this way.

v. 3b: Equally human and natural is it that joyful acknowledgement should broaden out. The hearers say 'how wonderful' and their awed astonishment gives them fresh confidence. Here awe and trust belong closely together.

The sentence in 3b aptly illustrates the use of the Hebrew imperfect, which can have both a past meaning, like the imperfect of classical grammar, and a future one. So 3b could equally well be translated by a past tense: 'Many saw and feared . . .'. In this instance, it cannot be said that one rendering is right and the other wrong. The past tense would correspond to the narrative form of vv. 1–3a, but the structure of the psalm seems to indicate that the future would be preferable as forming a bridge to what happens in the final verses. What 3b forecasts actually takes place through the proclamation of vv. 9–10.

v. 4: The reason for the exclamation here is provided by the affirmation of trust in v. 3b; as far as its contents are concerned, it resembles Psalm 1. The opposition between God and the idols is not a product of the psalm's structure – indeed it is foreign to it – and is never met with in other individual psalms of praise. It could be a parenthetical exclamation of the psalmist himself or a reader's marginal note. In any case it is an interjection and the psalm would lose nothing were it not there.

v. 5: This verse is directly linked with v. 3, as the praise of god intimated in 3a. But it differs from v. 3 in that here the psalmist joins himself to the others who have also experienced such wondrous deeds. At the same time, the narrative praise of God based on verbs passes over into the descriptive based on nouns: 'Many are thy wondrous deeds . . .'. Like Psalm 31: 19, this verse is an expression of awed astonishment. When the speaker reflects in wonderment on God's thoughts as well as His deeds, he brings together the individual memorable events and the abiding certainty that God thinks of us, as in v. 3b. Reflection on all this leads him to recognize that God is incomparable, as is said in Isaiah 40: 18, 'To whom will you liken God?', words which also occur in a context of the praise of God. As He is incomparable, so also is He immeasurable, man cannot number His deeds and thoughts. This attitude to God's thoughts and deeds is in clear contrast to any striving after a knowledge of God which aims to achieve a conceptual language, by means of which thinking about those deeds and thoughts would be possible.

vv. 6-8: To understand these difficult verses, we must first premise a contrast motif here, such as we meet elsewhere, especially in Psalms 50 and 51 – not sacrifice, but praise. To summarize it very briefly, what is being said is: 'not sacrifices, vv. 6-8, but praise, vv. 9-10, I will offer to thee'. We see this contrast motif clearly and unambiguously in the first and third lines of v. 6: 'Sacrifice and grain offering thou dost not delight in, burnt offering and sin offering thou dost not require'. Since these clauses are the two units of a verse in parallelism, it follows that the intervening line 'ears thou hast dug for me' is a later addition, as F. Crüsemann holds. The addition is to be understood as that of a reader who recognized here the prophetic tradition's contrast between sacrifice and obedience, as found for example in 1 Samuel 15: 22, where we have the same expression as in 6a: 'Has the Lord delight in . . .'. In Psalm 40, however, the contrast 'not sacrifice – but praise' means the same as it does in Psalms 50 and 51.

v. 7: This verse expands v. 6: 'Then (that is, if thou didst
require it) I would have said, "Lo, I come".' Because this is
difficult to understand, many commentators read the verb
as a Hiphil instead of a Qal and render: 'Lo, I bring'. This
emendation suits the sense but it remains problematic
because 'I bring' has no object. In favour of retaining the
existing text is the fact that the expression 'I come' is
frequently used on occasions when a sacrifice is brought,
for example, Psalm 66: 13. Hence the words, 'Lo, I come'
represent an abbreviated offering formula.

But the second line is even more difficult: 'in the roll of
the book it is written of me'. By 'the roll of the book', the
Law cannot be meant, though this is how it is commonly
understood, for then the 'of me' would make no sense.
Some commentators suggest that this 'roll of the book'
contained the thanksgiving song which the psalmist brings
as his offering.[55] But this explanation also has its problems.
Nowhere else in the Psalter do we find anything similar and
hence the meaning of the clause remains obscure.

v. 8: V. 8 connects with v. 7a: Didst thou require sacrifices,
I would give thee them, I only wish to do what pleases thee.
In the second line, _tōrā_ is to be understood in its wider sense
of 'instruction' or 'direction'.

vv. 9-10: Vv. 6-7 are concerned with what God does not
want, that is, by way of a thankful response from the one
He has delivered. V. 8 leads on from this: 'I will do what
pleases thee, O God', and what the psalmist does we learn
from vv. 9-10. Therefore it follows that these verses are to
be translated in the present tense.[56] F. Crüsemann
understands vv. 8-9 as speaking of a past occasion and
concludes from this that vv. 12-17, along with vv. 1-11,
originally comprised a single psalm. But vv. 9-10 are a

[55] This is the opinion of G. Bornkamm, J. Hermisson and F.
Crüsemann, who adduce parallels from the history of religions.

[56] See D. Michel, _Tempora und Satzstellung in den Psalmen_, 1960, p. 93
f., who understands the perfect in v. 9 as a declarative perfect 'in
conformity with the structure of the whole section'.

promise or vow of praise; this is a component of the narrative psalm of praise and nowhere else is it represented as occurring in the past. It is, however, possible that, after vv. 12-17 were added, vv. 9-10 were understood as referring to the past.

The psalm has no opening introduction: 'I will . . . ' (see comment on v. 1). All the more strongly do these closing verses emphasize the readiness to carry the praise further. The emphasis is also seen in the carefully thought out pattern of these verses: the first and last lines both end with 'the great congregation'. The three intervening lines present a chiastic structure, formed from the positive and negative formulae 'I tell – I do not restrain – I do not hide – I speak'. The object of these verses is always identical but always differently formulated. This strong emphasis, stylistically so clearly underlined, must be designed to give special prominence to 'the great congregation'. The reason is that the praise of God's deeds, which arose from the experience of one pious individual, extends to reach the great congregation and is echoed there (v. 3b). One may suspect a mild polemic against the legalistic piety that developed in the post-exilic period, when the 'scribes' achieved a dominating position. For in this psalm it is the 'laity', the ordinary folk, who make known what God has done, the deeds which this faithful and gracious God has done in their own day, which are available for all and about which the 'theologians' cannot lay down the law. When the psalmist stresses so powerfully that he will not hide God's saving help in his heart and will not conceal His steadfast love and faithfulness, he is perhaps hinting at a contemporary trend which was threatening to silence the simple piety of laity.

v. 11: This final verse is a petition such as often occurs at the end of a psalm of praise. It fully conforms to v. 3b: from praise grows trust.

Psalm 66: 13–20: I will pay thee my vows

13   I will come into thy house with burnt offerings;
     I will pay thee my vows,
14   that which my lips uttered
     and my mouth promised when I was in trouble.
15   I will offer to thee burnt offerings of fatlings,
     with the smoke of the sacrifice of rams;
     I will make an offering of bulls and goats.

16   Come and hear, all you who fear God,
     and I will tell you what he has done for me.
17   I cried aloud to him,
     and he was extolled with my tongue.
18   I had thought in my heart
     that God had not heard me.
19   But truly God has listened; he has given heed to the
     voice of my prayer.

20   Praised be God, because he has not rejected my
     prayer
     or removed his steadfast love from me!

Text

v. 18: the Massoretic text has 'if I saw wickedness'; with
        many parallel passages, read *'anī 'āmartī*.

Structure

Verses 13–20 of Psalm 66, which form a single independent
individual psalm of praise, are preceded by a descriptive
psalm of praise, in fact a liturgical hymn, which in vv. 10–12
recount a divine act of deliverance for Israel. The joining
together of the two parts makes good sense – the
worshipping community's song of praise is followed by the

similar song of the individual when he offers a sacrifice in fulfilment of his vow. The structure of vv. 13- 20 is extremely simple and clear. The introduction, vv. 13-15, is a sacrificial text spoken when a sacrifice in fulfilment of a vow is to be offered. The speaker recalls the distress in which the vow was made, v. 14, and lists the sacrificial gifts he is going to offer, v. 15. In vv. 16-20, sacrifice is followed by praise, consisting of a narrative of distress and deliverance and a brief shout of praise, v. 20.

vv. 13-15: With the words 'I will come into thy house', the sacrificial text begins. The pilgrimage from daily life to the Temple links the scene of a disaster, a catastrophe or a sick-bed with the place where the congregation assembles for worship. Outside the Temple, an individual in deep distress has made a vow; now he will redeem it in the Temple in a service of worship. Such a vow or promise made in distress is a fundamental human phenomenon, which is met with in many different religions over thousands of years and is still a living phenomenon today, even though officially frowned upon. Such a vow or promise is completely misunderstood when it is frowned upon on the grounds that it is, so to speak, doing a deal with God, as though a man were to think that, by means of it, he can buy his deliverance. On the contrary, the psalms testify that, by means of it, life's depths and heights are bound together. When someone in the depths holds on to God and promises Him something, then, when he keeps this promise, a link is forged; in the moment of isolation a path opens up which has a meaning and has a goal.

In his distress, the psalmist had promised to offer sacrifice and praise and in this psalm he does both, vv. 13-15 (sacrifice) and vv. 16-20 (praise). There is a difficulty, however, if we compare Psalm 66 with Psalm 40, and with Psalms 50 and 51 as well. Psalm 40, as we saw, states that God does not want sacrifice but rather praise, while here both are clearly considered to be well pleasing to Him. The difference can only be explained by the different periods at which the respective psalms originated. Vv. 13-15 of this psalm belong to a time when Israel's sacrificial cult was still intact and was still an essential and significant part of worship. The rejection of sacrifice presupposes the destruction of the Temple and the exile. This raises further questions but we cannot embark on them here. Only one observation is necessary: the fact that Psalm 66 takes a positive attitude to sacrifice and Psalm 40 a negative one shows that those who transmitted the psalms deliberately allowed both views to stand side by side and did not try to correct or reverse Psalm 40 by Psalm 66. And this indicates that they were able to think historically, even though in a way different from us. Both views made good sense for their own time.

v. 15: The list of animal sacrifices in v. 15 obviously does not imply that one man would offer all of them on a single occasion. Rather, the verse enumerates a wide variety of animal sacrifices which could be offered, because the psalm was intended to be recited by a wide variety of individuals.

vv. 16-19: As part of the offering by which he fulfils his vow, the psalmist narrates before the others what he has experienced. This is just sketched here, so that it can apply to the many. But basically the story is always the same. The summons in v. 16 could accompany the recital of any other history, but here a particular individual wants to narrate what God has done for him. What happened in his case is concentrated in the marvellous transformation from lament to praise (compare Psalm 22), although he himself had doubted that deliverance was possible. But the real turning-point was when God turned towards him again, v. 19.

v. 20: The verse represents the concluding praise of God. Only when we have read and pondered the psalm many times do we perceive how all of it, sentence by sentence, from 'I come' through 'Come and hear all of you', leads up to this final shout of praise and in it reaches its goal.

Psalm 116: Snares of death encompassed me

1   I love – for Yahweh has heard my voice of my
        supplication,
2   because he inclined his ear to me,
        and in my days I call on him.
3   Snares of death encompassed me
        and nets of Sheol befell me.
        I found trouble and sorrow.
4   Then I called on the name of Yahweh:
        'O Yahweh, save my life!'
5   Gracious is Yahweh and just,
        our God is a merciful one.
6   Yahweh preserves the simple.
        I was brought low, and he helped me.

7   Return, my soul, to thy rest,
        for Yahweh has done good to thee.
8   For thou hast snatched my soul from death,
        my eyes from tears, my feet from falling.
9   I can walk before Yahweh in the land of the
        living.
10   I believed when I said: 'I am deeply afflicted',
11   I had thought in my consternation: 'All men lie!'

12   How shall I repay Yahweh for all he has done for
        me?
13   I will lift up the cup of salvation
        and call on the name of Yahweh!
14   I will pay my vows to Yahweh
        before all his people!
15   Precious in the eyes of Yahweh is the death of his
        devoted ones.
16   O Yahweh, for I am they servant!
        I am thy servant, the son of thy maid.
        Thou hast loosed my fetters.
17   I will offer to thee sacrifices of praise
        and call upon the name of Yahweh,

18   I will pay my vows to Yahweh
       before all his people,
19   in the forecourts of the house of Yahweh,
       in the midst of Jerusalem.

Text

A preliminary note: The above translation of Psalm 116 is without any textual emendation and is also as literal as possible (thus, for example, 'Yahweh' instead of 'the Lord'). The intention is to demonstrate to the reader of the commentary by this example that the Psalter, and indeed the Old Testament in general, contains texts which, because of the way they have been transmitted, are no longer really comprehensible. The reader can verify for himself that some parts of the Psalter are fully understandable literally and without emendation, but that others are not. In the latter case, it is not just a question of individual words or phrases whose meaning is unrecognizable, but also of the sentence order, which often has clearly been disturbed.

A help towards understanding such a disrupted psalm text is the fact that the psalm category to which Psalm 116 belongs, the individual narrative psalms of praise or thanksgiving psalms, has an amazingly consistent form. From this, we can attempt a reconstruction which makes possible a better understanding of the text. In the case of Psalm 116, scarcely any textual emendations are necessary and only a couple of transpositions. These will be discussed in the detailed commentary that follows.

Structure

All the individual parts or units of the narrative psalm of praise are here and clearly visible, and the psalm contains no later additions (see the reconstruction at the end).

vv. 1-2: Something has been lost at the beginning of our text, as is also indicated by the lack of a title. The first half-line consists only of the verb *āhabti*, 'I love', without an object and with no connection with what follows. From the rest of v. 1 and v. 2, which contain an introductory summary, we can conclude, with Gunkel, that a sentence with a cohortative in the first person singular must originally have stood at the beginning: 'I will . . . for Yahweh has heard . . . '. However, we meet such a sentence in v. 14: 'I will pay my vow'. The same sentence returns subsequently in the form of a brief conclusion at v. 18. That the same sentence should occur twice in such short succession is improbable, and it is for this reason that v. 14 is lacking in the Septuagint. If the words 'I will pay my vow' are transferred from v. 14 to v. 1, not only does this fit in with the structure of the psalm, but placing the same sentence at both beginning and end (the latter amplified by specifying the setting) produces the stylistic device known as 'inclusio', that is, the self-contained section vv. 1-18 is 'included' between the same clause which occurs at the beginning and the end. Inclusio in fact is frequently found in narratives.

The ground for the psalmist's decision to pay his vow is provided, in the brief introductory summary of what he has experienced, vv. 1b-2, by a single sentence: God has heard my supplication! In v. 2b 'and in my days' should be emended to 'on the day when . . . '

vv. 3-4, 10-11: The report of distress and deliverance succeeds the introductory summary. V. 3 is the report of distress, v. 4 the beginning of the report of deliverance. V. 3 uses traditional language in speaking of the distress, compare Psalm 18: 4-5. Death is understood as a force that intervenes in human life, entangling man in 'nets' and 'snares'. V. 4 follows on directly: in peril of death, the psalmist called on God's name. But vv. 10-11, which are out of context in their present position, also belong to the narrative of distress, as their contents show, especially the opening words of v. 11, 'I had thought . . . ', *'ani 'āmarti*;

compare, for example, the same words in the same context at Psalm 31: 22 (Heb. 23). In vv. 10-11, as frequently in the narrative of distress, alongside the attack by the power of death there also appears the attack by men (the enemies or the wicked). But the text of v. 10 is confused and its meaning can no longer be recovered. It is possible that the complaint: 'when I said: I am deeply afflicted' could have been misunderstood by the psalmist's enemies as a confession of wrong- doing, and v. 11, unamended, could have this meaning (with 11a, compare Psalm 31: 22). But v. 10a, 'I believed when I said', remains difficult and invites emendation. The Septuagint has ἐπίστευσα, διὸ ἐλάλησα, 'I believed, and so I spoke', which Paul cites at 2 Corinthians 4: 13.

vv. 4, 16: With v. 4, there begins the narrative of deliverance with the plea in distress, which, significantly, is actually quoted: 'O Lord, save my life!'. The same exclamation 'O Lord', 'ānnāh yhwh, recurs in v. 16 but it makes no sense in the context there. As Gunkel saw, v. 16 is in fact the continuation of v. 4, which gives the following text: 'Then I called on the name of the Lord: "O Lord, save my life!", v. 4, "O Lord, for I am thy servant; I am thy servant the son of thy maid"', v. 16. Two convincing arguments can be adduced for this rearrangement. First, the words 'for I am . . .' represent the element of the petition the object of which is to influence God to intervene. The second argument arises from the last line of v. 16: 'Thou hast loosed my fetters', which makes no real sense in v. 16 as it stands. But if v. 16 is placed after v. 4, then, according to the pattern of the narrative of deliverance, v. 4 and the two first lines of v. 16 are part of the plea in distress, which is succeeded by the deliverance itself, the account of which begins with the last line of v. 16. In other words, the three parts of v. 16 find their correct position and their true meaning as part of the narrative of deliverance and hence as the continuation of v. 4.

When in v. 16 the speaker backs up his plea on the ground that 'I am thy servant', he is appealing to the bond between master and servant, as constituting a relationship in which first and foremost the master is the one who protects, and provides for, his servant, compare Genesis 24. When he adds 'the son of thy maid', he has in mind the succeeding generations who, long before him, have acknowledged God as their master and put their trust in Him.

vv. 8-9: However, the single sentence 'Thou has loosed my fetters' at the end of v. 16 is by itself inadequate as a narrative of deliverance – perhaps something like 'and freed me from the snares' has fallen out after it. Vv. 5-7 cannot be its continuation since they are not in narrative form. But vv. 8-9 are an unmistakeable narrative of deliverance (they are almost the same as Psalm 56: 13). These verses breathe the glad sigh of relief of one delivered from death: 'Thou hast snatched my soul from death, my eyes from tears, my feet from falling'. This 'thou hast' is answered by 'I can', 'now I can', 'I can walk before the Lord in the land of the living'. V. 9 is particularly characteristic of the psalms' understanding of man. 'I can walk' – that he was delivered and set free does not mean the psalmist's attaining a different status or position, for there is no word for freedom in the Old Testament and being free is not understood as a state of life. Rather, freedom means that he can go on, that he is able to take further steps, that new possibilities can open out for him. And this is more closely defined. The steps he takes are, literally, 'in the face of the Lord', that is, in an abiding mutual relationship which is part of real life.

vv. 5-7, 15: That v. 9 closes the narrative of deliverance can be seen not only from the content but also from the rhythm. According to the structure of the psalm of praise, at this point narrative praise should give way to descriptive praise speaking of God's activity in comprehensive fashion, and this is in fact the case in vv. 5-7. On grounds of content, v. 15 also belongs here; its present position between vv. 14 and 16 is difficult, but it makes an excellent transition from vv. 8-9 to 5-7. 'Precious in his eyes is the death of his devoted ones', that is, He has a concern for their death, as Psalm 72: 14 shows. This verse looks back to the report of

deliverance, and to v. 8a in particular, but now God's
concern for life under threat is widened to include all the
pious. Vv. 5, 6a lead on to the praise of the gracious and
merciful God and vv. 6b and 7 turn back again to the
psalmist's own experience; his anguish in the face of death,
v. 3, his affliction, v. 10, and doubt, v. 11, are all now
behind him. Clearly this section is concluded by v. 7.

vv. 12–13, 17–18: In line with the psalm's structure, the
final section renews the promise of praise. The question of
v. 12 which begins the section, 'How shall I repay . . . ?'
(compare Isaiah 38: 15 which also occurs in a psalm of
praise) expresses the psalmist's emotion before the
greatness of the gift he has received; no thanks he could give
would measure up to it.

But something he can do, for he knows that God's
pleasure is that the life He has given back should be life with
Him. This is what the psalmist is saying, in psalm language,
in vv. 13 and 17. That these two verses are the two units of
the concluding vow, and so go closely together, becomes
clear when what are now the intervening verses 14–16 are
placed where they properly belong. Vv. 13 and 17 join
together the two chief aspects of worship, word (13b and
17b) and sacrament (13a and 17a), prayer and sacrifice. But
the repetition of the second line of 13 in 17b serves to
emphasize the prominence of the word. 'To call on the
name of the Lord', *qārā' bešēm yhwh*, is an ancient formula
evidenced in the patriarchal narratives, for example Genesis
12: 8. We must not conclude that it represents a particular
kind of formal prayer, rather it is the verbal expression of a
turning to God which begins with the invocation of His
name. So it includes not just the praise of vv. 13–17 but also
the plea of v. 4. The other aspect of worship, represented by
vv. 13a and 17a, is the sacramental, the sacrifice. The term
'sacrifice of praise', *zebaḥ tōdāḥ,* can mean either a sacrifice
consisting of the praise of God or the sacrificial meal, that is,
a shared offering, when a vow was discharged. Here,
parallel to v. 13a, the latter is intended, and it is referred to in
Psalm 22: 26. Both food and drink are part of the sacrificial

meal, so the 'cup of salvation', literally, 'cup of saving acts', means the beaker of wine drunk in the sacrifice of praise.

vv. 18-19: Through the sacrificial ritual referred to in vv. 13, 17, the psalmist discharges his vow by carrying out what he had promised God to do. What he has announced in v. 1 (= 14), is now accomplished. The conclusion of the psalm, according to the proposal put forward earlier, repeats the opening verse but adds to it the information about the place where the vow is to be discharged, in the forecourt of the Jerusalem Temple, 'before all God's people'.

Some final comments: In what has gone before, we have given a daring exegesis of Psalm 116. In its favour is the fact that the proposed transpositions produce a psalm in which every sentence makes sense in its position and that the criterion for the transpositions is the well–attested structure of the individual psalm of praise. But we should at least attempt to answer the question of how the psalm has reached us in its present form. We cannot recognize any overall plan or deliberate purpose in the existing verse order, which must have come about quite mechanically. But the hypothesis that it results from mistakes in copying is not a satisfactory explanation either. Possibly the psalm was first inscribed on a large clay potsherd – or on two or three – (compare the comment on Psalm 40: 7) and then laid up in the Temple. The sherd was subsequently broken, and when the contents were transcribed on to a roll they were arranged in the wrong order. In support of this explanation, we have seen that the opening is broken off at v. 1 but preserved intact in v. 14 and that, in particular, the position of vv. 8-9, 10-11, 15, 16 shows these verses to be separate fragments. Further, v. 16 can only be understood as a fragment, because, as we have also seen, v. 4b comes immediately before its first line, its final line, 'Thou hast loosed my fetters' is followed by v. 8, and vv. 13 and 17, which are now separated by vv. 14-16, belong together.

The hypothesis of such transpositions and the explanation of them is no more than that. But anyone who seeks to interpret this psalm must assume that it has the structure of the psalm of praise, which is assured by the parallel psalms of the same type. We append our proposed reconstruction for comparison with the translation provided above:

Proposed reconstruction of Psalm 116

Introductory summary

v. 14: I will pay my vows to the Lord before all his people,

v. 1b: for he has heard the voice of my supplication,

v. 2:   yea, he inclined his ear to me on the day when I called.

Narrative of distress and deliverance

v. 3:   Snares of death encompassed me
        and nets of Sheol befell me,
        I found trouble and sorrow

v. 10: I believed (?) when I said: 'I am deeply afflicted',

v. 11: I had thought in my consternation: 'all men lie!'

v. 4:   Then I called on the name of the Lord:
        'O Lord, save my life! 16a: O Lord, for I am thy servant. 16b: I am thy servant, the son of thy maid.'

v. 16c: Thou hast loosed my fetters, freed me from the nets.

v. 8:   Thou hast snatched my soul from death, my eyes from tears, my feet from falling.

v. 9:   I can walk before the Lord in the land of the living!

Praise of God

v. 15: Precious in the eyes of the Lord is the death of his devoted ones.

v. 5:   Gracious is the Lord and just, our God is a merciful
        one.
v. 6:   The Lord preserves the humble.
        I was brought low, he helped me.
v. 7:   Return, my soul, to thy rest,
        for the Lord has done good to thee.

Renewed vow of praise

v. 12: How shall I repay the Lord for all
        that he has done for me?
v. 13: I will lift up the cup of salvation
        and call on the name of the Lord.
v. 17: I will offer to thee sacrifices of praise
        and call on the name of the Lord,
v. 18: I will pay my vows to the Lord
        before all his people,
v. 19: in the courts of the house of the Lord,
        in the midst of Jerusalem.

Psalm 138: I give thee thanks with my whole heart!

1   I give thee thanks with my whole heart,
    before the gods I will make melody to thee.
2   I bow down in thy holy temple,
    and praise thy name for thy steadfast love and thy
        faithfulness;
    for thou hast exalted thy name
    above all that is recounted of thee.

3   On the day I called, thou didst answer me,
    my strength of soul thou didst increase.

4   All the kings of the earth shall praise thee, O
        Lord,
    when they hear the words of thy mouth.

5   And they shall sing of the ways of the Lord,
       for great is the glory of the Lord.
6   For the Lord is high and regards the lowly;
       and the haughty he knows from afar.
7   Though I walk in the midst of trouble,
       thou dost preserve my life.
       Thou dost stretch out thy hand against the wrath of
            my enemies,
       and thy right hand delivers me.
8   The Lord will further my cause;
       thy steadfast love, O Lord, endures for ever.
       Do not forsake the work of thy hands!

Text

v. 2:   for the last word, *šima'kā*, 'thy tidings', 'what is
        recounted of thee', is to be read instead of *'imratekā*,
        'thy word'.

Structure

The structure of the psalm is loose and one can observe how
the strict form of the individual psalm of praise broadens
out. The psalm is introduced by the resolve to praise of vv.
1-2a, with an expansion in 1b. The narrative of distress and
deliverance in vv. 2b-3 is very short and overlaps with the
opening summary. There follows in vv. 4-5a a summons to
the kings of the earth to praise Yahweh, which elsewhere is
a unit of the descriptive hymn of praise, and the same
applies to the praise of God which now follows in vv. 5b-6.
After an expression of confidence in vv. 7-8a, the psalm is
rounded off by a petition, linked with a brief word of praise,
in v. 8b.

The psalm represents a transitional stage between the
narrative praise of an individual and the liturgical psalm of
praise of the congregation. It shows that the two could be
easily assimilated to one another.

vv. 1-3: Leaving aside the expansions contained in these verses, the psalm begins as follows: 'I give thee thanks with my whole heart, I praise thy name for thy steadfast love and faithfulness; on the day I called, thou didst hear me, my strength of soul thou didst increase'. This opening corresponds with that of the individual psalm of praise we have so far discussed; identical or very similar clauses are also met with there. Here we have as an expansion: 'Before the gods I will make melody to thee, I will bow down in thy holy temple; for thou hast exalted thy name above all that is recounted of thee'. Bowing down, as attesting awe, takes place within the Temple itself; by contrast the ceremonies in connection with vows are carried out in the forecourt, Psalm 116: 19. The interior of the Temple is also indicated by the reference to the instrumental musical accompaniment ('make melody') and the mention of a tribunal 'before the gods'; by the latter are probably meant the heavenly beings who form the divine court, as in Isaiah 6. What is said about the glorification of God's name in v. 2b is also more in the manner of hymnic or liturgical praise.

vv. 4-5: an important feature of the narration of what God has done for him by the one who pays his vow is that the others who hear him join in his praise, so that it spreads from a single mouth into a wider circle. In vv. 4-5 this feature is modified in an unusual manner to conform to a characteristic of hymnic praise: the psalmist to some extent breaks out of the circle of his immediate hearers to picture the much wider circle of 'the kings of the earth' as taking up the psalm (usually in psalms of praise the kings are paralleled by the nations, for example, Psalm 72: 11). That the kings of the earth should laud Israel's God and sing of His works strikes us as rather absurd and almost grotesque, and not least in this case, where it is a question of what God has done in the intimacy of the personal life of an individual Israelite. So indeed it must look from the outside. Only the context of the descriptive praise of God, where these words properly belong, can give us access to what is meant here.

v. 6: This context is indicated in v. 6. Here we have the same phrase that occurs in the middle of Psalm 113; we shall discuss it in detail when we come to that psalm. At this point, we need only remark that the praise of God describing His majesty and graciousness has two aspects:

> 5b Great is the glory of the Lord
> 8b Thy steadfast love, O Lord, endures for ever!

When it speaks of God, that is, such praise always has in view the fullness of His being and the whole range of His activity. In the upward glance towards God in v. 6, the divine fullness is expressed by the two poles of God's enthronement in the heights and His mercy that regards the depths of human suffering. In this wide perspective, all humanity comes close together – mighty and powerful kings in God's sight are nothing but lowly, fallible men. When they set themselves up in overweening pride, there is One who marks them: 'the haughty he knows from afar'.

vv. 7-8: V. 7 could be read with v. 3; the contrast with the style of the intervening vv. 4-6 is clear. Now the psalmist recurs again to his personal situation. He has experienced God's marvellous act of deliverance, v. 3, and now he looks ahead to the course of his future life from which anguish and care will not be absent. But he can take the next step in confident trust: 'thou dost preserve my life'. He is also preserved in the face of enemies mightier than he, for God's hand is even mightier, v. 7b. The psalm closes with a petition in which the creature entrusts himself to his Creator: 'Do not forsake the work of thy hands!', compare Job 10: 8.

A final word: One of the finer points of this psalm is the intentional way in which the two sentences in vv. 5 and 8 which, in their praise of God, describe the divine being:

> 'Great is the glory of the Lord,
> Thy steadfast love, O Lord, endures for ever'

hold together the whole psalm under these two very different aspects.

DESCRIPTIVE PSALMS OF PRAISE OR HYMNS

Psalm 113: He who is seated on high, who looks far down

1   Hallelujah!
Praise, O servants of the Lord, praise the name of
    the Lord!

2   Praised be the name of the Lord from this time
    forth and for evermore!

3   From the rising of the sun to its setting
the name of the Lord is to be praised!

4   The Lord is high above all nations,
and his glory above the heavens!

5a, 6b Who is like the Lord our God
in heaven and on earth,

5b, 6a who is seated on high, who looks far down?

7   He raises the poor from the dust,
and lifts the needy from the ash heap,

8   to make them sit with princes,
with the princes of his people.

9   He gives the barren woman a home,
making her the joyous mother of children.

Text

v. 5:   the second two lines of vv. 5 and 6 are to be changed
round, as proposed in the apparatus of BHS and by
all commentators. VV. 5b, 6a are literally: 'who
causes to be seated on high, who causes to look far
down'.

v. 8:   the first verb should have the third person plural
suffix, instead of the first person singular.

Structure

In no other psalm can we recognize so clearly the difference between the narrative psalm of praise of an individual and the psalm of praise of a congregation assembled for worship; from its place in worship, the latter is also described as a hymn. In such psalms, it is not a question only of God's act of deliverance on behalf of an individual, but God is praised in the fullness of His divine being, including His deeds and His words. Psalm 113 is the basic example of a psalm of this type.

We have seen that, with the narrative psalm of praise, its kernel is a single sentence: 'Praised be God, who has done . . .'. The same is true also of the descriptive psalm of praise. When we leave aside all expansions, its kernel also consists of a single sentence, here: 'Praised be the Lord, who is seated on high and looks far down!' This sentence accords with the situation of worship, in which it is set, but, as a summons and the ground of that summons, it is also an independent verbal unit, with its own life.

Excursus: Language and Prayer. In the psalms, we come across a phenomenon which has too often been overlooked but which is of great significance for our secular world. Psalms of lament or praise have developed, as the result of a long and gradual process, from a single sentence. At a very early stage of its existence, what we call prayer only consisted of a single sentence. But in the main, this sentence took the form of a cry or an exclamation; exclamation preceded statement. In this early phase of human speech, the single independent sentence was the dominant influence on language. Communication was mostly achieved in single sentences, as indeed we still find is the case in situations of extremity, but which is no longer the case in normal life where a more extensive speech structure predominates.

In psalm prayer, we are still at the stage in which human speech was developing its real force and its real potentialities through independent sentences. That there are still prayers which project this early stage from a distant past into the present undoubtedly proves that the cry to God had for many thousands of years a fundamental significance for human existence, a significance which man could not explain from within himself. On the other hand, it proves that this kind of language, where speech consists only of a single sentence, is native to humanity. The cry to God – or, to put it another way, the cry to something outside oneself – cannot be got rid of. It is independent of any particular set of beliefs or any particular religion. However remote or hidden it may be, it still remains innate in humankind.

Psalm 113 begins in v. 1 with the imperative summons to praise characteristic of descriptive praise, which is continued by the jussive in vv. 2-3. Vv. 4-6 give the ground of this summons to praise. In the middle of vv. 4-6 stands the two-clause sentence vv. 5b, 6a, containing the reason proper for the praise of God, one aspect of which (majesty) is developed in vv. 4, 5a, 6b, the other (goodness) in vv. 7-9. This structure is clear and succinct; it indicates that the kernel of the psalm consists of the imperative summons to praise and the grounds for it, so that all the other sections can be identified as expansions or developments.

v. 1: The title of the psalm, *hallelujah*, identifies it as belonging to a collection of psalms with this particular title. The title coincides with the type of psalm to which it is attached; the imperative summons to praise is a feature of the descriptive psalm of praise or hymn. The word 'Hallelujah' has passed in its original form and language, via Greek and Latin, into many different languages and still remains current, as a summons to praise Yahweh that expresses something peculiarly characteristic of these ancient Israelite psalms.

Noteworthy also is the form of v. 1. The sentence 'Praise, O servants of the Lord, praise the name of the Lord' vibrates with the rhythm of an extended parallelism, where the first part contains the subject in the vocative and the second the object. The imperative summons to praise originated apart from the psalms and was originally in prose, like the liturgical summons 'Let us pray'; subsequently it was taken up into the psalms and developed into a poetic form. The 'servants of Yahweh' here are not priests or Temple singers; rather, the whole congregation is being called to praise by this summons. They are God's servants because they serve Him with their whole being and this is the meaning of the term as it is employed in the book of Deuteronomy in particular. By the 'name of Yahweh' is meant His fame, what is recounted of His deeds.

vv. 2-3: In v. 2 the imperative is continued by a jussive, as often happens; the sense is the same, so that the summons to praise goes on through vv. 2-3. It is expanded by what is said about the range of the praise; in v. 2 it is given temporal extension, in v. 3 spatial: 'from this time forth and for evermore' – 'from east to west'. The call to praise does not die away inside the walls of the Temple; God's praise has within itself an impulse to spread out into the recesses of time and the whole expanse of space. It knows no boundaries, for the One who is to be praised is the Creator of all who holds everything in His hands. Here we can see both how descriptive praise resembles narrative praise and how it differs from it. In both, the praise of God is to spread further, but in narrative praise only to the circle of those to whom God's saving act is recounted, while in descriptive praise it spreads to embrace the whole expanse of space.

vv. 4-9: Similar considerations apply to the grounds for praise given in vv. 4-9. Vv. 4-6 sing of all that God is and all that He does. But those who praise God know what He is like and what He does from their own experience, vv. 7-9; these latter verses correspond to what we find in narrative praise.

vv. 5b, 6a: In the middle of the psalm occurs the two-member sentence in which the praise of God is supremely concentrated: 'who is seated on high – who looks far down'. The entire Old Testament, indeed the whole Bible, tells us what this verse means! It is a statement of the two poles which mark respectively God's being and work, that is, the verse speaks of God by picturing, as it were, the two poles of a magnetic field. God's being can only be spoken of in conjunction with the other pole of His activity. The Old Testament knows nothing of God as a transcendent being who could be defined by His static attributes or characteristics. When here God's majesty and His goodness or steadfast love are spoken of, these are not to be understood as inactive divine attributes: the polar structure of the verse speaks rather of God's activity, which the two poles we have mentioned define. God's majestic seat on high, a phrase which sums up all that can possibly be said of divine transcendence, is inseparably bound up with His looking far down into the depths, as that is further pictured in vv. 7-9. But with neither is it a question of 'God as He is in Himself' but of God in relation to His creation, His people and His 'servants'.

vv. 4, 5a, 6b: Here we have the development of what is meant by God's majesty. The controlling expression of v. 4 is 'God is high above . . .', which could also be translated as 'God is higher than . . .'. What this implies is more closely defined by 'above all nations', v. 4a, and 'above the heavens', v. 4b, which refer respectively to the two realms of history and creation. In 4b, the subject of the clause is 'his glory' or 'his honour'. The word *kābōd* thus means glory that is revealed in action, and from this it is clear that God's transcendence, His being seated on high, v. 6a, is not to be understood in a local sense as though it denoted a place where He is enthroned. The statement is metaphorical: 'high' here means what we mean when we speak of high office. V. 4 says that God is the Lord of creation and the Lord of history. A local understanding of God's seat on high is also excluded by the phrase, 'his glory *above* the heavens'. To confine God to a particular place is impossible. So when the Bible speaks of God's 'dwelling place', again the term is metaphorical. Such a mythical or metaphorical expression is in danger of restricting God to our own apprehension of Him, but what is further said of God's

majesty in vv. 5a, 6b prevents us taking it in this way: 'Who
is like Yahweh our God in heaven and on earth?'. This is
another expression of wonderment, and the wonderment
results from the recognition of God's incomparability. That
God is incomparable, that there is no-one like Him, is a
precisely defined statement, but one to be taken literally,
about the being of God Himself. There is no standard
against which we can measure God; He cannot be classified
according to any of our criteria or descriptions, by any of
our terms or concepts. V. 6b further defines the statement
of God's incomparability by the words: 'in heaven and on
earth'. These two words occur in the opening verse of the
creation account in Genesis 1; together they express
completeness, and they sum up the created whole. In the
entire creation, there is nothing equal to God, nothing that
can be compared with Him. Hence the Old Testament
contains no theoretical concept of God – He cannot be
comprehended, and no representation of God – He cannot
be portrayed. When His majesty is spoken of, this means
that nothing and no-one is as He is. Nothing at all could be
said of God were it not for the further fact that 'he looks far
down', whereby His majesty comes into contact with the
reality we know.

vv. 7-9: V. 6a is expanded by vv. 7-9. God looks far down
to help those who cry to Him from the depths. God's
transcendence is from the start linked with His looking far
down, the two go together. His transcendence makes it
possible for God to 'oversee' and so to turn towards
sufferers, it enables Him to intervene as Lord of creation
and Lord of history, for nothing can withstand Him.

Two examples from the great army of sufferers are
picked out, the distress typical of a man and the distress
typical of a woman in those days. By the mention of man
and woman here, what is intended is this: just as the
expression 'heaven and earth' signifies the whole creation,
so man and woman stand for all humanity as created by
God. Here too Psalm 113 knows of no boundaries to God's
mercy, He is there for all sufferers.

God, as He looks down from the height into the depths, directs His actions to those in the depths, the poor and needy. That is the experience of which the psalms of lament and the narrative psalms of praise speak. Someone stuck in the dust and mire has found that God has helped him and that he has again achieved an honoured position, v. 8. A woman like Hannah the mother of Samuel, 1 Samuel 1-2, has found that when, after enduring childlessness for a long period, she cried to God in her distress, she became a joyous mother of children, v. 9. Such apparently minor human experiences of how suffering can be transformed are what awaken the praise of God, where we hear again of the God who is seated on high and looks far down.

Psalm 33: His word – His work

1   Rejoice in the Lord, O you righteous!
     Praise befits the upright.
2   Praise the Lord with the lyre,
     make melody to him with the harp of ten strings.
3   Sing to him a new song, play skilfully on the
     strings, with loud shouts!

4   For the word of the Lord is upright;
     and all his work dependable.
5   He loves righteousness and justice;
     the earth is full of the goodness of the Lord.
6   By the word of the Lord the heavens were made,
     and all their host by the breath of his mouth.
7   He gathered the waters of the sea as in a goat-
     skin;
     he put the deeps in storehouses.
8   Let all the earth fear the Lord,
     let all the inhabitants of the world stand in awe of
     him.
9   For he spoke, and it came to be; he commanded and
     it stood forth.
10   The Lord brings the counsel of the nations to
     nought;

he frustrates the plans of the peoples.
11   The counsel of the Lord stands for ever, the
     thoughts of his heart to all generations.
12   Blessed is the nation whose God is the Lord,
     the people whom he has chosen as his heritage!

13   The Lord looks down from heaven,
     he sees all the sons of men;
14   from where he sits enthroned he looks forth on all
     the inhabitants of the earth,
15   he who fashions the hearts of them all,
     and observes all their deeds.
16   A king is not saved by his great army;
     a warrior is not delivered by his great strength.
17   The war horse is a vain hope for victory,
     and by its might it cannot save.
18   But the eye of the Lord is on those who fear him,
     and on those who hope in his steadfast love,
19   that he may deliver their soul from death,
     and keep them alive in famine.

20   Our soul waits for the Lord;
     he is our help and shield.
21   For our heart is glad in him,
     because we trust in his holy name.
22   Let thy steadfast love, O Lord, be upon us,
     even as we hope in thee.

Text

v. 7:   instead of *kannēd*, 'dam', read *kannōd*, 'goat-skin'.
v. 17: read the Niphal, *jimmālēṭ*, instead of the Piel.

Structure

To determine the structure of Psalm 33, the psalm clearly must be compared with Psalm 113, for the structure of the former forms an expansion of the latter. The two main sections are the same: the imperative summons to praise of vv. 1-3, and then the grounds for praising God, vv. 4-19, corresponding to Psalm 113: 1-3 and 4-9. The summons to praise of vv. 1-3 consists of a string of imperatives but here, unlike Psalm 113, the verbal praise is to be accompanied by musical instruments. The ground of praise is introduced here with 'For', and then, in both psalms, follow statements in praise of God, but these are considerably expanded in Psalm 33. The polar statement of God's majesty and mercy in v. 5, corresponding to Psalm 113: 5b, 6, is expanded in v. 4 by paralleling His word – His work. God's majesty (Psalm 113: 4-5a) can be spoken of in various ways; here it is seen in the fact that He is Creator, vv. 6-9, and Lord of history, vv. 10-11. Vv. 13-14 and 18-19 tell of God's gracious condescension and correspond closely with Psalm 113: 6a, 7-9.

By comparison, all the remaining verses are expansions. V. 12 is a grateful reflection, in between the two sections that deal with the divine majesty and goodness. In vv. 15-17, God's downward glance has two aspects: it is directed both towards those who depend on His goodness, v. 15, and towards the powerful, vv. 16-17. Two concluding sections are added, an avowal of confidence, vv. 20-21 and a request for blessing, v. 22.

In his commentary, H. Gunkel has this to say about the structure of Psalm 33: 'When we stress the fact that the number of verses corresponds to the number of letters in the Hebrew alphabet, it becomes understandable that the thought process is rather loosely worked out and that the psalm consists of individual groups of ideas which stand more or less side by side . . . Hence commentators dispute as to how the psalm should be divided'. But the structure of the psalms is not intellectually thought out; it is determined by events. The structure is entirely clear and each part, as with Psalm 113, is meaningfully connected with the whole.

vv. 1-3: The worshipping congregation is the recipient of the call to praise. By the pious (literally, 'the righteous') and the upright (compare Genesis 17: 1) is not here meant a group differentiated from others but the worshipping congregation as a unity, as it actually is. Six different words are employed in the call to praise of vv. 1–3. Each of them has its own proper individual meaning but here they have all become simply different descriptions of the praise of God. Hence the two terms *tōdāh* and *tehillāh*, narrative and descriptive praise respectively, have much the same sense, since both denote praise of God. In this and other respects, Psalm 33 shows itself to be relatively late in its present form. In Psalm 66 too, we meet the same assimilation of the narrative and descriptive psalm of praise to make one single psalm. But *tōdāh* and *tehillāh* here are synonyms for 'praise', not for 'giving thanks', since *tehillāh* cannot mean the latter.

v. 1: For the psalm's late date argues also the reflective line v. 1b: 'Praise befits (or, becomes) the upright', so similarly Psalm 92: 1; that is, praise is right and proper for them, it is something that is part of their life. The fact that 1b gives the ground for the call to praise, at the same time throws light on the character of the imperative form; the description of it in Latin grammar, 'mode of command', is only applicable to a fraction of its usages. Here it indicates an urgent request which can only be meaningfully addressed to a group all of whom belong together and of which the one who makes the request is also a member. This challenging call is especially characteristic of the speech of children: 'Come, let's . . . '

v. 2: In the summons 'Praise . . . with the lyre', the verb *hōdāh* is assimilated to the verb *hillēl*. In its original meaning, *hōdāh* can only happen in words, because narration is part of it (see p. 168 f. above). For this reason, musical instruments are never mentioned in narrative psalms of praise, but they properly belong to *hillēl*, the liturgical hymn. By the parallelism of v. 2, both verbs, *hōdū* ('praise' in words alone) and *zammerū* ('make melody', always with musical accompaniment), are linked with musical instruments. This means that here the accompanying instruments have become part of the procedure for praising God.

What is more, we see here a precise understanding of the rôle of musical instruments in worship, as we also find in Psalm 150. When they become part of the means by which men give God praise, it means that they themselves participate in the act of praise, albeit in a subordinate capacity. Perhaps we should see this as a distant analogy with the summons to praise God addressed to the creation in Psalm 148. Instruments made by human hands also bear the stamp of creatureliness and by that very fact they can serve to extol God. The boundless possibilities of musical sound extend the range of the praise sung by human voices, now amplified by the instruments human hands have made. From the viewpoint of the history of religions, we may suppose that instrumental music originally had a magical function, but in Israel's worship this has been completely superseded by its function as praise of God.

v. 3: 'Sing to him a new song . . .': the 'new song' here is to be understood in the light of Psalm 40: 3, for which see the comment on p. 182 above. The new song arises from a new experience, but it has become a figure of speech, employed even where it no longer makes any clear sense in its context. The word *terū'āh*, properly '(loud) sound' or 'blaring (of trumpets)', was originally a battle alarm or victory cry and later came to mean the ringing sound of the instruments, especially the horns, employed in liturgical ceremonies.[57]

vv. 4–5: Corresponding to the polar combination of divine majesty and benevolent activity as aspects of God's being in Psalm 113, here word and work appear together. God's work (the historical books) and His words (Law and prophets) between them subsume all that God means for the world, for His people and for each individual, and hence both belong together. God's word is praised as 'upright',

---

[57] See P. Humbert, *'La terou'ā', analyse d'un rite biblique*, 1946.

His work as 'dependable', but both adjectives say the same
thing: that one can rely on both, hold to both.

In v. 5, alongside God's goodness, *ḥesed*, which knows
no bounds and fills the earth, though in a sense somewhat
different from Psalm 113: 4, 5a, there is introduced the
frequently occurring pair of terms 'righteousness and
justice', *ṣedāqāh ūmišpāṭ*. The One enthroned on high,
Psalm 113: 5b, is king but also judge: 'he loves
righteousness and justice' and as judge he enforces them.

Vv. 4–5 illustrate how the descriptive psalm of praise
tends to speak of the totality of the divine life, to include in
its praise the whole being and work of God. We could label
this a systematizing tendency. But in contrast to systematic
theology, which proceeds from a conceptual understanding
of God, the language about God in the psalms of praise,
when it systematizes and combines, is only to be
comprehended when it is seen as carrying further what is
said about God's work in narrative praise. In short, the
descriptive psalms of praise expand on what has already
been said about God's work in the narrative psalms of
praise.

vv. 6–9: Now the activity of the majestic and gracious God
is unfolded through a description of His majestic work as
Creator, vv. 6–9, and Lord of history, vv. 10–12. Vv. 6–9
are divided as follows: vv. 6 and 9 are concerned with the
work of God's creative word, while, in between, v. 7 deals
with God' activity as Creator and v. 8 with His effect on
humankind.

Behind the two lines of v. 6, which both lay stress on
creation through the word, the priestly account of creation
in Genesis 1 is clearly recognizable. V. 9 again gives
expression to the majesty and wonder of the creative
activity of God's word.[58] If one compares the account in
Genesis 1 with vv. 6–9 of Psalm 33, one is struck by how
close they are to each other, and not least by the fact that in

---

[58] For a fuller discussion, see the commentary on Genesis 1 in C.
Westermann, *Genesis 1-11*, translated by J.J. Scullion, 1984.

both praise is seen as the appropriate way of speaking of God as Creator. For Genesis 1 too is dominated by the praise of God, as appears particularly from the phrase, 'and it was good', which interweaves the whole account.

Awe must be the keynote of praise, as v. 8 says expressly: 'Let all the earth fear the Lord'. If this verse is read as a unit of the whole psalm, one can perceive how the author amplifies the summons to praise of vv. 1-3 in the call here for reverent awe before the Creator. The paralleling of the earth – its inhabitants means the response of awe is to come not only from men but also from all creation, as Psalm 148 says.

For the author of Psalm 33, it is impossible to speak of the Creator except on the basis of awe. Discourse about Creator and creation cannot be divorced from awe and merely carried on at the level of rational argument, where one can ask whether the universe was created or whether it evolved. A mere dogmatic statement of fact that God made the world or that the world was made by God misses the point of what the Bible has to say.

That the Old Testament does not confine itself to any one picture of how the world was made again reveals the limits to human understanding of creation. While vv. 6 and 9 highlight creation through the word, v. 7 pictures the world as being made in the same sort of way that human beings make things: God gathers the waters of the seas as in a goat-skin, compare Psalm 78: 13, he locks up the deeps (as) in storehouses, compare Job 38: 22. Setting bounds to the sea is viewed here as a handiwork, corresponding to the way in which in Genesis 1 God's creative handiwork stands alongside creation through His word, without any logical connection between them.[59] But v. 7 also hints at the mythical picture of the taming of a chaos monster, as at Isaiah 51: 10; *tehōmot*, akkadian *tiāmat*, 'deeps', is originally a mythical concept. Genesis 1 does not obliterate this older picture by its account of creation through the word; the former retains its expressive force alongside the latter.

---

[59] Westermann speaks of a 'word' account and an 'act' account in Genesis 1: see his commentary referred to in footnote [58] above.

vv. 10-12: Vv. 10-12 tell us that the Creator is also the Lord of history, but this lordship is only suggested by stating its opposite. The divine blueprint for history is set over against the designs of the nations. This juxtaposition can only give a brief indication of the author's meaning. It is noteworthy that here we no longer have the contrast between the superior might of the warrior God and the inferior power of Israel's enemies, as was the case at an earlier epoch, for example at the time of the Song of Deborah in Judges 5; the antithesis is presented in a more abstract and reflective manner. When God 'frustrates' the plans of the nations, what is meant are plans conceived in overweening pride, of which, for example, Assyria is accused in Isaiah 10; when v. 11 says that God's plans stand for all generations, it means that they also survive any catastrophes that befall His people. This is how we are to understand the exclamation of v. 12: 'Blessed is the nation . . .', compare Psalm 40: 4. The people whom He has chosen can hold fast to Him through all the disasters of their history, compare v. 4. V. 12 is both intentionally connected with v. 8 and also rounds off the section vv. 6-11.

vv. 13-19: These verses amplify the praise of God's goodness in v. 5. Vv. 13 and 14 are in parallelism and describe how God looks down from the height on mankind, as in Psalm 113: 6a. The expressions 'from heaven – from where he sits', as is also the case in Psalm 113, do not indicate location but refer to what immediately follows. Three verbs are used for God's 'looking down' on men, in order to assure those being addressed that nothing can disturb His kindly observation of them. Here there is a direct connection with v. 18, but the amplification of the theme in vv. 15-17 is intended to explain more fully what is involved in this looking down; it is an expansion typical of descriptive praise.

vv. 15-17: Because such praise is always concerned with the whole of God's activity, one statement is often balanced by its corresponding opposite: 'He puts down the mighty from their thrones – he exalts those of low degree'. To what has been said about God's looking down, vv. 15-17 add that thereby He tests mankind. He knows their thoughts and actions, for they are His creation, v. 15. Behind this statement lies a concept frequently met with in many religious systems, for example, that of the eye of Horus in Egyptian religion.[60] No-one can hide his deeds and his heart from God, because, as is said here and in Psalm 139, men have been made by God: 'he who fashions the hearts of them all and observes all their deeds'. We see here that the creation of the world and the creation of humanity are originally distinct themes in the Old Testament. The creation of the world opens God's majesty to view, as in vv. 6-9 here; the creation of man, on the other hand, is linked with God's gracious care.

In vv. 16-17, God looks down from on high not only on the misery of those who hope in Him, vv. 18-19, but He also sees the others, the mighty and powerful who trust in their own strength, vv. 16-17. When the verb 'deliver' is specially emphasized in these verses – it occurs four times in different words – it is saying that even the mighty will one day fall, something that, in a somewhat different way, the prophets had also said.

vv. 18-19: These verses connect with v. 14. God's eye is on those who fear Him and hope in His steadfast love. It is to give more weight to these words that the amplification in vv. 15-17 was introduced. Its effect is to make clear that fear of God and hope for His aid are possible in the face of the direst threat, in contrast to what is said in vv. 16-17. What is more to be relied on is God's regard for those in the depths of suffering.

So the two lines of v. 19 sound loud and long a reverberating final note, in which the psalm's call to praise reaches its goal. In the first line, 'to deliver their soul from death' is the goal of God's looking down from on high, v. 14, seen as the deliverance of the one who calls on Him in

---

[60] See R. Pettazzoni, *The All-Knowing God,* 1956.

deadly peril, through the course of events with which the narrative songs of praise are concerned. The second line joins preservation to deliverance, the constant to what happens but once. God's intervention to deliver from distress is not just a once for all act. On the single act there supervenes constant and everlasting care, on deliverance preservation; so from deliverance, Exodus 1-15, there develops history, Exodus 16 ff.

vv. 20-21: Properly speaking, the psalm of praise ends with v. 19. Vv. 20-21 are an epilogue, consisting of an avowal of confidence, compare Psalm 40: 11. The God who has saved from deadly peril will continue to make provision, says v. 19b. In this way, the psalmist can look to the future, trusting in God's protecting care. 'He is our help and our shield' can be said by the one who cries in distress, but also by the one who has been delivered as he regards his future. Hence the psalm's final word is one of joy: 'our heart is glad in him' – joy which is grounded in confidence 'because we trust in his holy name'.

v. 22: This verse is not part of the psalm proper but a liturgical response to it from the congregation. It is a request for blessing, picking up the concluding vv. 20-21.

It is possible that vv. 20-22 were added to bring up the number of verses to the number of letters in the Hebrew alphabet.

Psalm 66: 1-12: Through fire and through water

1   Make a joyful noise to God, all the earth;
2   sing the glory of his name;
     give to him glorious praise!
3   Say to God, 'How thy deeds compel to awe!
     So great is thy power that thy enemies cringe before
          thee.
4   All the earth worships thee,

and sings praises to thee, sings praises to thy name.'

5   Come and see what God has done:
his deeds strike men with awe.

6   He turned the sea into dry land;
men passed through the river on foot;
let us mightily rejoice in him,

7   who rules by his power for ever,
whose eyes keep watch on the nations –
the rebellious cannot exalt themselves against him!

8   Bless our God, O peoples,
let the sound of his praise be heard,

9   who has kept us among the living,
and has not let our feet slip.

10   For thou, O God, hast tested us;
thou hast tried us as silver is tried.

11   Thou didst bring us into prison;
thou hast put chains on our thighs;

12   thou didst let men ride over our heads;
we went through fire and through water;
yet thou hast brought us forth to a spacious place.

Text

v. 2: after *sīmu*, add *lō*.

v. 6: instead of *šām*, 'there', which is impossible by reason of the following cohortative, read the infinitive absolute *sāmōaḥ*.

v. 11: the translation 'prison' is uncertain.

v. 12: with the Versions, read *rewāḥāh*, 'spacious place', instead of *rewājāh*.

Structure

The succeeding verses 13–20 form an individual psalm of praise (see above, p. 186). Vv. 9–12 closely resemble a communal psalm of praise. Vv. 1–8 are a descriptive psalm of praise dominated by imperatives in vv. 1-5, 8 (and hence an 'imperative psalm'), which introduce the two narrative psalms of praise; the whole is a liturgical composition made up from three psalms of praise.

The frame for vv. 1-8 is the imperative call to praise of vv. 1-2, expanded by 3-5 and 8. The ground of the call to praise is the praise of God's majesty, v. 3 (perhaps 3-5) and v. 7, and the praise of His act of deliverance, v. 6. The basic structure is the same as that of such descriptive psalms of praise as Psalms 113 and 33, but freely adapted. The imperative call to praise of v. 8 rounds off v. 1-7 and introduces 9-12. The latter are narrative communal praise; v. 9 is a stock formula, vv. 10-12 look back to a sorrowful testing by God, divided into distress, 10-12a, and deliverance, 12b.

vv. 1-2: This is the opening of a liturgical psalm of praise in the form of a succession of calls to praise in the imperative.

vv. 3-4: These calls to praise are continued in v. 3 by the imperative 'Say . . . !'. Singing, with instrumental accompaniment,[61], and speaking are here all viewed as one; articulate speech is a necessary element of the praise of God. Hence the congregation is summoned to praise God's majestic work by uttering the words: 'How awe compelling (literally, 'how terrible') are thy deeds!'. Here God's majestic work is confined to His work in history, as is stipulated in the continuation vv. 9-12.

Because the whole psalm deals with history, 'all the world', vv. 1, 4, 8, is summoned to praise the Lord of history. This is no hymnic hyperbole; rather, we see here a characteristic feature of ancient Israel's worship which, unhappily, Christian worship has almost entirely lost. God is taken seriously as Lord of history, as He is in the whole of the Old Testament. The division of mankind into various nations, Genesis 10, depends on God's work of creation and

---

[61] 'Sing' in v. 2 of the translation can also mean 'make music'.

the blessing there: 'be fruitful and multiply'. In the historical books, God is concerned not only with Israel but also with the nations, and the same applies in even greater degree to the prophets. And in Apocalyptic God's concern for His people once again becomes one with His concern for all humanity. This is what gives Israel's worship that broad horizon which enables the nations also to be called to praise: 'Bless our God, O peoples!'

v. 5: 'Make a joyful noise – say – come!' – the nations are here summoned as witnesses to what God has done. The deliverance from Egypt and the return from exile are historical events which have happened before the eyes of the nations and to which they can testify, as Deutero-Isaiah expressly states, Isaiah 41: 5. In this connection, it is important to observe that God's acts of judgment and condemnation, just as much as His saving acts, can be described as 'awe compelling', vv. 3 and 5. Both aspects of God's activity in history are awe compelling. God's act of deliverance at the Sea, Exodus 14–15, is only hinted at, but the very fact that it only needs to be so briefly touched on shows how alive it remained for centuries in Israel's traditions. The rejoicing once provoked by that great deliverance still echoes and does not fall silent: 'Let us rejoice in him!'

v. 7: The psalm now returns once more to the praise of the divine majesty; v. 7 continues vv. 3-5. It is an amazingly bold step when God's watching over the ways of men is expanded to include His work as Lord of history: 'his eyes keep watch on the nations'. This sentence challenges all absolutist political claims: One alone is in overall control, One alone governs everything and everybody. Here the psalm comes close to the message of Deutero-Isaiah. In any case, this sentence has been confirmed, incontestably if only in part, by the whole course of world history up to the present day. There has never yet been a political power which has ruled over all men.

vv. 8-12: Since, in form and content, v. 8 belongs to the category of descriptive praise, it is an appropriate conclusion for vv. 1-7, but it also serves as an introduction to what follows in vv. 9-12. With v. 8 we may compare Exodus 18: 10, where the Midianite Jethro praises God for His deliverance of the Israelites from the power of the Egyptians.

v. 9: V. 9 contains the praise of a group of people who have been delivered but the words are so general that they could be spoken by a single individual; hence v. 9 can be taken as the introduction to vv. 13-20 as well as to vv. 9- 12.

vv. 10-12: These verses consist of a narrative of the people's distress, vv. 9-12a, and of their deliverance, 12b. The narrative of distress is further divided into a summary interpretation of the time of need as a time of testing, v. 10, and a description of the people's sufferings, vv. 11-12a. However, God's purpose in allowing His people to endure such hardship was not to torment or punish them. In God's plan, the time of suffering was aimed at testing the nation: as Gunkel writes, 'Through suffering "in the furnace of affliction" (Isaiah 48: 10), God wanted to establish whether or not Israel would be faithful to Him'. Such an interpretation of the time of suffering takes it for granted that whatever hardship an individual or community has to undergo is to be attributed to God. In the story of Abraham, suffering in personal life is interpreted as a test from God, Genesis 22: 1.

So it is possible to continue to address God in the description of the sufferings: 'thou, O God . . . thou hast'. Only a few examples are provided: imprisonment, v. 11, threat from the elements of fire and water, v. 12aβ, and the shame of subjugation, of being reduced to profound degradation, which is what is meant by the words of 12a α: 'thou didst let men ride over our heads'.

Then the account of the deliverance can be summed up in a single sentence: 'yet thou hast brought us forth into a spacious place!'. With these words of deliverance, the section vv. 9–12 reaches its goal. The section is given unity by the address to God which binds all its clauses together: 'Thou hast . . . '. Only because He had himself gone with them through the depths can those who have been saved take it as self-evident that their deliverance was an act of God. They had experienced suffering as God's 'strange work', but yet as *His* work. This persevering in fellowship with God through all disasters, 'through fire and through water', is characteristic of Israel's religion.

Psalm 145:
I will sing of thy wondrous works!

A Song of Praise of David

1   I will extol thee, my God and King,
      and bless thy name for ever and ever.

2   Every day I will bless thee,
      and praise thy name for ever and ever.

3   Great is the Lord, and highly to be praised,
      and his greatness is unsearchable.

4   One generation shall laud thy works to another,
      and shall declare thy mighty acts.

5   Of the glorious splendour of thy majesty they shall
        speak,
      of thy wondrous works they shall sing.

6   They shall proclaim the might of thy terrible acts,
      thy mighty acts they shall relate.

7   They shall pour forth the fame of thy abundant acts
        of deliverance,
      and shall sing aloud of thy righteousness.

8   The Lord is gracious and merciful,
      slow to anger and abounding in steadfast love.

9   The Lord is good to all,
      and his compassion is over all that he has made.

10   All thy works shall praise thee, O Lord,
      and all thy saints shall bless thee.
11   They shall extol the glory of thy kingdom,
      and tell of thy power,
12   to make known to the sons of men thy mighty
         deeds,
      and the glorious splendour of thy kingdom.
13   Thy kingdom is an everlasting kingdom,
      and thy dominion endures throughout all
         generations.
      The Lord is faithful in all his words,
      and gracious in all his deeds.
14   The Lord upholds all who are falling,
      and raises up all who are bowed down.

15   The eyes of all look to thee,
      and thou givest them their food in due season.
16   Thou openest thy hand,
      thou satisfiest the desire of every living thing.
17   The Lord is just in all his ways,
      and kind in all his doings.
18   The Lord is near to all who call upon him,
      to all who call upon him with a pure heart.
19   He fulfils the desire of all who fear him,
      he also hears their cry, and saves them.
20   The Lord preserves all who love him;
      but all the wicked he will destroy.

21   My mouth shall speak the praise of the Lord,
      and let all flesh bless his holy name for ever and
         ever!

Text

v. 5:   here, and in v. 6b, the verbs are to be read as plurals,
        following the Versions.
v. 13: after v. 13 (the first two lines), there should be a
        verse beginning with *nūn*, but this is lacking in the

Massoretic text. A verse beginning with *nūn* is to be supplied, following the Versions and the apparatus of BHS (the last two lines of v. 13).

Structure

The psalm is an acrostic; the verses begin with the successive letters of the Hebrew alphabet. Because this is an artificial scribal mode of composition, the psalm must be a written document of the later period, as the swarm of repetitions also indicates. Nor, for this reason, can we expect to find a clear psalm structure in it. What is clear is that the author wished to produce a psalm of praise – hence its title *tehillāh*, 'song of praise' – but he had to adapt the arrangement to fit the alphabet. In spite of this, the psalmist succeeded in producing a meaningful structure corresponding to that of the psalm of praise. The final v. 21 combines the resolve of an individual to praise God with a summons to 'all flesh' to bless His name and, in this way, the verse connects with the beginning of the psalm, 21a with v. 1 and 21b with vv. 4-7. The beginning and end of the psalm show that it is an individual song of praise with which the praise of the worshipping congregation has been deliberately combined. Framing the psalm at its beginning and end by a clause with virtually the same meaning represents the literary device of inclusio. From this, we can conclude that the author consciously planned the intervening text also.

The psalm which is thus framed by its opening and closing verses praises God in His majesty, v. 3, and in His goodness, vv. 8 f. The divine praise in this psalm is structured by the same polar contrast that we have already seen in Psalms 113 and 33. The praise of God's majesty, v. 3, follows immediately on the introduction, vv. 1-2. The section between v. 3 and v. 8 f. is an amplification of the call to praise, with the jussive replacing the imperative. The call to praise is resumed again in vv. 10-12. Then there follows once more the praise of God's majesty, specified as His kingly rule, 13a, and of His goodness, 13b–14, the latter being expanded in vv. 15–19. This expansion carries the praise of God a stage further: God's goodness is at work to bless, vv. 15–16, and to save, vv. 18–19. The intervening v. 17 returns again to the other aspect of God's activity, His justice and judgment. V. 20 is a final wish, which properly belongs to the individual lament, modified here to become an expression of praise. This verse is perhaps an addition made to satisfy the requirements of the acrostic form.

vv. 1–2: From the fact that this psalm, clearly in its content a liturgical psalm of praise, is also marked as the song of praise of an individual by its opening, vv. 1–2, and by its close, v. 21a, we can perceive that a development has occurred, of which traces are visible in many other passages elsewhere in the Old Testament. What has happened is that fellowship with God has been shifted into the realm of personal piety. In the later period, the Psalter became a book for private devotion, although without losing its former character, as is shown most clearly by Psalm 119, which is also an acrostic, and also by Psalm 1. We can also recognize this development in Psalm 145 from the way in which in it the imperative call to praise is replaced throughout by the jussive. Furthermore, this development is visible even in the way the individual verses are formulated.

The psalm begins with the words: 'I will extol thee, my God and King'. They recall the psalms in which God is celebrated and praised as king, Psalms 93; 95–100. These are liturgical psalms; when God is extolled as king, it is the worshipping congregation, as the people of the king, which is in view. It is in this setting that the royal title of God has its true meaning. But, at the time when Israel was still a nation, an individual never invoked God as his king. In the second line of the verse, the psalmist says: 'and (I will) bless thy name for ever and ever', le'ōlām wā'ed, a strong expression coined for use in the psalms of the worshipping congregation, for worship continues from generation to generation. The expression is almost too excessive for a single individual with his limited lifespan; by contrast, v. 2a: 'every day I will bless thee' is quite fitting for him. Here we see an important tendency applicable to every religious tradition: when social changes occur, the language of a past age continues in use unaltered, but it quickly loses its original vigour and may even become incomprehensible.

v. 3: God's majesty is extolled: 'Great is Yahweh and highly to be praised'. What does it mean when the psalms praise God in His greatness and sublimity? Never in any sense are they thinking of greatness and majesty in themselves. In terms of the human body, to be outsize is something negative, even something grotesque. Nor do the psalms mean 'greatness of spirit' as we might use the expression in speaking of a great writer or thinker. What is meant by greatness in this verse is made clear by its second line: 'his greatness is unsearchable', which can only mean that God's acts and thoughts, that is, His plans and designs, are inexhaustible. By God's greatness, then, what is meant is God as seen in His relationship with . . ., God as seen in His potential for acting on . . . , God is great in reference to creation, to humanity, to the individual. To acknowledge this greatness and hence to praise God in His great and majestic sublimity is itself also to recognize and accept the limitations of humanity and all the rest of creation. Praising God's greatness is necessarily to reject any acknowledgment or glorification of human greatness of whatever sort, political or spiritual. Up to a certain point, the glorification of human achievement – honouring a great man or acclaiming political authority – can run concurrently with the praise of God's greatness. But beyond this point, when the glorification of human greatness and power oversteps its limit and overweening greatness receives excessive adulation, then it is no longer of service to human society but actually endangers it. Seen thus, the praise of God's majesty and greatness in the psalms has an important function in the life of the individual and the community.

vv. 4–7: These verses are a modification of what is properly the imperative call to praise, compare Psalms 113 and 33. The numerous variations and repetitions serve to heighten and underline the summons to praise. First and foremost, these verses corroborate what has been said earlier about God's greatness, that this greatness does not indicate God as He is in Himself, nor does it represent a picture or 'concept of God' that men make for themselves but it consists in God's work and activity – v. 4 'thy works' . . . 'thy mighty acts'; 5 'thy wondrous works'; 6 'thy terrible and mighty acts'; 7 'thy abundant acts of deliverance'. Such an accumulation of terms to describe God's activity is only found here in the whole Psalter. They all refer to God's action in history and the aim of the summons ('they shall' . . .) is that the memory of His past deeds may be preserved for the future. V. 4: 'One generation shall laud thy works to another' – it is to speak, testify and relate, 'pour forth the fame of thy acts', vv. 5–7. Here the praise of the divine greatness involves keeping alive a historical continuum during which God has done great and wonderful things. What preserving the continuity of God's action in history can mean is shown by Psalm 80, which once again should be carefully compared with Psalm 145. Here speaks an understanding of history which sees it as one continuous active process, 'active' because God is active. As the result of the secularizing of the concept of history by the Enlightenment this understanding of history has become completely lost to us.

v. 8–9: These two verses should be taken together with v. 3; they are the kernel of the psalm of praise. God is praised in His majesty and in His goodness. The fact that the two always stand *next* to one another in psalms of praise, so that God's being is always extolled only in juxtaposition with His goodness, means that God can never be brought under one single idea. If one were to say of God only one of these two things, one would not be speaking of the real God. God cannot be brought under a single concept; the juxtaposition we have noted can also be seen as a sequence, for God's work is work in history.

The words of v. 9, splendid in their width and universality: 'The Lord is good to all, and his compassion is over all that he has made', are misunderstood if they are taken as a statement of fact that would be capable of verification. Both the psalms of lament and the psalms of praise would themselves be enough to refute such a view. Rather, v. 9 is saying that compassion knows no bounds, that it embraces all catastrophes without exception. The same can be said of Jesus' compassion for the suffering and the outcast.

vv. 10–13a: In these verses the call to praise is continued, hence v. 10 could be joined to v. 7. But what is new here is the wider range of the call: 'all thy works', a thought which emerges even more clearly in vv. 15–16. All creation joins with the worshipping congregation to praise God, 'all thy works – all thy saints', v. 10. Psalm 148 amplifies this juxtaposition and we may also compare Psalm 19 with v. 11.

The second new feature of vv. 10–13a is what is said of God's kingly rule: 'the glory of thy kingdom', v. 11, 'thy kingdom – thy dominion', v. 13. In this matter, Psalm 145 is close to the psalms about the kingship of God, Psalms 93; 95–100. In the latter the concept is developed in more detail, here only this much is said: God's kingship is above all the quintessence of what it means to rule, and God's rule both makes all-embracing provision for each one of His subjects – the king is the mediator of blessing – and endures throughout all generations, v. 13a.

vv. 13b–14: Vv. 13b–16 continue the praise of God's goodness; they belong together with vv. 8–9. V. 13b again parallels God's words and deeds, but it also amplifies the praise of God's goodness by saying that His words are 'faithful', one can rely on them; in this we catch the echo of God's promises, the story of which constitutes the entire Old Testament. V. 14 further adds that His mercy cares for those bowed down and fallen, as in Psalm 113: 7–9.

vv. 15-20: The last section of the psalm is a carefully worked-out amplification of the praise of God in two parts, vv. 15-16 dealing with God as the source of blessing and vv. 18-19 dealing with God as saviour.[62]

vv. 15-16: God's blessing is universal, embracing the whole creation. God's provision of nourishment for men and animals refers to His creation of the means of life, Genesis 1: 29-30; 2: 9, 16.

v. 17: In between the verses dealing respectively with God's work in blessing and deliverance, v. 17 picks up again the other aspect of God's activity. 'Widely as his mercy flows', the God of grace is always the God of justice and thus too the Judge – His grace never 'comes cheap'.

vv. 18-19: The saving work of God is expressed in the psalm language of distress and deliverance. Vv. 18-19 recount the cry from the depths, the lament that God is far away, His turning to those whose plea He hears and His intervention which brings them the aid they implore. Both verses show, again in a new way, how lament and narrative praise become part of liturgical praise.

v. 20: Properly speaking, the psalm ends with v. 19. V. 20 is a closing psalm verse which, in the form of a wish or request, often marks the end of a psalm of lament; here, however, it is changed to a statement in praise of God, which makes sense in the context of what has gone before in that it again picks up the contrast of v. 17 between the two sides of God's activity. We find the contrast in the Magnificat, Luke 1: 46-55, in the middle of which both God's majesty and His goodness is praised, vv. 49-50, and which then goes on: 'he has put down the mighty from their thrones, and exalted those of low degree', v. 52.

---

[62] For the relationship between deliverance, or salvation, and blessing, see C. Westermann, *Theologie des Alten Testaments in Grundzügen*, 1978, Teil II, III.

v. 21: For this verse, see the introductory paragraph in the section on Structure above. In this conclusion, the author once more combines his own praise of God with that of the wider circle to which he is aware of belonging.

Psalm 29: Ascribe to the Lord!

1   Ascribe to the Lord, ye sons of gods, (1)
      ascribe to the Lord glory and strength, (2)
2   ascribe to the Lord the glory of his name; (3)
      worship the Lord in holy array. (4)

3   The voice of the Lord is upon the water, (5)
      the Lord, upon many waters; (6)
      the God of glory thunders. (7)
4   The voice of the Lord is powerful, (8)
      the voice of the Lord is full of majesty. (9)
5   The voice of the Lord breaks the cedars, (10)
      the Lord breaks the cedars of Lebanon. (11)
6   He makes Lebanon to skip like a calf, (12)
      and Sirion like a young wild ox. (13)
7   The voice of the Lord flashes forth flames of fire.
         (14)
8   The voice of the Lord shakes the wilderness, (15)
      the Lord shakes the wilderness of Kadesh. (16)
9a   The voice of the Lord makes the hinds to calve,
         (17)
      and the kids to be born out of due time. (18)

10   The Lord sits enthroned over the flood; (19)
      the Lord sits enthroned as king for ever, (20)
9b   and in his palace all cry, 'Glory!' (21)
11   May the Lord give strength to his people! (22)
      May the Lord bless his people with peace! (23)

Text

v. 2:   instead of 'in holy array', H.-J. Kraus in his

commentary translates 'when he appears in holiness', from a similar word occurring in Ugaritic. But this requires an emendation of the Hebrew text.

v. 6:   instead of *jarkidēm*, *jarkēd* is to be read with the apparatus of BHK.

v. 9b: this is to be read after v. 10.

Structure

This psalm is, to a remarkable degree, a poem of strange but marvellous beauty. The principle that a psalm can only be understood as a whole is especially important when we seek to interpret Psalm 29.

It has a verse form which we meet nowhere else: the only close analogy is Psalm 93. This verse form has been described as climbing or step parallelism. It could also be described as extended parallelism, since the second and third lines complement and complete the first, as, for example, with the three opening lines here:

> Ascribe to the Lord, ye sons of gods,
> ascribe to the Lord glory and strength,
> ascribe to the Lord the glory of his name!

But to describe the psalm in this way is inadequate, since the verse form in question does not predominate throughout the whole of the psalm: alongside it we meet simple, usually synonymous, parallelism as well, for example in lines 8-9, 10-11, 12-13. The peculiarity of the verse form lies in the frequent alternation between groups of three and two lines (so lines 1-3, 5-7, 14-16, 19-21 are triads, and lines 8-9, 10-11, 12-13, 17-18, 19-20 are dyads), while, in addition, we have the free-standing single sentence lines 4 and 21 where, as a result, the parallelism is broken The consequence of this particular verse form is that it gives the separate line greater weight than it would have as a unit of parallelismus membrorum. The relative independence of the individual line is what gives the psalm its distinctive character and differentiates it from the rest of the Psalter; this is the reason for the above arrangement and enumeration of the psalm in separate lines rather than by verses.

Once one has recognized the close connection between its beginning and its end, the structure of the psalm becomes clear. It begins with a summons in the imperative, but to homage, not praise, lines 1-4. The conclusion, lines 19-21, clarifies what the summons involves: homage is to be paid to the enthroned King, lines 19-20, and this is done, line 21. The intervening section provides the reason for the summons to homage by means of a description of God's royal majesty, lines 5-18. He shows His majesty in the storm, and so the middle section is divided according to the phenomena of a storm, thunder, lines 5-13, and lightning, 14-18. The opinion of many commentators that something has fallen out before v. 9a is incorrect, rather v. 9b = line 21 is certainly to be read after v. 10. V. 11, lines 22-23, is a request for blessing, which was subsequently appended to the psalm to make a liturgical conclusion.

vv. 1-2: The summons to homage is issued by means of two verbs in parallelism: ascribe – worship or fall down. Only, the first verb, *hābū*, is subsequently repeated twice, amplifying the thought and giving the clause a solemn mounting rhythm. Those addressed are the 'sons of gods', that is, the gods who are to pay homage to the divine King, as v. 10 shows. We have here a picture of a heavenly court, where homage is paid to the divine King by subordinate deities, who appear, though somewhat differently, in Isaiah 6 and in many other passages. This picture must have its origin in polytheism, but since God was also honoured as king in Israel, as we see especially in Psalms 93; 95-100, the idea of adopting this picture to describe the homage to Israel's divine King easily suggested itself. Numerous passages show that this is what happened: the beginning of Psalm 29 is paralleled in part by the words of Psalm 96: 7 ff.:

Ascribe to Yahweh, O families of the peoples,
ascribe to Yahweh glory and strength,
ascribe to Yahweh the glory due to his name.
Worship Yahweh in holy array,
tremble before him all the earth!

The agreement between these passages strongly suggests
that we are in the presence of a prescriptive formula. The
summons in the imperative, with the grounds for it which
follow, corresponds to the other liturgical psalms of praise;
what is different here is that in the entire psalm we do not
meet one syllable of praise, in contrast to the descriptive
psalms of praise, including Psalm 96, and in this respect too
Psalm 29 is peculiar.

vv. 3-9: Just as vv. 2-3 are dominated by the verb *hābū*,
'ascribe', so vv. 3-9 are dominated by the noun *qōl*, 'voice'.
The repetitions of this one dominant word create a
powerfully poetic effect. The device of frequently repeating
the same word is also rare elsewhere in the Psalter.

This part gives the grounds for the summons of vv. 1-2.
It is divided into 'thunder', vv. 3-6, and lightning, 'flashes
forth flames of fire', v. 7-9a. Homage is paid to the storm
God, and in contrast to the other psalms of praise, it is
confined to this aspect of the deity.

vv. 3-6: God's voice is the voice of thunder (the second line
of v. 3 is to be read after the third). It is said of it that it is
'upon the waters', in place of which v. 10 has 'over the
flood', meaning the primaeval waters, as in Genesis 1: 2, for
such is the sense of the Hebrew word *mabbūl*, translated as
'flood'. The nominal sentence of the second line of the verse
(line 6) assumes the verb of the third line (line 7), 'thunders',
but the phrase 'upon many waters' indicates the lordship
clearly brought out in v. 10. God is victor over the flood and
He erects His throne over the defeated chaos power. This is
only suggested here but it obviously lies in the background.
The deity is called 'God of glory', *'el hakkābōd*, as in Psalm
24, which is also a psalm of homage.

vv. 4-6: These verses describe the effect of God's thunderous voice. Corresponding to the style of the psalm, v. 4 picks up v. 3 again, but adds the predicates 'powerful' and 'full of majesty'. The power and the majesty of this voice shake the created order: mountains quake – storm and earthquake often occur together – trees are uprooted and shattered. Such great power has the voice, that even what is most solid, the 'everlasting mountains', must reel and totter at its sound. The function of the comparisons, 'like a calf', 'like a young wild ox', is to strengthen the effect. God's voice is so mighty that it can splinter huge and lofty trees!

The repeated mention of the Lebanon range, for which Sirion is only another name, does not refer to just any mountain, but rather the psalm originated in an area where both the Lebanon and the wilderness of Kadesh, v. 8, were known and visible to all.

vv. 7-9a: 'The voice of the Lord flashes forth flames of fire', that is, the lightning flashes which embody the same majestic power: the God of thunder flashes forth flames of fire. The mention together of mountains and wilderness indicates a whole by naming its two extremities, as often occurs; what is meant is the entire surface of the earth. In the same way, the 'hinds' and 'kids' of v. 9a belong together with the trees of v. 5; what is meant are animals and plants in general. The art of the poet is visible when the shaking of the mountains and plains or deserts is followed by the shaking of animals: God's majestic power disrupts all creation.

vv. 10, 9b: V. 9a closes the section which describes the thunderous mighty voice and 9b should follow v. 10. As H.-J. Kraus points out in his commentary, the final verses 10, 9b revert to the beginning of the psalm. For the first time here, homage is said to be for the King, the king enthroned in his palace where his servants pay him homage. God 'sits enthroned over the flood', the ancient idea, rooted in myth, that the palace of the victor God is erected on the primaeval flood, now subjugated and rendered impotent.

In ancient art, the royal palace is often depicted standing above lines of waves which represent the flood. God has become the ruler of the hostile elements, and His lordship will be everlasting: 'The Lord sits enthroned as king for ever'. V. 9b corresponds to the opening summons 'Ascribe to the Lord the glory of his name', v. 2. The summons is answered when 'in his palace all cry, "Glory"', which makes clear the meaning of *'ēl hakkābōd* in v. 3. This conclusion to Psalm 29 makes it abundantly clear that God is a king and is to be honoured as king. The premise for this idea is the fact that, in the ancient world, the political institution of kingship always had something sacral about it – kingship could only be sacral kingship and a merely political and secular kingship would have been a contradiction in terms. An echo of this ancient concept can still be heard in the very word 'Majesty'.

v. 11: V. 11 does not really belong to the psalm itself, as can be spotted from the difference in language and metre. It is a liturgical request for blessing such as occurs at the end of many psalms. But the later addition of this request for blessing to this particular psalm is of special significance. Psalm 29 differs from the other psalms of praise in that the worshipping congregation, representing the nation, never appears in it. God's relation to creation is the single dominant element and nothing whatever is said about human beings. Hence, when this psalm was taken over into worship, v. 11, with its reference to God's relationship to His people, was deliberately appended: 'give strength to his people . . . bless his people'. This is a clear sign that Psalm 29, with its unusual characteristics, could not have originated in Israel.

Hence something needs to be said about its background from the standpoint of the history of religions. H.L. Ginsberg was the first to suggest that it was originally a Canaanite psalm which Israel took over, and he has been followed by the majority of commentators. In favour of this hypothesis is the fact that, as our discussion has shown, the psalm displays many distinctive features which do not occur in the other psalms of praise. The addition of the concluding request for blessing too may indicate that those who collected the psalms together were also conscious of the difference. More particularly, Psalm 29 evidences a whole list of Canaanite, and especially Ugaritic, parallels.

There is abundant evidence for Baal as the Canaanite storm god.[63] In the text *Ashirat and Baal*, Baal is spoken of as the storm god in language very similar to Psalm 29:

'And he will make his voice ring out in the clouds,
by flashing his lightning to the earth.'[64]

The mighty divine voice is also regularly extolled in Babylonian psalms, where 'the word' constantly recurs as the dominant feature, for example:

'The word that makes heaven above to tremble,
the word that makes earth beneath to totter . . . '

In addition, there is a whole list of verbal parallels. The 'sons of gods', *benē 'ēlīm* addressed in v. 1 of Psalm 29 occur in the same rôle in a prayer to the Canaanite deity El:

O El! O sons of El!
O assembly of the sons of El!
O meeting of the sons of El!'[65]

We have seen above that the expression in v. 2 'in holy array' *bᵉhadrat qōdeš*, may have a Canaanite background, though this is by no means certain. Lebanon and Sirion are paralleled in a Ugaritic text just as they are in v. 6 and the term 'wilderness of Kadesh', v. 8, is found in Ugaritic documents, as is the concept of God enthroned as king over the ocean. v.10.[66]

There is ample evidence that a hymn, psalm or liturgical song can be adopted by one religious community from

---

[63] See W. Beyerlin, *Near Eastern Religious Texts relating to the Old Testament*, 1978, pp. 185-221, especially pp. 206 ff.

[64] Beyerlin, *op. cit.*, p. 209.

[65] Beyerlin, *op. cit.*, p. 222.

[66] For the details, see the commentary on Psalm 29 in H.-J. Kraus, *Psalmen*, pp. 235 ff.

another, as has often happened between Catholics and
Protestants. Many Israelite psalm motifs also occur in the
environment of the ancient Near East. The peculiar thing
about Psalm 29 – and here it differs, for example, from
Psalm 96 – is that a Canaanite psalm could be taken up in
Israel's worship with apparently hardly any alteration. The
reason this could easily happen is because the
tetragrammaton runs through the whole psalm; it occurs
twice in each of the verses 1–5. When the name Yahweh
replaced that of the Canaanite storm god Baal or Hadad, the
effect on the Temple congregation was that the divine name
became resonant with all that the name Yahweh meant for
them. For them Yahweh was not just a storm god but the
God who 'worketh all things in all'. Then it became
perfectly possible to accept what the two religious systems
had in common, awe in the presence of the Creator and His
word of power, recognition of God as king and homage
paid to Him in worship. It cannot be denied that, in later
stages of religious development, where the rational element
came to assume a dominant rôle, especially in the area of
doctrine, awe before God's majesty and its effects in
creation largely receded into the background or even
entirely disappeared. It is this awe before God's majesty
which Psalm 29 can still mediate to us today.

Psalm 103: Praise the Lord, O my soul!

1   Praise the Lord, O my soul;
      and all that is within me, praise his holy name!
2   Praise the Lord, O my soul,
      and forget not all his benefits,

3   who forgives all thy iniquity, and heals all thy
          infirmities,
4   who redeems thy life from corruption,
      who crowns thee with steadfast love and mercy,
5   who fills thy life with goodness,
      so that thy youth is renewed like the eagle's.

6   The Lord works saving acts, and justice for all who
       are oppressed.

7   He made known his ways to Moses,
       his acts to the people of Israel.

8   The Lord is merciful and gracious,
       long suffering and abounding in steadfast love.

9   He will not always chide,
       nor will he keep his anger for ever.

10 He does not deal with us according to our sins,
       nor requite us according to our iniquities.

11 For as the heavens are high above the earth,
       so great is his steadfast love toward those who fear
         him;

12 as far as morning is from night,
       so does he remove our transgressions from us.

13 As a father pities his children,
       so the Lord pities those who fear him.

14 For he knows our frame;
       he remembers that we are but dust,

15 As for man, his days are like grass;
       he flourishes like a flower of the field;

16 for the wind passes over it, and it is gone,
       and its place knows it no more.

17 But the steadfast love of the Lord is from everlasting
       to everlasting,
       and his faithfulness to children's children,

18 to the pious who keep his covenant
       and remember to do his commandments.

19 The Lord has established his throne in the
       heavens,
       and his kingdom rules over all.

20 Praise the Lord, O you his messengers,
       you mighty ones who do his word.

21 Praise the Lord, all his hosts,
       his ministers that do his will.

22 Praise the Lord, all his works,
       in all places of his dominion.
       Praise the Lord, O my soul!

Text

v. 8: 'long suffering', properly 'slow to anger', as in RSV.

v. 11: the second verb should be read as *gābah* to correspond with the first verb.

v. 20: the three final words are omitted as a doublet.

Structure

The imperative summons to praise of vv. 1-2, perhaps 1-5, and vv. 20-22 forms the framework of the psalm. Hence it is recognizable as a descriptive psalm of praise or hymn, but equally, from the psalmist's address to himself in vv. 1 and 22, as an individual psalm of praise. Psalms of praise of this latter type are structured by the praise of both God's majesty and His goodness, but here the structure shows that only v. 19 praises God's majesty and the rest of the psalm, vv. 3-18, deliberately confines itself to praise of God's goodness. Vv. 3-5 are marked by a chain of participles and make the transition from the summons to praise, the ground for which they provide, to the main body of the praise of God itself, which begins with the finite verbs of v. 6. Vv. 6-7 celebrate God's deeds for His people, vv. 8-18 His concern for the individual human life, in particular for the one who utters the call to praise in vv. 1-2. Vv. 8-18 amplify the two aspects of the introductory vv. 3-8, God's pardoning grace in vv. 8-13, corresponding to v. 3, and His perpetual goodness compared with the limitations of human existence in vv. 14-18. Again, one can only marvel at the clarity and logic of the structure down to the smallest detail:

```
   1-2

        3-5                6-7
                     8-18  ⎰ 8-13
                           ⎱ 14-18
        19
   20-22
```

In this respect, it must be explained that in ancient Israel what we call the arts were largely identical with the art of words, and so Psalm 103 also was planned, down to each individual clause, to be a pellucid and carefully formed work of art. Every unit of it is linked to all the others, every similarity and dissimilarity is intentional. From the first line, 'Praise the Lord, O my soul', the psalm wends its way to the final identical line; the recurrence of the summons at the very end rounds off a coherent whole which, from start to finish, has unfolded from this summons. The final summons contains in itself all that is embraced within both summonses.

vv. 1-2: The address to the psalmist's own self is to be understood as an assimilation to the style of the hymn, which is characterized by an introduction in the imperative: an introduction 'I will praise . . . ', or similar words, would be in keeping with the individual psalm of praise. In fact, the whole psalm links together individual praise with hymnic motifs, vv. 6-7, 19, 20-22a. The summons to praise here is no doubt to be identified with the resolve to praise, but the imperative gives a festive and liturgical air to the psalm. Both verses together form an extended parallelism. In the first, God's 'holy name' is emphasized; God's name stands for what He means for those who invoke Him. The continuation in v. 2 echoes the vow of praise from the psalm of praise of an individual who recounts the benefits he has received from God – they may not be forgotten!

vv. 3-5: These verses are marked by a chain of participles which do not just follow one another automatically; v. 3 juxtaposes God's forgiveness and His healing, v. 4 His deliverance or redemption and His blessing. The succession of these six verbs, forgive-heal-redeem-crown-fill-rejuvenate, serves to convey, in a compelling fashion, how God's actions thus pictured in the song of praise embrace the whole of a person's being. It is not speaking of an abstract forgiveness of sins but of the whole man, redeemed and renewed in body and soul.

vv. 6-7: That the praise of God should embrace all His
actions is characteristic of descriptive praise and so next
after the introduction what God has done for His people is
extolled: 'The Lord works saving acts', 6a, which embrace
the nation's whole life; the miracle at the Sea is recalled, 7a,
but also God's championing of the oppressed within the
nation, 6b.

vv. 8-18: But the main part of the psalm deliberately
concentrates on the praise of God's goodness and mercy. It
divides under the two aspects of human existence for which
God in His goodness shows concern, fallibility and
finitude. It conforms of set purpose to the introduction in v.
3, vv. 8-13 developing 3a and 14-18 developing 3b.

vv. 8-13: This section divides as follows: v. 8 praises God's
mercy, with this v. 9 contrasts His anger, to which,
however, He sets limits; v. 10 describes how mercy brings
about forgiveness of sin, while vv. 11-13 round off the
praise of the divine mercy by two comparisons from two
different spheres of life.

vv. 8-9: V. 8 stands at the centre of the psalm; the entire
psalm develops what it has to say of God's mercy. In no
way does it do away with God's wrath but it limits it. Wrath
in the Old Testament is not an emotion of a supernatural
being. As the action of a power judging and condemning, it
is a necessary part of reality. Did God' wrath not exist, His
goodness too would have no value; were God not judge,
history would become unbalanced. For God's anger is His
reaction to corruption, to all that threatens life; the very
force of His wrath upholds life. Only against this
background can we understand what it means when the
author of the psalm extols God's mercy as yet more
powerful and more permanent, knowing no bounds, v. 17.
'His anger is but for a moment but his favour is for a
lifetime', Psalm 30: 5.

v. 10: This verse illustrates how the preponderance of mercy operates. If God requited man in accordance with the amount of his sin, one could only despair. But God's logic is not ours; He does not square accounts with us, His grace always overtips the balance.

vv. 11-13: The two comparisons here, one drawn from the created world, vv. 11 f., the other from human life, v. 13, make the same point. Creation's immeasurableness, shown in the dimensions of height and breadth, of the vertical and the horizontal, serves to extol the divine immeasurableness. The comparison from human life says the same thing from a different point of view. The love of parent for child, 'as a father pities his children', recognizes no limits. The same comparison is expanded into a parable in Luke 15; there too the objections of the elder brother underline mercy's illogicality.

The reader should now again study for himself the self-contained section vv. 8-13, the section which forms the heart of the psalm, and then he will see clearly how, as it ascends from v. 8 to v. 11, it takes shape as a literary work of art.

vv. 14-18: Vv. 8-13 look at human life as restricted by sin; vv. 14-18 look at the limits set to it by finitude, at how it is cut short by death. Plainly the author has Genesis 3 in view. This second section is divided into two parts. The first sets out the motif of transitoriness by means of comparisons, vv. 14-16, while by contrast the second extols the goodness of the God who cares for His servants, vv. 17-18.

vv. 14-16: This part provides the justification for what has been said just before: God takes pity on sinful man because He knows how transitory and how vulnerable is the human frame. Vv. 14-16 are really a motif from the psalm of lament, representing the lament for transitoriness which is itself a development of the 'I' lament (see the comment on Psalm 90 above). The one who laments remonstrates with God: thou well knowest how frail man is! The two

comparisons in 14b and 15-16 are also characteristic of the
lament for transitoriness, compare Psalm 90: 5-6; Job 14:
1-12. V. 14b: '. . . that we are but dust', a comparison all
the more effective because of its brevity, recalls Genesis 3:
19. Greater emphasis is laid on the more detailed second
comparison, vv. 15-16. In it the rising and falling of the arch
of human existence is pictured. The comparison with grass
and flower brings out the extreme brevity of life's span,
'men's days'; its brevity and frailty are seen precisely in the
light of their opposites, growth and blossoming. But v. 16
presents yet another motif: 'for the wind passes over it'.
Frail and destined for death as it is, human life has to face
still further threats. As the hot desert wind can quickly
wither a newly opened flower, so human life is exposed to
forces which can bring about sudden death and sufferings of
all kinds. Here the connection between vv. 14-16 and 8-13
becomes clear: it is effected by the words of v. 14, God
knows the human frame. He has pity not only for sins but
also for the suffering of men faced with the inevitability of
physical death. Death, here as elsewhere, is not just the end
but a force, projected into life itself.

vv. 17-18: The 'but' which introduces the closing section of
vv. 8-18 is not there merely to emphasize the contrast
between God's everlasting goodness and human
transitoriness, but to make clear that human transitoriness
and vulnerability still remain in God's embrace. What this
means is only brought out in the following lines. The
comparison of vv. 15-16 ended with the words: 'and its
place knows it no more'. After his death, a man is quickly
forgotten, but God's goodness, that enfolded and sheltered
his life, 'is from everlasting to everlasting'. It carries on into
succeeding generations 'to the pious who keep his
covenant'. The one who, in this psalm, praises God knows
that, in this transitory life, he shares in a reality which does
not pass away.

v. 19: It is this participation of an individual transitory
human life in life that endures which now recalls the speaker

to the wide horizon of God's dominion and to the other aspect under which God is to be praised. To praise of His goodness is now finally added praise of His majesty, seen in His all-embracing kingly rule – 'for thine is the kingdom, the power and the glory'. Here it should be noted that to speak of God as king is also to draw a comparison. No one can ever understand God's universal reign, it cannot be comprehended intellectually. It can only be spoken of as the author of this psalm speaks of it, in terms of awe and praise.

vv. 20-22: So the psalm ends as it began, with the summons to praise. But there is a difference: at the beginning, the author had only summoned himself to praise but now the call broadens out to embrace the whole creation.

Those summoned in vv. 20-21, the messengers, the ministers, the mighty ones and the hosts who do God's will and word, all really belong to the comparison of God with a king, v. 19; a king has messengers and servants, a court and an army. So, in the Old Testament, we frequently read descriptions, in language that comes close to that of myth, of the courtiers surrounding God's throne, for example Isaiah 6; Job 1-2. What is meant is that all the authorities and powers in creation stand ready for God's service.

In v. 22a, the call to praise is again issued briefly to the whole created order, 'all his works', a theme developed in Psalm 148, which should be referred to in explanation of v. 22. Here all that need be said is that summoning all creation to praise means that the whole created order only has significance as being made by God. We human beings cannot get to the bottom of the mystery of creation. But of one thing we can be certain: there is a connection between the individual's turning to his Maker in his grief and guilt and the 'return' of the whole universe to its Creator, of whom and to whom is all that has been made.

vv. 22b: After his call to creation in all its breadth and fullness, the author returns to what he has said at the beginning of the psalm. He can never forget what good things God has done for him: 'Praise the Lord, O my soul!'

Psalm 104: Thou art clothed with honour and majesty

1   Praise the Lord, O my soul!

     O Lord my God, thou art very great!
     Thou art clothed with honour and majesty,
2   who coverest thyself with light as with a
        garment,
     who hast stretched out the heavens like a tent,
3   who hast built thy dwelling on the waters,
     who makest the clouds thy chariot,
     who ridest on the wings of the wind,
4   who makest the winds thy messengers,
     fire and flame thy ministers.
5   Thou didst set the earth on pillars,
     so that it should never be shaken.
6   Thou didst cover it with the deep as with a
        garment;
     the waters stood above the mountains.
7   At thy rebuke they fled;
     at the sound of thy thunder they took to flight.
8   The mountains rose, the valleys sank down
     to the place which thou didst appoint for them.
9   Thou didst set bounds which they should not
        pass,
     so that they might not again cover the earth.
10   Thou makest springs gush forth in the valleys;
     they flow between the hills,
11   they give drink to every beast of the field;
     the wild asses quench their thirst.
12   On their banks the birds of the air have their
        habitation;
     they sing among the branches.

13 From thy abode thou waterest the mountains;
    the earth is satisfied by thy clouds.
14 Thou dost cause the grass to grow for the cattle,
    the plants for the service of man,
15 that he may bring forth food from the earth,
    and wine to gladden the heart of man,
    oil to make his face shine,
    and bread to strengthen man's heart.
16 The trees of the Lord are watered abundantly,
    the cedars of Lebanon which he planted.
17 In them the birds build their nests;
    the stork has her home in the cypresses.
18 The high mountains are for the ibex;
    the rocks are a refuge for the badger.
19 Thou hast made the moon to mark the seasons;
    the sun knows its time for setting.
20 Thou makest darkness, and it is night,
    when all the beasts of the forest creep forth.
21 The young lions roar for their prey,
    seeking their food from God.
22 When the sun rises, they get them away
    and lie down in their dens.
23 Man goes forth to his work
    and to his labour until the evening.

24 O Lord, how many are thy works!
    In wisdom hast thou made them all;
    the earth is full of thy creatures.

25 Yonder is the sea, great and wide,
    which teems with things innumerable, living things
        both small and great.
26 There go the ships,
    and Leviathan which thou didst form to sport in
        it.
27 These all look to thee, to give them their food in due
        season.
28 When thou givest to them, they gather it up;
    when thou openest thy hand, they are filled with
        good things.

29   When thou hidest thy face, they are dismayed;
     when thou takest away their breath,
     they die and return to their dust.
30   When thou sendest forth thy breath, they are
        created;
     and thou renewest the face of the ground.

31   May the glory of the Lord endure for ever,
     may the Lord rejoice in his works,
32   who looks on the earth and it trembles,
     who touches the mountains and they smoke!

33   I will sing to the Lord as long as I live;
     I will make melody to my God while I have my
        being.
34   May my poem be pleasing to him,
     for I rejoice in the Lord.
35   Let sinners be consumed from the earth,
     and let the godless be no more!

     Praise the Lord, O my soul!

Text

v. 4:   the two last words are to be read as *lahat 'ēš*, with
          the Septuagint.
vv. 5-6: the two verbs in these verses are to be read as
          second person singular.
v. 10:   perhaps the word 'waters' should be added to the
          second line.
v. 13b: the text is uncertain; it is literally 'with the fruit of
          thy work'.
v. 19:   'thou makest', reading the participle.
v. 24:   the line 'in wisdom hast thou made them all' should
          perhaps be transposed to the end of v. 25.
v. 29:   the words 'and return to their dust' are possibly an
          addition.
v. 35:   'Hallelujah' at the end of v. 35 is the title to Psalm
          105.

Structure

Psalms may be prayers, hymns or poems, and Psalm 104 is certainly the last. The author himself describes it as such in v. 34, as a poem that he offers, which is poetry and praise in one. The framework in vv. 1 and 35 is that of an individual's praise of God and the intervening passage from its beginning to its end is a praise of the Creator. Praise of the Creator is an element of descriptive praise of God (compare, for example, Psalm 33), as appears also from vv. 1, 24, 31 and 35 of this psalm, which show that praise of the Creator, as a formal motif, is not unknown to it. But otherwise the author feels free to express the Creator's praise in his own way. One is tempted to add: according to his own free imagination, but that would not really be correct, for there is a difference between the way we understand the writing of the poetry and the way the Bible understands it. Praise of the Creator is not something that the author of Psalm 104 can think up for himself. He can unfold it through his own poetry but it remains something he has inherited from his predecessors. So, line by line, behind the verses of Psalm 104, the creation account of Genesis 1 is visible, often in detail, but always in such a way that the poem remains its author's own.

The introductory and concluding imperatives in vv. 1a and 35 reflect the psalm of praise, as does the praise of God's majesty in vv. 1b, 24, 31, here expressed as a wish, and 32. This is developed into the praise of the Creator in vv. 2–30, while praise of the Lord of history is echoed in v. 35a; this whole section is a free adaptation of Genesis 1. It extols the Creator of heaven, vv. 2–4, and earth, v. 5, and vv. 6–9 are reminiscent of the beginning of the creation account in Genesis. The author speaks of mountains, valleys and springs, vv. 8, 10, of the beasts of the field, that is, the land animals, and the birds, vv. 11–12, 17–18, of the rain and the plants, vv. 13–16, of sun and moon, day and night, vv. 16–23, of human beings, vv. 14–15, 23 and of sea and ships and the great and small denizens of the ocean, vv. 25–26. All this leads up to awed praise of the Creator, vv. 24, 31, who

provides life-sustaining food for all His creatures, vv. 27-
30. There are many striking parallels between Psalm 104
and Akhenaten's[67] hymn to the sun.[68]

v. 1a: This psalm can clarify for us one aspect of what the
Psalter and the whole Old Testament means by praising
God. To see how it does this, we must take together the
verses that express praise:

> 1 Praise the Lord, O my soul!
> 31 May the Lord rejoice in his works!
> 34 I rejoice in the Lord
> 35 Praise the Lord, O my soul!

The works of creation of which the psalm speaks bring joy
to the one who recounts them. Delight in them unites God
with man and man with God, and praise of God gives voice
to this joy. Saying 'yes' to God, or greeting Him, is one
with rejoicing in His creation. Here above all Psalm 104
chimes in with the creation account of Genesis 1, where the
creative acts are accompanied by the phrase: 'and God saw
that it was good'; the word 'good' here includes what we
mean by 'beautiful'. When Genesis 1 says: 'and God saw the
light that it was good' and Psalm 104 says: 'light is the
garment thou wearest', in both phrases the One who
created the light is being praised.

v. 1b: 'Thou art clothed with honour and majesty' –
throughout the entire ancient world words like majesty,
highness or honour are properly terms for deities and the
divine. They were transferred to the king inasmuch as he
shares in them through the sacral character of his kingship.
These terms for the king do not imply that men are seeking
to get above themselves, rather they indicate the
paramountcy of the divine. The same applies to the term
'greatness'; it is a term intended for God, not for man.

[67] Akhenaten, also known as Amenophis IV, reigned from 1365-1348
B.C.
[68] Translation and commentary in W. Beyerlin, *Near Eastern Religious
Texts*, pp. 16-19.

When someone, as here, says to God: 'O Lord my God, thou art very great', he means a greatness which man cannot comprehend or measure, which he can only sense in action. By contrast, men invariably enjoy greatness only to a limited degree.

vv. 2-4: Here God's majesty is revealed by the dimensions into which it extends. The infinite heavens are God's work, the immense sea is for Him the place on which He dwells, the elements stand ready to serve Him.

vv. 5-9: These verses describe creation's very beginnings. In them, we meet reminiscences of Genesis 1 but also of a mythical battle, as a result of which the sea is dammed up; this mythical battle is found in Babylonian creation myths and also in Job 38 and Psalm 77: 16. It is noteworthy how in this psalm the account of the beginnings of creation, vv. 5-6, merges imperceptibly into the description of creation as it now is, vv. 10 ff,; both are inseparable.

vv. 10-18: In what follows, we no longer have a succession of creative acts but a description of the unity and harmony of the world God has made. This indicates the transition to the praise of the Creator in His works, praise which at the same time vibrates with human delight in the beauty of the created world. Psalm 104 is a description of nature, of much the same kind as we find in the Romantic poets; the difference is that the description of nature in Psalm 104 is also directed to praising God, so that here it sounds entirely 'natural' when instead of saying, for example, 'I heard a brooklet rustling . . . '[69] our author says: 'Thou makest springs gush forth in the valleys . . . '. But this in turn leads to a further difference: in our psalm, man and the rest of creation are closer to one another: 'The trees of the Lord are watered abundantly, the cedars of Lebanon which he planted', v. 16. As in Genesis 1, the provision of nourishment for both men and animals goes together, vv.

---

[69] 'Ich hört' ein Bächlein rauschen', the first line of the well-known poem *Wohin?* by Wilhelm Müller (1794-1827).

14–15, and we see the same awareness of this in the way v.
23 follows on from vv. 21–22.

vv. 19–23: The circuits of sun, moon and stars determine
the rhythm of all life. The list of created things in vv. 10–18
is succeeded by the alternation of day and night, the blessed
rhythm which maintains the creation in being, as we see in
Genesis 8: 22, and from which all that is made receives the
breath of life.

vv. 24–30: At this point, the author pauses in wonder and
awe: 'O Lord! . . . '. What he has earlier described has
moved him deeply; now his emotion finds expression in the
invocation of God's name. From this, we can see that the
invocation of God's name has a real and necessary part to
play in human life; not even unbelievers can avoid crying 'O
God!'. What it means thus to call on God is brought out in
the three following verses: 'how many are thy works!', the
earth is full of them!, where the word 'many' corresponds
to the 'very great' of v. 1. But this does not mean an amount
that can be reckoned numerically, though the adjective
'many' immediately makes us think in terms of numbers.
But this is to impoverish the meaning of the word. What it
means here is 'multifarious', 'manifold' (as RSV): God's
works in all their abundance are understood as having a
potential beyond anything we can conceive. This in turn
reveals the Creator's wisdom: 'in wisdom hast thou made
them all', a wisdom that infinitely surpasses all science and
all knowledge.

vv. 27–28: V. 24 has its continuation in v. 27, the words
'these all' of v. 27 refer to 'thy creatures' of v. 24. In vv.
25–26 the author amplifies what has gone before by
describing the sea and its denizens, and in vv. 27–30 the
rhythm of life and death is added to the rhythm of day and
night, vv. 19–23. In this section, the closeness of creature
and Creator is again depicted with inimitable skill, which
one can pursue sentence by sentence. 'These (all living
creatures) look to thee' – the language is very naïf, not to say

primitive, yet at the same time very profound. If one takes the words superficially, one can ask: What does it mean to say that a fish or a mosquito looks to God for its food? But one must have more confidence in our author's abilities. If his words are taken seriously, it will be seen from the final line of this section 'thou openest thy hand', that in vv. 27-28 the author is employing a comparison, which indeed is only suggested but still clearly recognizable. He is describing how the farmer feeds his animals and this leads him to conclude: We cannot comprehend how God nourishes all His creatures, we can only express it in a comparison.

vv. 29-30: So this comparison shows us that the life of every creature depends on its Creator. But the same is equally true of the death of every creature. Life comes to an end for all: 'when thou takest away their breath, they die'. The rhythm of life and death is joined to that of day and night; to survive, creation also needs the former. The author's description of animal birth leans heavily on the story of the creation of man in Genesis 2: 'When thou sendest forth thy breath, they are created', and so we are to understand that all organic existence derives from the Creator's life force. In such simple language, even the birth of a lamb or the emergence of a butterfly is traced back directly to the Creator of all living things.

This astonishing section ends with the words: 'and thou renewest the face of the ground'. Here we can grasp what the Bible is really meaning when it speaks of the Creator. Whoever is not convinced that the Creator is the One who daily renews the earth through the universal rhythm of life and death has no true comprehension of Him.

vv. 31-32: This final part begins with a wish that God's glory as revealed in His works may endure for ever in spite of the catastrophes which will continue to shake the earth. The destructive aspect of God's activity is pictured here with reference only to volcanic eruptions and earthquakes; the author is telling us that also in them this aspect of the divine activity is manifested. But this aspect of God's activity also affects human beings, who are also God's creatures, in that among them are the wicked, destructive of peace and dishonouring God. These are not overlooked in the praise of the Creator in the psalm, but the author merely expresses the wish that they may be consumed from off the earth, v. 35a. The conclusion of the psalm represents a promise of praise, v. 33; the praise which the author has struck up in his psalm is to determine his whole life. Linked with the promise of praise is the wish: 'May my poem be pleasing to him!'. These few words are of significance as indicating a new stage in Israel's cultural development; the speaker is not simply one unit of the worshipping congregation, he is also the author of a poem and he knows it. But his work is throughout enfolded in the praise of God, for which he calls in both the first and the last line of his psalm.

Psalm 19: 1-6: The heavens are telling

1   The heavens are telling the glory of God;
     and the firmament proclaims his handiwork.
2   Day to day pours forth speech,
     and night to night declares knowledge.
3   There is no speech, nor are there words;
     their voice is not heard;
4   yet their voice goes out through all the earth,
     and their words to the end of the world.
     . . . ..
     In them he has set a tent for the sun,
5   which comes forth like a bridegroom leaving his
        chamber,
     and like a strong man runs its course with joy.
6   Its rising is from the end of the heavens,
     and its circuit to the other end of them;
     and there is nothing hid from its heat.

Text

v. 4a   (Heb. 5a): for *qawwām*, 'their line', read *qōlām*, 'their voice'.

v. 4b   (Heb. 5b): 'in them' refers to 'the heavens' of v. 1. Probably something has fallen out between 4a and 4b (Heb. 5a and 5b).

v. 6   (Heb. 7): 'to', reading *'ad*, instead of *'āl*.

Structure

The psalm is continued in vv. 7-14, a unit consisting of an encomium of the Law, corresponding to Psalm 119; so v. 7: 'The Law of the Lord is perfect'. The unit vv. 7-14 is a later addition, see the commentary on Psalm 119, p. 292 ff. below. The fact of this addition suggests that the first part, vv. 1-6, is no more than a fragment. V. 1 shows that the fragment is a psalm in praise of the Creator, but it has neither the regular introduction nor conclusion, containing the summons to praise. In contradistinction to such psalms as 148 or 104, only the heavens and the sun are referred to ; both parts, vv. 1-4a and 4b-6, deal with these, but something seems to have fallen out between them. There is no good reason why the heavens and the sun alone should be mentioned, nor does this correspond to the pattern of the praise of the Creator elsewhere in the Psalter, which again indicates that we have before us only a small fragment of a longer creation psalm, the remainder of which has disappeared.

vv. 1-2: The terms 'heavens' and 'firmament' are synonymous, as are the corresponding verbs 'tell' and 'proclaim'. What they tell or proclaim is God's glory manifest in His works. V. 2 adds that God is seen at work in the rhythm of day and night. The heavens are not to be understood as a static object, a matter for investigation, but to be viewed in their constant change as night succeeds day. What the heavens are telling and proclaiming is not only what happens in the alternation of day and night, but everything else that occurs in and through the heavens from dawn to dusk. The tale and the proclamation are continuous: 'Day to day pours forth speech'. This continuous 'proclamation' day by day and night by night is meant to indicate that the story of God's glory is never to be interrupted; it does not appear just here and there, it is the perpetual accompaniment of the history of the cosmos through thousands of years.

These verses define, in a very profound manner, what is involved in the creation's praise of the Creator, compare Psalm 148; that praise echoes God's creative work. And because God is still Creator through all the centuries, the echo goes on reverberating: 'Day to day pours forth speech'.

vv. 4–5: The two following verses expand on what is meant by this continuous praise. They are the product not of intellectual speculation but of deep emotion. The sort of 'telling' and 'proclaiming' we find here is something unfamiliar to us, very different from the ideas those expressions usually suggest to our minds. For 'their voice is not heard', there are no words for us to hear. Yet their voice goes out to the ends of the earth – here we meet the same extension of praise to the horizontal from the vertical, v. 2, as in Psalm 113: 2 and 3. Commentators on these verses have often spoken of 'creation as revelation' here, from which a 'natural theology', a theologia naturalis, could be derived. But what Psalm 19 is saying at this point has nothing to do with revelation, quite apart from the fact that a general concept of revelation is unknown in the Old Testament. When the heavens tell of the glory of God, they are not conveying information about Him: 'there is no speech, nor are there words'. Rather, they are extolling and glorifying Him in the way Psalm 148: 1 calls on them to do.

vv. 5b–7: How the heavens and the sun are to do this is clarified in the second part of the psalm, vv. 5b–7, namely, that they can do so just by being there. For the radiant and delighted language of vv. 5b–7 simply describes the course of the sun from its rising to its setting. But when these verses show what the sun's circuit and setting meant for the author of the psalm so that he was able, by means of a comparison, to express in words the radiance of sunrise, they provide the answer to the question of how the sun and the heavens can speak words that fill time and space, although 'their voice is not heard'.

The deeper reason why such psalms as 19 and 148 could emerge in ancient Israel is that man's relationship to God and the relationship of the other creatures to their Creator could be described by the same words: the rôle of both in that relationship is to praise, to extol, to magnify. When the fundamental relationship with God came to be thought of in terms of 'believing', this vision of the oneness of creation was inevitably lost, for to believe is what neither the sun nor the heavens can do.

Psalm 148: From the heavens – from the earth

1   Hallelujah!
     Praise the Lord from the heavens, praise him in the
          heights!
2   Praise him, all his angels,
     praise him, all his hosts!
3   Praise him, sun and moon,
     praise him, all you shining stars!
4   Praise him, you highest heavens!
     and you waters above the heavens!
5   Let them praise the name of the Lord!
     For he commanded and they were created.
6   He established them for ever and ever,
     he fixed their bounds which cannot be passed.

7   Praise the Lord from the earth.
     you monsters and all deeps,
8   fire and hail, snow and mist,
     stormy wind fulfilling his word!

9   Mountains and all hills, fruit trees and all cedars!
10   Beasts and all cattle,
      creeping things and flying birds!
11   Kings of the earth and all peoples,
      princes and all rulers of the earth!
12   Young men and maidens together, old men and
         children!
13   Let them praise the name of the Lord,
      for his name alone is exalted;
      his glory is above earth and heaven.
14   He has raised up the horn of his people,
      praise for all his devoted ones,
      for the children of Israel, a people near to him.

      Hallelujah!

Text

v. 14:   instead of 'people of his nearness', read *qerobājw*,
         'near to him'.

Structure

Psalm 148 belongs to the category of imperative psalms,
that is, psalms of praise in which the summons to praise in
the imperative is dominant. In this case, one unit of the
descriptive psalm of praise has become a complete psalm in
its own right, as we have seen happens with other psalm
motifs. The main component of the descriptive psalm of
praise, the praise of God's majesty and goodness, is only
hinted at incidentally, in vv. 13 and 14. Imperatives make
up the main part of the psalm and divide it into two sections:

vv. 1-6: Praise the Lord from heaven . . .
vv. 7-12: Praise the Lord from the earth . . .

In these two sections, the heavenly and earthly creatures
respectively are summoned to praise their Creator.

vv. 1-6: The praise of God tends to broaden out in the course of the Old Testament. The reason for this is that God's praise is viewed as joy finding words. Joy has a tendency to spread out to others so that they can join in it, as we see from the parable of the woman who has found her lost coin. When a many-throated song of praise, with its instrumental accompaniment, resounds in an act of worship, it cannot be confined within the walls of the Temple. As H. Gunkel writes: 'It is not enough for the pious congregation by itself to sing the chant of praise; it is fitting for God's universal dominion that all creatures should add their voices to the joyful song'.

Let us return for a moment to what we said above about Psalm 19. It is the praise of God that unites man with the rest of creation, for the praise of the creatures is their response to their creation, as Genesis 1 already shows. This gives to Israel's worshipping congregation the revolutionary, and barely comprehensible, potential to extend the call to praise from the liturgy to include all creation, and thus to address all creation in that call. This is not the exaggeration of poetry or liturgical rhetoric, but simply the consequence of an awareness that all created things are, like man, made by God and so can react, like man, to their creatureliness by the response of praise. This they do simply by the fact of their existing, as Psalm 19 shows.

The twofold division into vv. 1-6 and 7-13 is meant to indicate the creation as a whole. So to indicate a whole under two aspects and by employing two parallel terms is characteristic of Hebrew linguistic usage. The first and most important example is the description of the universe as 'heaven and earth' in Genesis 1: 1. In Psalm 148, as in Genesis, 'heaven and earth' means the entirety of creation, and the call to praise applies to the whole of it. The psalm mentions the heavenly beings, v. 2 (compare again Isaiah 6), the stars and planets, v. 3, the heavens and the waters above the heavens, v. 4, and Genesis 1: 7. This last passage helps to explain why the word for heaven in Hebrew is a plural, or, strictly, a dual. It is not a numerical plural, as was recognized when at a later date the concept of seven heavens grew up, but the so-called 'plural of extension'. Thus it describes the vast expanse of the heavens and what is higher even than the heavens, the waters above the heavens.

In v. 5, the imperative of v. 1 is succeeded by a jussive and then the reason why praise should be offered is stated, namely that all have been brought into being by God's creative word, as in Genesis 1. Here it is made clear that the praise of the creature is to be understood as its 'response' to its having been made. The words of v. 6: 'He established them for ever and ever' are not asserting the eternity of the world but, in accordance with the way the expression is employed in Hebrew, the continued existence of the world that God has made, within the limits He has set for it, as is said in Genesis 8: 20-22.

vv. 7-13: The creature's praise is to resound to the Creator from earth just as from heaven. It is noteworthy that in Psalm 148 heaven as well as earth belongs to the realm of created existence. Heaven here is no mythical other-world, for a locally conceived 'other-world' is unknown to the Old Testament.

vv. 7-8: Summoned to praise are the 'monsters and all deeps', v. 7. It is striking that it is just these who head the list. Not merely the bright and benevolent side of creation is called to praise but the whole creation, including all that is terrible, frightening or inimical in it, and so the elements in v. 8 are to be understood as both fostering and hindering human activities. Here we see that the 'praise of God' to which they are called is not to be measured by human standards.

vv. 9-10: In the following verses it is the created world of man's immediate environment that is summoned, mountains and hills, fruit trees and forest trees, wild and domestic animals, 'creeping things', that is, insects, and birds, in fact what we call nature. But Psalm 148 has an understanding of nature different from ours. The secular world view which grew up with the Enlightenment set man and nature over against one another. Two possible ways for man to deal with nature developed side by side: on the one hand, by means of science and technology, man makes nature into an object that he investigates and exploits, on the other hand, he makes it into the object of aesthetic contemplation and lyrical description. For Psalm 148 and the Old Testament in general a quite different outlook is decisive: on the one hand is God the Creator, on the other the whole created order which derives its existence from Him and is preserved in being by Him. All that exists is one in creatureliness. Man emancipates himself from the rest, when he makes all other created existences into objects which he then has at his disposal. In our generation, for the first time since the Enlightenment, people have been forced to recognize that the objectifying of nature has reached a point where it is endangering humanity as a whole. We are faced with the question of whether a fundamental change can come about without recognizing how dubious is the notion of objectifying nature at all.

vv. 11-12: Along with all other creatures, humanity is summoned to praise God. The list of people in these verses goes from top to bottom, first the great and mighty of v. 11 and then the ordinary folk, young and old alike, in v. 12. What the author wants to say here is clear: high and low are alike God's creatures and life in community can only be healthy when ordinary people, as well as kings and presidents, are conscious of this and act accordingly. Over against God, they are all on the same level and before Him no-one is of greater or lesser worth than anyone else.

But the author has another purpose in the way he enumerates mankind. After listing the animals, wild and domestic beasts, insects and birds, in v. 10, he turns at once to the kings and princes of the earth. What they have in common with all other living creatures is more important than the dignity of their status – they have to die just as all the rest.

vv. 13-14: The gap between creature and Creator is again brought out in the closing verses. They give a ground for the call to praise different from that at the end of the first section, vv. 5 f., and one which is directed to mankind in particular: 'Let them praise the *name* of the Lord'. This assumes that the name can be uttered, that human beings can call on God's name, Genesis 4: 26, and this name is decisive for what God means for man and the whole creation. But there is also a gap here: 'his name *alone* is exalted'. The Creator's majesty befits One only.

As a whole, the psalms of praise extol God's majesty and goodness. The conclusion of Psalm 148 shows that praise of the Creator involves praise of God's greatness, and so v. 14 adds this other aspect of the praise of God by referring to the deeds He has done in His people's history. The final verse introduces the circle of worshippers, 'the children of Israel, a people near to him'. The call to praise which begins and ends the whole psalm rings out in Israel's worship.

Psalm 8: What is man?

To the choirmaster: according to the Gittith. A Psalm of David.

1   O Lord, our ruler, how majestic is thy name!
Thy majesty reaches to the ends of the earth,
thy glory above the heavens.

2   Out of the mouth of babes and sucklings
thou hast founded thy power in despite of thy foes,
to still the enemy.

3   When I look at thy heavens, the work of thy fingers,
the moon and the stars which thou hast set on their course;

4   What is man that thou art mindful of him,
and the son of man that thou dost care for him?

5   Yet thou hast made him little less than God,
and thou dost crown him with glory and honour.

6   Thou hast given him dominion over the works of

thy hands;
thou hast put all things under his feet,

7   all sheep and oxen, and also the wild beasts,
8   the birds of the air, and the fish of the sea,
whatever passes along the paths of the sea.

9   O Lord, our ruler,
how majestic is thy name in all the earth!

Text

The meaning of the musical direction *'al haggittīt* in the title is unknown.

v. 1   (Heb. 2): the words *'ašer tenāh*, defy understanding. On account of the parallelism, the word *'adartekā*, parallel to *hōdekā*, is proposed here.

v. 2   (Heb. 3): the last word 'and the avenger' is probably an addition.

Structure

Earlier we saw that in Psalm 77, the psalm of lament was further developed in a meditation on God's works and we noted especially there v. 3: 'I think of God . . . I meditate'. We find the same thing in Psalm 8: 3: 'When I look at thy heavens . . . ', but here meditation develops from praise of God. Frequently, a moment of awed wonder interrupts the course of psalms of praise, for example, Psalm 31: 19: 'O how abundant is thy goodness . . . '. Such awed reflection dominates Psalm 8: v.1, 'how majestic is thy name . . . ', v. 5, 'what is man that thou . . . '. It also determines the psalm's structure. Psalm 8 does not exhibit the structure of a psalm of praise, but it should not therefore be categorized as a ' mixed psalm'; rather, it is praise of God developed into an awed meditation on the created being, man. To this corresponds the fact that the setting of the psalm is not one of worship and hence it contains no call to praise, and that its structure does not correspond to that of any of the psalm categories, although it embodies many psalm motifs. Rather, the structure of Psalm 8 is determined by its thought content.

The psalm begins in v. 1a with the exclamation of awe from the praise of God, which is then carried further by a meditation on the contrast described in vv. 1b-2. Then follows another awed meditation. vv. 3a-4a, again carried further by the contrast in vv. 3-4. V. 5 is the conclusion drawn from this meditation, carried further in vv. 6-8. In v. 9, meditation turns back into the praise of God from which it emerged.

v. 1-2: In v. 1, the author joins in the praise of the Temple congregation; this is that unit of praise to God in majesty which we meet with in many psalms. But what follows in v. 2 no longer corresponds to what follows this unit in the psalms which extol God in majesty. It opens the author's meditation: this majestic God can be bothered with puny human beings! The author pictures to himself a newborn infant, a tiny helpless baby. Within this little being, the Lord of heaven and earth has established his strong power! Some highly fanciful explanations have been proffered for this verse, but its plain and simple meaning is found in the contrast between vv. 1 and 2. As J.J. Stamm puts it: 'Psalm 8: 2 deals with ordinary children, whose crying shows that they are capable of surviving to become a bulwark against the enemy'.[70] The contrast between v. 1-2 implies, without explicitly stating, the distinction between the creation of the world and the creation of man. Already the infant's cry displays God's creative power, already God there 'founds his power', in the way that, as we find elsewhere, He does great things by means of small, compare 2 Corinthians 12: 9. Luther's translation too, 'thou hast prepared praise for thyself', compare Matthew 21: 16, has a certain justification, for the Hebrew word for 'power' or 'strength', 'ōz, can also mean 'praise' in some contexts.

[70] RSV translates in v. 2: 'thou hast founded a bulwark because of thy foes'.

When it is said that this power is established against the enemies, the latter must mean those who deny God's power, that is, the wicked or godless of the late period who are often accused of just this. But only here in the Bible are we shown how merely the crying of a tiny human baby can silence the godless man.

vv. 3–4: Here we have the second contrast, which clearly rests on the distinction between the creation of the world and the creation of man. These two verses show beyond doubt that Psalm 8 is a verbal or poetic meditation. The meditation was triggered off by gazing on the heavens, the sun, the moon and the stars. The effect on individuals of gazing at the heavens especially on a spring day, and at the starry sky at night, has not changed since the psalm was composed some 2,500 years ago. Just so did the philosopher Kant gaze on the stars, ' . . . and the starry heavens above me', just so did the Romantic poets. Nor has scientific investigation of the physical world altered this at all. But people can react differently, depending on whether the sight of the starry heavens stirs them or not, whether or not it moves them to something akin to awe. The author of Psalm 8, who, when he gazes at the heavens above, can only be reminded of the Creator's greatness, thereby becomes conscious of how small man is – the same thought that occurs to many even today when they look up at the starry sky. And just as his gazing at the heavens can make him think of their Creator, so the same thought strikes him when he sees how tiny man is compared with the vast extent of the cosmos. What is man, he asks, that thou art mindful of him, that thou dost care for him? To understand these words, one must observe that the verbs employed here occur in psalms of lament, and particularly in the petition there for God to return again, as for example in Jeremiah 15: 15: 'O Lord . . . be mindful of me and visit me!'. These verbs are directed to man under threat and in need of help, to man who is as vulnerable as a tiny baby, v. 2. This is what the author sets before us to reflect on and wonder at, that it is the same God who made the boundless

universe who also cares for every tiny individual human
being.

vv. 5–8: After v. 4, we must imagine the author pausing for
some time in his meditation and then going on to a new
train of thought in v. 5: It is not only, great God, that thou
carest for man in his need, thou dost even endow him with
such great potentialities! Among these, one in particular is
picked out. Within vv. 5–8, 6–8 are to be understood as
explaining v. 5: 'thou hast made him . . . ', v. 5, in that
'thou hast given him', v.6–8. 'Little less than God' refers to
God in action; the meaning is, thou hast given him a share in
an office for which God is also responsible, namely,
dominion over other creatures, the animals, vv. 7–8. Here
there is a clear reference to the commission given by God to
human beings when He created them, Genesis 1: 26. We
find this difficult to understand, and not only because
industrialization has led to man's control over the material
world becoming more significant and extensive. No doubt
at the back of the idea here is the fact that human civilization
only became possible because of the domestication of
animals. But the author also has in mind the present in
which he lives. He feels a sense of wonder, that a man can be
in real contact, through will and word, with the animal
world which is so very different from himself, that his voice
can so bridge the gap between himself and the animals that
an animal will follow him, listen to him and obey him. The
author sees in this one of the highest of human capacities,
which puts in the shade all man's technical capabilities.
Even if we cannot entirely go along with this, it is worth
more than a second thought, when we consider how at the
present time humanity is destroying more and more animal
species.

v. 9: At the end the psalm recurs to its beginning. The value
put on man in v. 5 is reminiscent of a line from Sophocles'
Antigone: 'Much is there passing strange; nothing
surpassing mankind'. The meditation on humanity in this
psalm grows out of that praise of God which is also its final
word.

Psalm 139: Thou knowest me

1   O Lord, thou searchest me and knowest me!
2   Thou knowest when I sit down and when I rise
        up;
    thou discernest my thoughts from afar.
3   Thou searchest out my path and my lying down,
    and art acquainted with all my ways.
4   Even before a word is on my tongue,
    lo, O Lord, thou knowest it altogether.
5   Thou dost enfold me behind and before,
    and layest thy hand upon me.

6   Such knowledge is too wonderful for me,
    too high for me to attain it.
7   Whither shall I go from thy spirit?
    or whither shall I flee from thy presence?
8   If I ascend to heaven, thou art there!
    If I make my bed in Sheol, thou art there also!
9   If I took the wings of the morning
    and dwelt in the uttermost parts of the sea,
10 even there thy hand would seize me,
    thy right hand grasp me.
11 Were I to say: 'Darkness shall cover me,
    and the light about me be night',
12 even the darkness would not be dark to thee,
    the night would be bright as the day.

13 For thou didst form my inward parts,
    thou didst knit me together in my mother's
        womb.
14 I praise thee, that I am so wonderfully made,
    yea, wonderful are thy works!
15 Thou knowest my soul right well, my frame was
        not hidden from thee,
    when I was being made in secret,
    intricately wrought in the depths of the earth.
16 Thy eyes beheld all my days;
    in thy book were written, every one of them,

the days already formed for me, when as yet there
    was none of them.
17 How unfathomable to me are thy thoughts, O
    God!
    How vast is the sum of them!
18 If I would count them, they are more than the
    sand;
    were I to come to the end, I would still be with
    thee.
19 O that thou wouldest slay the wicked, O God,
    and that men of blood would depart from me,
20 men who maliciously defy thee and abuse thy
    name!
21 Should I not hate them that hate thee, O Lord?
    Should I not loathe them that rise up against thee?
22 I hate them with perfect hatred;
    I count them my enemies.

23 Search me, O God, and know my heart!
    Try me, and know my thoughts!
24 And see if there be any deceitful way in me,
    and lead me in the way everlasting!

Text

v. 12: the two final words 'darkness is as light' are an
    addition.
v. 16: read *kol- jāmaj*, 'all my days'.
v. 20: reading *jamrūka* and *nissā'ū*, with the apparatus of
    BHS.

Structure

This psalm too is reflective meditation, expanding a single
psalm motif, the protestation of innocence which is an
element of the individual lament. To this motif belongs the
appeal to God: 'Thou knowest that I am guiltless!'. Such an

appeal forms the framework of the psalm: v. 1, 'O Lord, thou searchest me . . . ', v. 23, 'Search me, O God, and know my heart!'. The situation in which this appeal is made is when an individual is protesting his innocence (compare Psalms 7; 35; 37; 69), as we find in v. 24a: 'And see, if there be any deceitful way in me'. Vv. 19–22 speak of the opponents who falsely accuse him. However, into this framework there is introduced something completely different, a meditative amplification of the opening clause, 'thou knowest me'; this meditation is a praise of God, in which the speaker, carried away by awe and wonderment, extols his Creator. Vv. 2–5 say that his life, and all that happens in it, lies open to God and the same thought is reflected on further in vv. 7–12, in which he says that there is nowhere he can hide from God. In between these two sections, v. 6 represents a momentary pause in face of the wonder of God's omniscience. Vv. 13–16 give the reason why the author feels as he does by means of a meditation on his own creatureliness, while vv. 17–18 again pick up v. 6 and close the section with praise meditating on the Creator of mankind.

v. 1: The protestation of innocence, with its appeal to God, 'thou well knowest that I am innocent!', arises from the situation of direst distress in which the guiltless speaker finds himself, a situation clearly recognizable also in vv. 19–22, where God is invoked against his enemies. But, with v. 2, this situation vanishes completely from view. The author breaks free of it as he reflects on the words of this verse, and by his meditation he is released from his fears. Here we learn something of importance for what the psalms meant for ancient Israel. The psalms not only had their place in Temple worship, but they also accompanied the people as they returned from worship to their daily lives. They reflected on the words of the psalms and, in doing so, they discovered in them things which delighted and amazed them and things they had not hitherto understood. In any event, the words of the psalm were important for them and exercised their minds. Hence we meet a meditation on a phrase from a psalm as the main part of Psalm 139.

vv. 2-5: Such a meditation is also of interest from the standpoint of psychology. The one who thus meditates asks himself: What do the words before me really mean? And he finds the explanation when he is able to see them as tangible realities in the circumstances of daily life. Whether he sits down or gets up, whether he goes out or lies down, God knows and is involved. God knows all his ways, all his thoughts, all his deeds and words. In realizing this, the author makes an important point; an individual can say to God in prayer, 'O Lord, thou knowest me', but he has not in fact said anything as long as the words remain for him an abstract theological formula. It is only when he spells out what these words mean for his actual life that it dawns on him what he has really said.

vv. 7-12: And so the next step in the meditation is also understandable psychologically. The author asks himself: But what if I am unwilling to accept what I have realized? What if I am unwilling for God to go with me in every step I take? It is only when he reflects in this negative way on the words he has uttered that their meaning becomes clear to him. I cannot myself possibly escape from my existing situation even 'if I took the wings of the morning and dwelt in the uttermost parts of the sea'. Now the author realizes that there is another present reality and another knowledge beyond what man can imagine for himself. And this means that I cannot myself possibly escape from God, 'the darkness would not be dark for thee'. This gives a sense of complete security, v. 5, 'thou dost enfold me behind and before and layest thy hand upon me'.

vv. 13-16: A third train of thought leads the author to ask: But how can this be, what is the reason for it? And the answer is at hand: I am God's creature. But again this simple conclusion is not enough for him, and again he has to spell it out in the circumstances of his own life, 'for thou didst knit me together in my mother's womb'. There follows an equation of birth from a human mother with the birth of the human race from Mother Earth, a primaeval myth of the origin of mankind. This is only hinted at in the words 'intricately wrought in the depths of the earth', but it would have been understood at once by those who originally heard the psalm. The equation of his own birth with the beginnings of humanity enables the author to make sense of the story of the creation of man: its goal is that the individual should understand himself, here and now, as a being created by God.

Not only does the author think of his birth in v. 13; he has also before his eyes the whole course of his life from birth up to now. Hence his reflection moves from the horizontal 'thou art acquainted with all my ways' to the vertical: thou wast with me from the very beginning and even when my infant frame had only just emerged from my mother's womb 'thy eyes beheld all my days'.

vv. 6, 14, 17f.: So the author's meditation finally reaches its conclusion in deeply felt praise by three routes. He is certain of what he has discovered but he cannot comprehend it: 'such knowledge is too wonderful for me', vv. 6, 17, 18. His incomprehension draws him to look to the Creator, v. 14; it is the work of the Creator that he is so wonderfully made. What a great gap there is between the conclusion reached by our author's reflections and that reached by a self-confident theology which interprets the psalm's message in such abstract terminology as 'divine omniscience and omnipresence', a heading given to this psalm by many commentators! But so to entitle it is to fail to understand it.

vv. 19-21: The reflective amplification comes to an end at v. 18. With vv. 19-21, we return to the framework of the psalm of lament, in which the protestation of innocence is followed by the speaker's request to God to annihilate his enemies who have unjustly accused him.. His enemies are equally God's enemies, v. 21, and so the pious man concludes that he must hate the wicked who hate God; he stands on the side of God over against them. At the time of the psalmist, this appeared an inevitable consequence, because this life was the arena where the issue between pious and godless had to be decided. Here we see the limitations of the faith of the psalms. A change first occurred when Christ died as well for the godless, for God's enemies, and asked forgiveness for them from the cross.

vv. 23-24: The psalm ends as it began. The psalmist is confident in the outcome of God's testing of him. But at the same time he entrusts his whole life to the Creator who knows him, and his trust in Him is boundless. 'Thou dost enfold me behind and before, and layest thy hand upon me', v. 5.

LITURGICAL PSALMS

By liturgical psalms are meant those in which there can be recognized a service of worship combining words and ritual actions. This is easily observable in the alternation of the speakers between two groups or between officiant and congregation, or by the change from summons to compliance with it. Hence a variety of rites and ceremonies appear, such as prostrations, processional shouts, circumambulation of the altar, entering the sanctuary, executing ceremonies of blessing or consecration and offering sacrifices of various kinds (compare Deuteronomy 26).

Psalm 118: This is the day which the Lord has made

1   O praise the Lord, for he is good;
    his steadfast love endures for ever!

2   Let Israel say, 'His steadfast love endures for ever'.

3   Let the house of Aaron say, 'His steadfast love endures for ever'.

4   Let those who fear the Lord say,
    'His steadfast love endures for ever'.

5   Out of my distress I called on the Lord;
    the Lord answered me and set me free.

6   With the Lord on my side I do not fear.
    What can man do to me?

7   The Lord is on my side to help me;
    I shall look in triumph on those who hate me.

8   It is better to take refuge in the Lord
    than to put confidence in man.

9   It is better to take refuge in the Lord
    than to put confidence in princes.

10 For dogs had surrounded me;
   in the name of the Lord I repelled them!

11 They surrounded me on every side;
   in the name of the Lord I repelled them!

12 They surrounded me like bees;
   in the name of the Lord I repelled them!
   (They were extinguished like a fire of thorns.)

13 They pushed me hard, so that I was falling,
   but the Lord helped me.

14 The Lord is my strength and my song; he has
   become my salvation.

15 Hark, glad songs of victory in the tents of the
   righteous:
   'The right hand of the Lord does valiantly,

16 the right hand of the Lord is exalted,
   the right hand of the Lord does valiantly!'

17 I shall not die, but I shall live,
   and recount the deeds of the Lord.

18 The Lord has chastened me sorely,
   but he has not given me over to death.

19 Open to me the gates of salvation,
   that I may enter through them to praise the Lord!

20 This is the gate of the Lord;
   the righteous shall enter through it.

21 I will praise thee, for thou hast heard me
   and hast become my deliverer.

22 The stone which the builders rejected
   has become the chief corner-stone.

23 This is the Lord's doing;
   it is marvellous in our eyes.

24 This is the day which the Lord has made;
   let us rejoice and be glad in it.

25 O Lord, save us, we beseech thee! O Lord, give us
   success!

26 Blessed be he who enters in the name of the Lord!

We bless you from the house of the Lord.
27 The Lord is God, may he cause to shine
upon us . . .
Bind the festal procession with branches, up to the
horns of the altar!
28 Thou art my God, and I will praise thee;
thou art my God, I will extol thee.

29 Praise the Lord, for he is good;
for his steadfast love endures for ever!

Text

v. 10: instead of *kol-gojim*, read *kī kelābīm*, 'for dogs'.
v. 12b: the text is in confusion and the translation only a
guess.
v. 13: the verb is to be read as third person plural.
v. 27a: this may be citing the blessing referred to in v. 26,
but the verse is incomplete and almost certainly 'his
countenance' should be supplied at the end.

Structure

Psalm 118 is a liturgical psalm, combining words and
actions, the latter in vv. 19-27. The kernel of the psalm is the
individual psalm of praise of vv. 5- 14, 17-18, expanded by
the citation from an ancient victory song in vv. 15-16. The
section vv. 5-18 is made into a psalm of praise of the
worshipping congregation by the introduction, vv. 1-4,
and the conclusion, v. 29; with these verses belong the
victory song added in vv. 15-16 and a number of clauses
expressing praise of God in the section of liturgical actions,
vv. 19- 27, especially in vv. 20-24. The individual psalm of
praise is complete but its various components are scattered
throughout the psalm: v. 5 is the introductory summary;
vv. 6-7 the expression of confidence, expanded in vv. 8-9;
vv. 10-13a a modified narrative of distress; vv. 13b-14,

17-18 the report of the deliverance and vv. 17, 21, 28 the vow of praise.

Vv. 19-27 could be described as an entrance liturgy, as is Psalm 24. But the succession of actions referred to here permits no more than a glimpse of it; it is only very briefly sketched and has probably been very much abbreviated. At the actual entrance, vv. 19-20, the verses were probably spoken alternately, v. 19 by those in the entrance procession, while v. 20 is the answer of a priest, or priests, from within the Temple, again compare Psalm 24. Vv. 21 and 28 are part of the individual song of praise, to which the congregation responds in vv. 22-24, picking up what its members have heard in the abbreviated prayer of v. 25. In vv. 26-27 the entrance liturgy is concluded by the blessing of those who have entered and the summoning of them to join in the cultic dance.

vv. 1-4: The imperative call to praise which, with its resumption in v. 29, frames the psalm, is divided in vv. 2-4 according to those being addressed, Israel, v. 2, the priests, v. 3 or the congregation, v. 4. At an early period, the call would probably have gone out to the tribes. The clause 'for he is good, for his steadfast love endures for ever' has already become a liturgical formula, as it has in Psalm 136 and commonly elsewhere.

vv. 5-14: It is not necessary to comment on the narrative psalm of praise in detail, since it corresponds to the pattern which we have examined earlier. Vv. 8-9 are a meditative amplification, of the kind we find, for example, in Psalm 34: 8b. The narrative of distress speaks of the threat from enemies in terms similar to those of Psalm 22: 12-16.

vv. 15-16: In these verses, praise of God for an act of deliverance for His people is added to the individual song of praise. It consists of a citation from a victory song of the same type as Judges 5, probably from Israel's early days. This fragment is evidence that there were once many more such victory songs than those that have been handed down to us.

vv. 19-27: Although this section is only abbreviated and allusive, it yet gives us some impression of how vivid and many-sided was ancient Israel's worship, full of jubilation, happy shouting and even dancing. Entry into the Temple, vv. 19-20, was a festal ceremony, accompanied by choirs singing alternately. The words of v. 22: 'The stone which the builders rejected has become the chief corner-stone', applied to Christ in Matthew 21: 42 and other passages, we can unfortunately no longer understand. While v. 21 belongs to the individual psalm of praise, v. 22 is connected with the victory song of vv. 15-16. Probably the comparison here is with the people of Israel: Israel, once rejected and humiliated by the nations, now gains new significance.

vv. 23-24: These verses bring together the mighty acts of God for His people and their celebration by its members.

v. 25: The celebration includes the appeal to God who seems far away, though it only appears in an abbreviated form in v. 25. It begins with the cultic cry 'O Lord!', *'ānnā' yhwh*. The repetition of this in both halves of the verse implies that the cry was repeated many times. In the two halves of the verse the petition for deliverance 'save us!' is linked with the petition for blessing, or more exactly for success: 'give us success!' – in both God's goodness, vv. 1-4, 29, will be experienced. From this cry in v. 25, we can more easily understand the curious change of meaning which the cultic cry 'Hosanna', *hōšī'āh na'* undergoes. Here the parallelism shows that it is still an appeal for God's help; by the time of Jesus' entry into Jerusalem it has become instead an expression of praise.

vv. 26-27: The festal entry concludes with the blessing from within the Temple of those entering the holy place. Probably here, as in Psalm 24, the blessing is given by a priestly choir. V. 27a probably indicates that the blessing was given in the words of Numbers 6: 24-26, but the quotation is broken off. The blessing is the response to the appeal to God of v. 25. The giving of the blessing is accompanied by a rite which the worshippers are summoned to perform, the festal circumambulation of the altar with branches in their hands, v. 27b.

vv. 28-29: V. 28 concludes the individual psalm; here the conclusion is taken up by the whole congregation. V. 29 repeats the shout of praise at the beginning: God's praise may never grow silent.

Psalm 24: Lift high the gates!

1 The earth is the Lord's and the fullness thereof,
   the world and those who dwell therein;
2 for he has founded it upon the seas,
   and established it upon the rivers.

3 Who shall ascend the hill of the Lord?
   And who shall stand in his holy place?
4 He who has clean hands and a pure heart,
   who does not lift up his soul to what is false,
   and does not swear deceitfully against his neighbour
       . . .
5 He will receive blessing from the Lord,
   and vindication from the God of his salvation.
6 Such is the generation of those who seek the Lord,
   who seek thy face, thou God of Jacob.

7 Lift up your heads, O gates,
   and be lifted up, O ancient doors,
   that the king of glory may come in!

8 Who is this king of glory?
   The Lord, strong and mighty,
   the Lord, mighty in battle.

9 Lift up your heads, O gates,

and be lifted up, O ancient doors,
that the king of glory may come in!

10 Who is this king of glory?
The Lord of hosts, he is the king of glory!

Text

v. 4: at the end of v. 4 'against his neighbour' is to be added with the Septuagint. Probably other requirements have here fallen out.

v. 6: in the first line, 'the Lord' should be added, and in the second 'thou God of Jacob' is to be read.

Structure

The psalm is in three sections: vv. 1-2 are part of a psalm of praise, representing an entrance song, vv. 3-6 are an entrance torah, compare Psalm 15, and vv. 7-10 the actual entrance. The whole psalm depicts and accompanies the processional entry of the ark into the Temple. This includes the 'torah liturgy' preceding the entrance, corresponding to Psalm 15, in the form of versicles and responses exchanged between pilgrims, v. 3, and priest, vv. 4-5, and a similar alternation at the entrance itself: the procession requests entry into the Temple for the ark, 'the king of glory', v. 7, the question comes from within: 'Who is this?', 8a and the answer is given, v. 8b. In vv. 9-10, the entrance dialogue is again repeated.

vv. 1-2: These verses are part of a liturgical psalm of praise, consisting of praise of God in majesty, v. 1, and the amplification of this to praise of the Creator and Lord of creation. We must assume that this extract takes the place of a complete psalm of praise. Through this psalm entry unit, the whole psalm is given a universal horizon: the One who enters the Jerusalem Temple is Creator and Lord of the world!

vv. 3-6: The entrance torah is concerned with the sanctity of the Temple as the place 'where God causes his name to dwell'. Not just anyone can enter, v. 3. It is noteworthy that in vv. 4-5 there is no question of rites of cleansing, no question of cultic impurity or violations of a tabu. Entry into the Temple is open to him 'who has clean hands and a pure heart'. This requirement is amplified by two more detailed precepts which reflect the commandments of the Decalogue. A comparison with Psalm 15 suggests that a number of other requirements would originally have been listed at this point. In what is mentioned, the sole concern is with the individual's inner disposition and his behaviour towards others, and this clearly shows prophetic influence on the psalm. V. 6 again repeats, in different words, the requirements for entry to the Temple: it is open to those who seek the Lord and His face. The verse does not describe an ethical or religious quality, but the trust which turns to God and the readiness to do His will. They are assured of what awaits them in the worship of the Temple: blessing for their daily life, for family and work, but also God's help when they approach Him in necessity, v. 5.

vv. 7-10: Here we reach the actual entrance into the Temple. These final verses are an impressive demonstration of how an ordinary, everyday happening can be transformed into a ceremony, even into a liturgical rite. It is what happens wherever a building, a fortress, a town or a temple is enclosed by walls and gates, and it involves four distinct and invariable stages: (1) the request for entry; (2) the question from inside: who are you? (3) the answer: we are so and so, and (4) the opening of the gates or the dismissal of those wishing to enter. This wholly mundane procedure is here made into a ritual by being transferred to the occasion of the arrival of a procession, in this case the procession carrying the ark, in front of the Temple. By this, it has lost its original function of reassuring those inside the walls. That we are now dealing with a ritual is shown especially by the repetition of the procedure in vv. 7-8 and 9-10.

Another sign that we have a ritual before us is the way that, in vv. 7 and 9, the gates are addressed and summoned, 'Lift up your heads' – presumably a portcullis is referred to – for this agrees with the style of rituals, as does the term 'ancient' or 'primaeval' applied to the gates. One of the pilgrimage party announces the arrival of a king who craves admittance: 'that the king of glory may come in'. What is indicated here is that in Israel the ark was carried in procession from its place in the Jerusalem Temple and brought back there in the same way, just as in processions of gods in Egypt and Mesopotamia the image of an enthroned deity was borne in procession from the temple and returned thither again. The ark was viewed as God's throne, though an empty one, and so the entry ritual was employed to glorify Israel's King. Instead of a simple answer to the query as to who it is who craves entrance, vv. 8a, 10a, the participants in the procession intone a chant of praise to the God who is with them, vv. 8b, 10b, extolling Him as the Lord of hosts, the mighty warrior King; so the psalm is rounded off with praise of God's majesty.

Excursus: Worship and History: This psalm illustrates, in a moving way, the influence of history on Israel's worship. The ark which David had transported to Jerusalem was a portable shrine of the early period when Israel had no town, no royal fortresses and no Temple. David's aim was to unite the traditions of the early period with the new form of worship in the royal Temple. Hence the ark was given a new interpretation as a royal throne and God was venerated as King. The procession with the ark took the place of the processions with the divine image characteristic of other religions. But eventually the royal stronghold and the royal Temple were destroyed and the ark disappeared. But the old Psalm 24 survived in the completely different circumstances of post-exilic worship, when there was no longer an ark or royal palace and the nation had become merely a province of a foreign empire. What remained was the praise of God from the worshipping congregation of those 'who seek thy face, thou God of Jacob'.

Psalm 122: Our feet have been standing within thy gates!

1   I was glad when they said to me,
         'Let us go to the house of the Lord!'

2   Our feet have been standing within thy gates, O
         Jerusalem!
         where those bound to her assemble,

3   Jerusalem, built as a city

4   to which the tribes go up, the tribes of the Lord,
         as was decreed for Israel,
         there to extol the name of the Lord.

5   There thrones for judgment were set,
         the thrones of the house of David.

6   Pray for Jerusalem's welfare, may thy tents be
         secure.

7   Peace be within thy walls,
         and security within thy houses.

8   For my brethren and companions' sake
         I will say, 'Peace be within thee'.
         For the sake of the house of the Lord our God,
         I will seek thy good.

Text

v. 3:   read the Qal with the Septuagint and for *jaḥdāw* read *jēḥad*.

v. 4:   before *lehōdōt*, *šām*, 'there', is to be added.

v. 6:   instead of 'who love thee' read *'ōhālajik*, 'thy tents'.

Structure

This is a very simple pilgrimage song, struck up at the moment when the pilgrims arrived before the Temple at

Jerusalem. It is divided into three parts: the arrival, vv. 1-2, the sight of the city, vv. 3-5, and the greeting to the holy city, vv. 6-8. Properly speaking, this is a completely secular song, the kind of popular folk-song that is everywhere sung on the course of a journey. With this psalm should be compared the similar Psalm 84.

vv. 1-2: The two opening verses present the ancient pattern, which is met with everywhere, of departure and arrival. The pilgrims have arrived before the city of Jerusalem and now that they have reached their goal they think back to when they set out. Now they are here and see city and Temple in front of them.

vv. 3-5: As they gaze on the city, they repeat to themselves its name, silently or aloud, and express what it means to them. Their first thought is for the present, vv. 3-4, their second for the past, v. 5. What is surprising is that both thoughts to which the pilgrims are moved are completely about secular matters. They think of all the people they will meet in the city and at the Temple: here there assemble out of the whole nation and its tribes those who have come together to praise the One who unites each to other as their common Lord.

And they also think: In this city stood the throne of David our king and of his royal successors! But for them the most important thing about the kingdom is that the 'thrones for judgment' were the seat of just government which guaranteed equity and peace.

vv. 6-8: Now the pilgrims salute the city before which they have arrived. This greeting is the purpose of the simple pilgrimage song, in the course of which the summons, v. 6a, passes over into the greeting itself in vv. 6b-8, which is wholly governed by the word šālōm: 'peace be within thy walls, and security within thy houses'. Then follows in beautiful and meaningful parallelism: 'For my brethren and companions' sake – For the sake of the house of our God'; here too, in conformity with the song's general character, it is the people standing before the Temple who are named.

This song also shows us what a greeting meant for ancient Israel. A greeting wishing peace can be bidden for a city as well, something that makes sense when we see how it arises from the situation which the psalm describes – the arrival of those coming from afar, vv. 1-2, their sight of the city, v. 3-5, and then the recognition that this is our city, vv. 6-8.

THE SONGS OF ZION

The Songs of Zion, whose theme is the preservation of the holy city in the face of enemy attack, are probably related to the pilgrimage songs. These psalms presuppose the choice of Zion, with its city and Temple, as the mountain of God. Many of the motifs in this psalm category, Psalms 46; 48; 76, 84, 87, go back to the pre-Davidic era, when Zion was still a Jebusite holy place.

Psalm 46: God is our refuge

1   God is our refuge and strength,
    a well proved help in trouble.
2   Therefore we will not fear
    though the earth should change,
    though the mountains shake in the heart of the
        sea;
3a though its waters roar and foam,
    though the mountains tremble with its tumult.
3b The Lord of hosts is with us;
    the God of Jacob is our fortress.

4   There is a river whose streams make glad the city of
        God;
    the Most High has sanctified his habitation.
5   God is in the midst of her, she shall not be
        moved;
    God will help her at break of day.
6   The nations rage, the kingdoms totter;
    he utters his voice, the earth melts.
7   The Lord of hosts is with us;
    the God of Jacob is our fortress.

8   Come, behold the works of the Lord,
    how he has wrought desolations in the earth.

9   He makes wars to cease to the end of the earth;
     he breaks the bow, and shatters the spear,
     he burns the shields with fire.
10   Be still, and know that I am God!
     I am exalted among the nations, I am exalted in the
         earth.

11   The Lord of hosts is with us,
     the God of Jacob is our fortress.

Text

v. 3   (Heb. 4): the refrain, as in vv. 7 (Heb. 8) and 11
       (Heb. 12) is to be added after this verse; it is needed
       in view of the preceding sentence in this verse.
v. 4   (Heb. 5): instead of 'holy', read *qiddēš*, 'he has
       sanctified', and then 'his' habitation.
v. 9   (Heb. 10): read *'agīlot*, 'shields'.

Structure

Psalm 46 is one of those psalms in which a single motif, in
this case the avowal of confidence, though here by the
nation, has been developed into an entire psalm, and the
process is particularly obvious in this psalm. It begins with
the motif in question, v. 1, which then runs all through it by
means of the refrain in v. 3, as amended, and vv. 7 and 11.
Thus the whole psalm is an expression of trust.

The refrain divides the psalm into three strophes, vv. 1-3,
4-7, 8-11. In the first, vv. 2-3 give the grounds for the
avowal of trust of v. 1: for this reason we will not fear, even
though a cosmic cataclysm should supervene. The second
strophe tells how confidence is preserved in spite of
threatening political catastrophe in the shape of an assault
by the nations on the city of God, the holy city encircled by
the river of life: God will repulse the attack. The third
strophe continues the second: the consequence of the

repulse of the nations' assaults is that God puts an end to wars and the nations are called upon to acknowledge Him as Lord.

vv. 1-3: The 'we' is the congregation assembled in Jerusalem for worship. They acknowledge that God is their refuge and their strength. He has proved Himself so to be throughout the nation's history and He can be relied on whatever may threaten in the future.

Luther translates v. 1 as: 'God is our refuge and strength, a help in the great ills that have overtaken us'. Grammatically, this rendering is impossible but it governs the way the whole psalm is understood in Luther's translation of it, namely as a word for present distress.[71] This understanding is even more pronounced in Luther's adaptation of the psalm, 'Ein' feste Burg', where he speaks expressly of 'all the ill that hath us now o'ertaken', which in turn results in the fighting tone of his famous hymn: 'And were this world all devils o'er . . . not they can overpower us'.[72] This understanding does not fit the psalm which sounds a note of quiet trust.

vv. 2-3: This trust will also hold firm even in the face of a future cosmic cataclysm. Behind the words of vv. 2-3 lies the idea of the primaeval chaos waters, as in Genesis 1: 2, which the Creator has tamed, compare Psalms 65: 7; 89: 10; 93: 3-4; 104: 6-9; Job 38: 11. Here the meaning is: even though chaos should break in upon us, we will not fear. The repeated 'though' in vv. 2b-3 seems to require a following clause to complete the thought, for otherwise the transition from v. 3a to 4 would be too abrupt. For this reason, the refrain of vv. 7 and 11 is to be added to make v. 3b, as proposed in the apparatus of BHS and accepted by almost all commentators. The term 'Lord of hosts', *yhwh ṣebāōt*, here describes God in majesty. In the parallel clause, 'the God of Jacob', equivalent to 'the God of Israel', describes

---

[71] Compare the translation of v. 1 in the Authorized Version: 'God is our refuge and strength, a very present help in trouble'.

[72] The quotations are from the translation by Thomas Carlyle.

the God who has proved to be a refuge throughout the nation's history.

vv. 4–7: The second strophe tells of an assault against the city of God by the nations. The river whose streams encircle the city recalls the paradisal river of Genesis 2: 10-14. Isaiah 33: 21 also speaks of this river[73] but here the reference is to the eschaton. The correspondence of primaeval time and end time[74] is presupposed both in vv. 2-3 and in 4-6. The sacred river which encircles it makes Jerusalem the eschatological city of God. God has consecrated her to be His dwelling place; she will not be moved because God is in the midst of her.

The assault of the nations against God's city, v. 6, is also pictured in eschatological terms, as it is also in Isaiah 17: 12-14: 'Ah, the thunder of many peoples, they thunder like the thundering of the sea'; and God's intervention to repulse them is similarly described in Isaiah 17: 13; 'but he will rebuke them, and they will flee far away'.

The words of v. 5b, 'God will help her at break of day', also refer to the nations' assault: dawn is the time of attack and the very first attack is broken by God. When vv. 2-3 and v. 6 employ the same verbs to depict the threat they each envisage, this indicates that both the cosmic threat and that of the assault by the nations are alike directed against the city of God at the time of the end; similarly, in Isaiah 17: 12 the thunder of the peoples is compared with that of that of the sea. Psalm 93 provides another parallel. Vv. 2-3 and 4-6 thus present two aspects of the same eschatological threat and the identical structure of both strophes again makes the same point. The assault of the nations on the city of God at the end of time will be on a cosmic scale, an attack which could drag creation down again to chaos. This is also what is signified by the figures of Gog and Magog in Ezekiel 38-39.

---

[73] See the comments on this verse in H. Wildberger, *Jesaja*, Vol. III, 1981.

[74] In German, 'Urzeit und Endzeit'.

Over against all this, the psalm sets peaceful trust in Israel's God, who has made the world and holds it in His hands.

vv. 8-11: The imperatives 'come, behold' must be addressed to the same people as the imperative 'Be still' of v. 10. It is the assembled nations who are being addressed, the forum where God's mighty acts are consummated, just as in Deutero-Isaiah, 'the coastlands have seen and are afraid', Isaiah 41: 15, and 'the Lord has bared his holy arm before the eyes of all the nations', Isaiah 52: 10. What God does is termed 'wreaking desolations' in v. 8, but this is not something negative but rather something moving and stirring. God will make wars to cease to the end of the earth by destroying the weapons of war, v. 9. Hence, from the way the third strophe succeeds the second, we have the following train of thought: the apocalyptic warfare, in which God breaks up the assault of the 'raging peoples' against His city, is to be followed by an era of peace when the nations finally cease to wage war. We find the same certainty about the future in Isaiah 2 and Micah 4, which also state that the weapons of war will be utterly destroyed. This peace will extend to the whole earth and embrace all humanity. And even though this eschatological peace still lies in the future, the certainty of its coming gives the congregation confidence here and now. 'Be still!' can mean abandoning the attempts to destroy by force the 'city of God', but it can also mean renouncing war altogether. In the face of God's mighty acts, the nations are challenged, as often in the book of Ezekiel, to acknowledge Him as Lord of all peoples.

This psalm was composed to be sung in the course of post-exilic worship. Prophetic influence can be traced in almost every line, especially that of late prophecy which is already on the way to apocalyptic. As a result, the psalm has also a strongly universalist tone; even when it equates confidence in God with confidence in the inviolability of God's city, it is still concerned with human destiny. Thus, its significance resides above all in this fact to which it witnesses: that God would finally bring wars to an end on earth was not only the message of a succession of prophets, it was also mediated afresh, through the worship of the post-exilic Temple, to every generation of worshippers as the basis of their sure and certain hope.

THE PSALMS OF BLESSING

The Psalter does not contain a specific group of psalms of blessing, for blessing is an act of worship and many liturgical ceremonies conclude with the giving and receiving of a blessing. The Psalter often mentions blessing in this particular context, for example Psalm 118: 26:

> 'Blessed be he who enters in the name of the Lord!
> We bless you from the house of the Lord.'

And similarly, Psalms 129: 8; 134: 3; 115: 12-15, while the object of the procession in Psalm 24: 5 is to receive a blessing. Blessing is frequently referred to in the 'Songs of Ascent' or pilgrimage songs, Psalms 120-134. Psalm 67 contains a request for blessing:

v. 1:   May God be gracious to us and bless us
        and make his face to shine upon us!
v. 6:   May the land yield its increase;
        May God, our God, bless us!
v. 7:   May God bless us, let all the ends of the earth fear him!

Psalm 65: 9-13 praises the operation of the divine blessing. While in all the above-mentioned passages the blessing is for the whole congregation, Psalms 91 and 121 both reflect the bestowal of blessing on an individual.

Psalm 121: I lift up my eyes to the hills

1   I lift up my eyes to the hills.
    From whence does my help come?
2   My help comes from the Lord,
    who made heaven and earth.
3   He will not let thy foot be moved,
    he who keeps thee will not slumber.
4   Behold, he who keeps Israel will neither slumber
    nor sleep.
5   The Lord is thy keeper;
    the Lord is thy shade on thy right hand.

6   The sun will not smite thee by day,
       nor the moon by night.
7   The Lord will keep thee from all evil; he will keep
       thy life.
8   The Lord will keep thy going out and thy coming
       in
       from this time forth and for evermore.

Text

v. 8:   'thy going out and thy coming in': it is typical of the
          language of the psalms that a term such as 'thy
          ways' should be given concrete expression by
          naming its two limits.

Structure

The psalm is formed on the pattern of an alternation of
speakers. Vv. 1-2 have a first person subject, vv. 3-8 are an
address in the second person. The same applies to Psalm 91,
where v. 2 is in the first person, while vv. 3-13 are an
address in the second person, and these two psalms also
correspond in content. The first speaker gives voice to his
trust in God, the second promises him God's protection and
guidance. We can therefore conclude that the psalm
represents the bestowal of a blessing on individuals in the
context of Israel's worship, no doubt on particular
occasions, such as before a journey or some other hazardous
undertaking. This personal reception of a blessing forms
the subject matter of Psalms 91 and 121 and probably this
rite is the background to Job 5.

v. 1-2: The words 'I lift up my eyes to the hills' do not refer
to one particular hill or to a hilltop shrine, but are more in
the nature of sign language. They are really saying only: 'I
lift up my eyes', but looking up towards a hill is so typical a
thing to do that its mention here serves, almost like a

comparison, to make the looking up a lively and vivid gesture.

The question, 'From whence does my help come?' may point to a preliminary question of the priest's, but, in the text as we have it, its effect is to underline the following sentence: 'My help comes . . . '. The fact that, as in Psalm 91, this avowal of trust precedes the bestowal of blessing, provides important evidence for how blessing is understood not only in the psalm but also throughout the entire Old Testament. The recipient shows that he does not just passively accept the blessing but receives it with a trusting heart. The help on which he relies comes from 'the Lord who made heaven and earth'. With every step he takes as he surveys the path before him, the speaker finds himself in the realm of the One who has created all things.

vv. 3–8: As a result, the priest gives him the blessing. Behind the words of the priest, we can recognize the blessing given to the worshipping congregation as laid down in Numbers 6: 24-26. But this blessing is no rigid formula; it can be varied according to the particular situation. In this case, the blessing is obviously bestowed at the start of a journey, the stages of which are listed, departure, v. 3, and arrival, v. 8, travelling by day and night, vv. 5-6, and the dangers when one lies down to sleep, vv. 3b, 4. When one reflects on the words of this blessing, one sees clearly how, with them, both giver and receiver commit the imminent journey, and all that is involved in it, into God's protecting charge, and how, when this happens, a man can truly 'go with God'.

PSALMS AND WISDOM

One group of psalms is frequently labelled as 'Wisdom psalms' but it is misleading to put all the psalms in question under this heading. Psalms have their origin and setting in worship. By contrast, 'Wisdom' belongs to a quite different, and originally secular, sphere, which has no relationship with worship. In the strict sense, there are not, and cannot be, any 'Wisdom psalms'.

There are, however, various reasons why Wisdom psalms are so designated:

1. Some Wisdom sayings have been included within the collection 'Songs of Ascent', Psalms 120-134, and only in this collection: Psalms 127: 1-2, 3-5; 128: 1-3; 4-6; 133: 1-3. Why this was done we do not know. Every one of these passages could equally well find a place in the book of Proverbs, for they are not psalms nor have they any relationship with them. That they were included in a psalm collection is connected with the fact that, in the later period, a religious Wisdom emerged which had much in common with the piety of the psalms.

2. What psalms and Wisdom had in common was the opposition we find in both between pious and godless, an opposition pictured in a large group of sayings in Proverbs and which is also an important component of the friends' speeches in the book of Job. It is met with as an added element in many individual laments, where the god-fearing man complains of the wicked who are oppressing him.

Psalm 37 represents a lament altered to become Wisdom instruction when it begins: 'Fret not thyself because of the wicked, be not envious of wrongdoers', and it goes on in vv. 3, 5, 7, 34, 37 to exhort the pious to trust in God, who will eventually punish the wicked and vindicate the pious:

> 'Commit thy ways to the Lord;
> trust in him and he will make all well', v. 5.

Psalm 1: Blessed is the man

1   Blessed is the man who walks not in the counsel of
      the wicked,
      nor stands in the way of sinners,
      nor sits in the seat of scoffers;

2   but his delight is in the law of the Lord,
      and on his law he meditates day and night.

3   He is like a tree planted by streams of water,
      that yields its fruit in its season,
      and its leaf does not wither.
      In all that he does, he prospers.

4   The godless are not so, but are like chaff
      which the wind drives away.

5   Therefore the wicked will not stand in the
      judgment,
      nor sinners in the congregation of the righteous;

6   For the Lord knows the way of the righteous,
      but the way of the wicked will perish.

This expression of pious Wisdom was prefixed as a kind of introit to the Psalter at a time when it had become not only a hymn-book for use in worship but also a book of personal devotion. The whole Psalter was thus to be understood in the light of the fundamental post-exilic opposition between pious and godless, whose divinely ordained destiny is presented in this psalm. The saying which proclaims their different fates, v. 6, is amplified in vv. 1-5, where vv. 1-2 describe the pious man, who has no fellowship with the godless but delights in God's word and busies himself with it continuously. The fate of each is shown by the two comparisons of the fruitful tree and the scattered chaff, vv. 3-4; and the wicked perish, v. 5. The extolling of the blessedness of the pious, with which the psalm begins, is also found at Psalms 41: 1 f.; 84: 12; 119: 1 f., and, in psalms of praise, at Psalms 34: 8 and 40: 4: 'Blessed is the man who makes the Lord his trust'.

3. Another feature common to some psalms and Wisdom is

meditation on human transitoriness. This is a further expansion of the lament over transitoriness and as such it becomes an independent unit in the form of a reflection on transitoriness, for instance in Psalms 39; 49; 50 and in Job 7; 9 f.; and 14. A good example is Psalm 39: 4-6, 11b:

> 'Surely every man stands as a mere breath!
> Surely man goes about as a shadow!
> Surely for nought are they in turmoil;
> man heaps up, and knows not who will gather!'

How meditation on transitoriness can become a main theme of Wisdom is seen in the book of Ecclesiastes.

4. A fourth common feature is devotion to the Torah. The Psalter evolved from a number of smaller collections and at one stage it embraced only Psalms 1-119 – a new collection, the 'Songs of Ascent', Psalms 120-134, begins with Psalm 120. The framework of this collection is formed by the two psalms which express devotion to the Torah, Psalms 1 and 119.[75]

Psalm 119: Thy Law

In Psalm 1, the pious man is described as the one who 'meditates on the Law (Torah) day and night'; precisely this is what occurs in Psalm 119, as also in Psalm 19: 7-14. It is not really a psalm but an act of devotion directed to the word of God. The psalm is an acrostic of 176 verses; it is divided into sections of eight lines and the opening letter of each of the lines of each section respectively is the same, so that the whole Hebrew alphabet is gone through.

> 11 With my whole heart I seek thee;
> let me not wander from thy commandments!

[75] The Hebrew term Torah is used here of set purpose in preference to the word 'Law'. The latter is an unsatisfactory rendering; Torah is nearer to what we mean by the word 'Bible'.

18 Open my eyes,
    that I may behold wondrous things out of thy
        law.
19 I am a sojourner on earth;
    hide not thy commandments from me!
33 Teach me, O Lord, the way of thy statutes;
    and I will keep it to the end.
50 This is my comfort in my affliction,
    that thy word gives me life.
64 The earth, O Lord, is full of thy goodness;
    teach me thy statutes!
67 Before I was afflicted, I went astray;
    but now I keep thy word.
73 Thy hands have made and fashioned me;
    give me understanding that I may learn thy
        commandments.
81 My soul languishes for thy salvation;
    I hope in thy word.
94 I am thine, save me;
    for I have sought thy precepts.
105 Thy word is a lamp to my feet
    and a light to my path.
114 Thou art my hiding-place and my shield;
    I hope in thy word.
140 Thy word is pure and upright,
    and thy servant loves it.
162 I rejoice at thy law
    like one who finds great spoil therein.
171 My lips will pour forth praise
    that thou dost teach me thy statutes.
175 Let my soul live, that I may praise thee,
    and let thy ordinances help me.
176 I have gone astray like a lost sheep;
    seek thy servant,
    for I do not forget thy commandments.

This poem of devout devotion witnesses to a Bible-based
piety which has been, and still is, of great significance both
for the Jewish and the Christian religion. God's word is

available in a book which is read reverently and devoutly. There are many psalm motifs in Psalm 119 but they have become isolated individual units in a way far removed from the organic unity of the true psalm. What we have is a Bible-based piety, where the individual saying, considered in its own right, is the object of individual devotion.

All the more strongly, however, does the real dominant motif emerge. This is the Law, and not just the Torah in the wider sense, which includes also the other divisions of the Bible, but, deliberately and specifically, the statutes and ordinances. Here we have the beginning of a Law-based piety, which sees the true word of God as being exclusively in those statutes and ordinances. A deep and genuine piety speaks to us here, but we cannot overlook the fact that it is directed solely and one-sidedly towards God's Law.

THE PSALMS AND JESUS CHRIST

The psalms are often printed along with the New Testament in a single volume, and this shows that, throughout the whole history of Christendom down to today, the psalms have been viewed as having a specially intimate connection with the New Testament. Historically, the reason for this is that the Psalter long remained the prayer book of the Christian congregations. Such it was for Jesus and the apostles and so it remained for many generations. The abiding value of the Psalter for Christians was also strengthened by the fact that the New Testament did not have a section containing prayers or hymns; hence the Psalter kept its particular value as a prayer book, and it was able to do so because nothing changed in respect of the fundamental constituents of prayer, however much the details might alter. But, in addition, there are three sets of passages in the psalms which link them directly with Christ and his work.

1. The first is the praise of the merciful God which is at the heart of the descriptive psalm of praise, as in Psalm 113:

> 'Who is like the Lord our God,
> in heaven and on earth,
> who is seated on high, who looks far down!'

These words directly foreshadow the coming of Christ, the event in which God's looking down on our lowliness from on high was realized: ' . . . he humbled himself, taking the form of a servant'. It is of this that our Christmas hymns sing:

> 'So that the sinner might find grace,
> Lord of the world, thou didst thyself abase.'[76]

---

[76] The original German is: '. . . damit der Sünder Gnad erhält, erniedrigst du dich, Herr der Welt.'

Dogmatic theology speaks of the divine condescension. In the infancy narratives of the gospel of Luke, this psalm motif passes over into the New Testament through the Magnificat, Luke 1: 46-55 and the Benedictus, Luke 1: 67-79:

> '. . . through the tender mercy of our God,
> whereby the dayspring from on high has visited us,
> to give light to those
> who sit in darkness and in the shadow of death.'

2. From the fact that God's looking down from on high was realized in Christ, it follows that Jesus was one who suffered and shared in the lament, the language of suffering. The gospels express this by their use of Psalm 22 in the passion narrative. The frequent quotations from this psalm in the passion narrative show that the evangelists recognized a connection between the two. That the cry of Jesus from the cross, Mark 15: 34, is in the words of Psalm 22 means that Christ has made the psalm's lament his own. He has descended into the depths of human suffering of which the psalm speaks. He knows the question asked by sufferers in all ages, 'Why?', 'How long?'. Psalm 22 is included in the passion narrative as representative of all psalms of lament (for its own special features, see the commentary above). We have already seen how Christ's suffering changes the petition against the enemies into an appearance before God on their behalf.

3. Psalm 22 is 'a lament turned round'; in its second part it passes over into praise for deliverance. When the evangelists employ Psalm 22 to interpret Christ's passion, they have in view the entire psalm where suffering and deliverance from suffering together make up the whole. In narrative psalms of praise, being saved from distress is often described as being snatched from the 'snares of death'. So, as in Psalm 22, when the sufferer's cry is answered, we read:

> 'For he has not despised
> or abhorred the affliction of the afflicted;

and he has not hid his face from him,
but has heard, when he cried to him',

in the same way, the first witnesses to the resurrection
proclaim a message of certainty that the cry from the cross
has been answered. The Easter message corresponds to the
narrative praise of the psalms; the words of Matthew 28: 10:
'Go and tell my brethren . . . ' allude to Psalm 22: 22. The
message of Jesus' resurrection takes its place, in the earliest
apostolic preaching, in the roll-call of God's mighty acts for
His people. And, just as in the psalms, the praise of God's
saving act in Christ has within itself the impulse to widen
out to the furthest distance.

The petition against the enemies

The Old Testament recounts a story which leads up to
Christ. Many psalms, such as Psalm 22, show this
particularly clearly. It is no accident, therefore, that, while
the author of Psalm 22 certainly pleads to be delivered from
his enemies, he utters no petition against them. Elsewhere,
however, in a whole range of psalms, we meet the petition
against the enemies, the request that God should annihilate
them, for example Psalms 2; 3; 5; 6; 7; 9; 10; 11; 12 ; 17; 58;
59; 109 and many others. We meet such a petition even in
the laments of Jeremiah, Jeremiah 12: 3; 15: 15; 18: 21-23;
20: 11. The reason for this petition for God's intervention
lies in the fact that in the Old Testament period, the time
before Christ, whatever happened between God and man
or between God and His people had to take place this side of
death: 'The dead praise not God'. Whose side God stood on
had to be seen in this life. If God was just, He had to
intervene in this life either for the pious or for their enemies;
no other alternative was conceivable. Therefore, as a pious
individual, a man could pray to God to destroy his enemies,
who were of course also God's enemies. In this life it had to
be shown on whose side God was.

The suffering, death and resurrection of Jesus Christ
break through this barrier. God was on the side of the loser,

the one who had been put to death. What had already been hinted at in the Servant Songs of Deutero-Isaiah now became a reality: here a human death made possible a life-bestowing work of God. The change thus brought about finds its expression in the gospels in Jesus' prayer from the cross for his enemies. Jesus' mission to suffer for others includes his enemies as well. So the petition against enemies is thereby eradicated from the prayers of God's people. The petition 'deliver us from evil', behind which lies the psalm lament, still remains, but, since Christ, no-one any longer needs to request God to destroy a fellow human being.

It only remains to point out that this change has even wider consequences. Many readers of the Old Testament are profoundly troubled when they find that in the historical books wars are so often waged in the name of God, that God is Himself described as a warrior, that men kill in their zeal for God. The justification for all this is that for a lengthy period in human history the religious, or worshipping, community was identical with the nation as a political unit. Such was the case with all religions at this period and from this standpoint ancient Israel was a nation like any other. But, in the course of Israel's own history, a change took place. In its Babylonian exile, Israel is indeed promised deliverance but not the restoration of its political power. Israel's promised king is to be a king of peace. The church built on the foundation of Christ's saving work is a congregation devoid of power, where suffering for others has a higher value than fighting against others. No-one is excluded from the church's intercession; what is wholly excluded from its prayer is petition against any other human society or any other human beings.

It is this change in the prayer against enemies which Christ brought about that made it possible for the psalms to become the prayer of Christians. Although petition against enemies is out of the question for Christians, the passages in the psalms where we meet such petitions remind us what had to happen before God's congregation could cease to be a group ranged against other groups and become a community for all humanity.

Index of Biblical References